The study of pottery in archaeology has become increasingly important over the last century, providing the archaeologist with information on many aspects of the past, including chronology, trade and technology. In recent years, scientific developments and statistical techniques have contributed still further to the analysis of pottery. *Pottery in archaeology* covers information obtained from over fifty years practical experience in the field and the latest research. As well as detailing the routine, but essential, tasks of handling pottery, the book examines the most recent research into the quantitative study and comparison of ceramic assemblages. This will be essential reading for students, field archaeologists and for anyone interested in working with pottery.

POTTERY IN ARCHAEOLOGY

CAMBRIDGE MANUALS IN ARCHAEOLOGY

Series editors

Don Brothwell, *University of London*
Graeme Barker, *University of Leicester*
Dena Dincauze, *University of Massachusetts, Amherst*
Ann Stahl, *State University of New York, Binghamton*

Already published

J. D. Richards and N. S. Ryan, *Data processing in archaeology*
Simon Hillson, *Teeth*
Alwyne Wheeler and Andrew K. G. Jones, *Fishes*
Peter G. Dorrell, *Photography in archaeology and conservation*
Lesley Adkins and Roy Adkins, *Archaeological illustration*
Marie-Agnès Courty, Paul Goldberg and Richard MacPhail,
Soils and micromorphology in archaeology

Cambridge Manuals in Archaeology are reference handbooks designed for an international audience of professional archaeologists and archaeological scientists in universities, museums, research laboratories, field units, and the public service. Each book includes a survey of current archaeological practice alongside essential reference material on contemporary techniques and methodology.

POTTERY IN ARCHAEOLOGY

Clive Orton
Institute of Archaeology
University College London

Paul Tyers
Institute of Archaeology
University College London

Alan Vince
City of Lincoln Archaeology Unit

PUBLISHED BY THE PRESS SYNDICATE OF THE UNIVERSITY OF CAMBRIDGE
The Pitt Building, Trumpington Street, Cambridge, United Kingdom

CAMBRIDGE UNIVERSITY PRESS
The Edinburgh Building, Cambridge CB2 2RU, UK
40 West 20th Street, New York, NY 10011–4211, USA
10 Stamford Road, Oakleigh, VIC 3166, Australia
Ruiz de Alarcón 13, 28014 Madrid, Spain
Dock House, The Waterfront, Cape Town 8001, South Africa

http://www.cambridge.org

First published 1993
Reprinted 1994, 1995, 1997, 1999, 2001

Printed in the United Kingdom at the University Press, Cambridge

A catalogue record for this book is available from the British Library

Library of Congress Cataloguing in Publication data
Orton, Clive, 1944–
    Pottery in archaeology / Clive Orton, Paul Tyers, Alan Vince.
        p.   cm. – (Cambridge manuals in archaeology)
    Includes bibliographical references and index.
    ISBN 0 521 25715 8
    1. Pottery. 2. Archaeology – Methodology. I. Tyers, Paul.
II. Vince, A. G. III. Title. IV. Series.
CC79.5.P6078 1993
930.1′028′5 – dc20   92–25814   CIP

ISBN 0 521 25715 8 hardback
ISBN 0 521 44597 3 paperback

CE

CONTENTS

FIGURES

xi

TABLES

PREFACE

An explanation of the events leading to the writing of this book may help to account for its structure and the thinking behind it. I was first approached to write it in 1981 while working as a Research Assistant at the Institute of Archaeology in London. I agreed to do so, and recruited the assistance of Dr Alan Vince, then working at the Museum of London's Department of Urban Archaeology. When the grant supporting my post was not renewed in 1982, I too moved to the Museum of London (Department of Greater London Archaeology). Here I found the pressures of work and bringing up a young family too great to allow time for writing, and in 1983 the project was shelved. In 1986 I returned to teach at the Institute of Archaeology, and in 1988 Dr Paul Tyers started work as my Research Assistant. This seemed to give a strong team and the opportunity for research and writing, and the project was revived. Complications arose when Alan Vince accepted a post at the City of Lincoln Archaeological Unit (some 130 miles north of London). They were resolved and in the summer of 1990 we agreed to proceed as follows. Alan Vince would write a practical manual or handbook on the processing, cataloguing and publication of excavated pottery (Part II, chapters 3–9), for the worker in the field feeling the need for step-by-step instruction. This part would be relatively free of theoretical justification and examples in the form of case studies, which were to be produced by Paul Tyers in Part III (chapters 10–17). Paul Tyers was also to carry out the bulk of the literature research, except for the history of pottery studies, which would be my responsibility. My rôle was to be overall co-ordinator, and to provide what were seen as the two difficult chapters on the history and value of pottery studies (Part I, chapters 1–2), which were intended to set the scene for the rest of the book. There would also be an Appendix containing specimen pro-formas and identification charts.

It did not work out so simply, of course. First, it ultimately seemed more appropriate that I should write chapter 13 on quantification, as this has been a subject close to my heart for over fifteen years. Next, I also took responsibility for chapter 14 on chronology, as much of the information was already assembled for teaching purposes. Finally, we found that the boundary between practice and theory was extremely difficult to draw, and some of the 'practical' text was moved to the theoretical section, particularly to the chapter on fabric analysis (chapter 11). At the same time, I rewrote parts of the manual to include topics which had fallen between my two co-authors. There has thus been a good deal of cross-fertilisation and it would be difficult to assign any chapter uniquely to one author.

Our personal backgrounds will probably be clear from our choices of examples. We are all mainly urban archaeologists, and have all worked at the Museum of London at one time or another. In our work we have specialised in pottery of the Roman and later periods. However, we no not believe that the approach to prehistoric pottery should be intrinsically different to that of any other period, although differences in modes of production should always be kept in mind (for any period, not just the prehistoric). Although we write about theory, this is not 'theory' as would be understood by many archaeologists, but theory about the nature of data and reasonable ways of handling them. We have thus concentrated on method and have tried to avoid nailing our colours to any particular theoretical mast. Fashions change, but the fundamental need to allow data to interact sensibly with theory remains.

The referencing of the book needs explanation. The literature on ceramic studies is vast: as early as 1910 it ran to over 600 pages (Solon 1910). We have therefore not tried to make an exhaustive bibliography on any topic. Rather, we have given a set of references that we believe adequately demonstrate the development of the topic and its current state of play. Omission of a paper from the bibliography does not mean that we regard it as unimportant, but simply that we did not need it to make a particular point.

The book is designed to meet the needs of various types of reader. Practical archaeologists will probably want to read Part II (chapters 3–9) first, but we hope that the question 'Why?' will prompt them to turn to the more theoretical aspects in Part III (chapters 10–17). For this reason, there are relatively few references in Part II, as we believe they would break the flow for the purely practical worker. Anyone who wants to do further reading can find the references in Part III. More general readers, who may be more interested in what archaeologists have done, and why, should perhaps start with Part III. For both, we hope that a desire to set their reading in context will encourage them to Part I (chapters 1–2). Possibly only students will read the book in order, cover-to-cover, although they might benefit by covering Part III before Part II. We would make a special plea for archaeologists who are not pottery workers to read chapter 2, even if they read nothing else in this book. One of our aims is to break down the barrier between those who work with pottery and those to whom it is an arcane study performed by rather strange people.

Clive Orton

ACKNOWLEDGEMENTS

To remember all the colleagues who have influenced one during one's career is a formidable task; for three careers it becomes almost impossible. Many of our ideas and beliefs about pottery took root in the heady days of the 1970s, when our specialist groups, the Medieval Pottery Research Group and the Standing Committee on Roman Pottery, were set up, and the pottery world seemed full of promise. It is ironic that they have come to fruition in this book at a time when pottery studies in the United Kingdom are at a low ebb, and many of our former colleagues have either lost their jobs or moved on to other things. We, some of the survivors, remember them with gratitude, and dedicate this book to them.

Some thanks are more tangible. Much of the research that underpins this book, and, we hope, sets it apart from its predecessors, has been funded by the Science Based Archaeology Committee of the Science and Engineering Research Council, and by the British Academy. We believe we are giving value for money and are grateful for the support. Many colleagues have generously allowed us to use unpublished datasets as 'test-beds' for our techniques; we thank Professors Martin Biddle and Michael Fulford whose data are used in the text, as well as the others whose data, although no less valuable, did not find space.

Many of the illustrations are not our own, and we thank the following for permission to reproduce them:
Academic Press (fig. 15.2), Professor Martin Biddle (fig. 13.5), the Boymans-van Beuningen Museum (fig. 2.2), the Trustees of the British Museum (figs. 1.4, 7.4, 8.1, 11.2 and A.4), Andrzej Buko (fig. 1.3), Chelmsford Museums Service and the Council for British Archaeology (fig. 15.4), CNRS, Paris (fig. 12.1), the Corinium Museum, Cirencester (fig. 8.3), the Colonial Williamsburg Foundation (fig. 14.3), Dr Michael Czwarno (fig. 6.2), Professor Michael Fulford (figs. 13.4 and 15.2), Andrew Gillam and the Society of Antiquaries of Newcastle upon Tyne (fig. 14.1), The Geographical Association (figs. A.5 and A.6), Hampshire County Museums Service (fig. 17.1), the Hampshire Field Club (fig. 14.7), Dr Colin Haselgrove (fig. 16.3), the Institute of Archaeology, University College London (figs. 8.2 and 12.2), Anne Jenner and International Academic Projects (fig. 7.2), Dr Morven Leese (fig. 12.6), Leicester University Press, Professor Colin Platt and Richard Coleman-Smith (fig. 2.3), Malcolm Lyne (fig. 2.1), Janis Mitchell and Thames

and Hudson Ltd. (fig. 4.1), Stephen Moorhouse (fig. 16.2), the Museum of London (figs. 6.1 (a) and (b), and individual drawings in figs. 6.3 and 7.1), the Oxford Architectural and Historical Society (fig. 15.3), Oxford University Press (fig. 1.2), Redactie Bulletin Antieke Beschaving (fig. 12.8), Dr Julian Richards (fig. 12.3), the Roman Society (fig. 14.8), Dr O. S. Rye (figs. 10.2 and 11.1), Harvey Sheldon (fig. 10.5), the Society for American Archaeology (fig. 12.7), the Society of Antiquaries of London (figs. 1.1 and 15.1), Dr Anthony Streeten (fig. 11.3) and the York Archaeological Trust (fig. 14.6).

The prolonged gestation of this book has seen three editors at Cambridge University Press. We thank Robin Derricourt for suggesting the book, Peter Richards for his support and forbearance during the difficult middle years, and Jessica Kuper for encouraging us to bring it to a conclusion.

PART I

HISTORY AND POTENTIAL

HISTORY OF POTTERY STUDIES

Introduction

Pottery tends to arouse strong emotions in archaeologists: they either love it or hate it. For some it has an indefinable fascination, and is potentially full of information, which has to be teased out of it by careful and painstaking study. At the other end of the scale, it is seen as the most common of archaeological materials, whose main functions are to slow down the real business of digging, fill up stores, and behave as an archaeological 'black hole' for post-excavation resources. Between these extremes there is a whole spectrum of opinion: some, for example, see pottery as an unavoidable chore, a material to be processed as quickly as possible before being reburied (either in the ground or in a store), a bit like low-level nuclear waste. A sign on a door in a museum 'Danger: pottery processing' satirised this view. Others take a more mystical view, believing the humblest sherd to be full of the most amazing information – 'Show them a piece of worn pottery and it's the rim of a centurion's favourite cup' (read in a local newspaper) – which only the pottery specialist, as some sort of *guru*, can unlock.

There is an element of truth and an element of caricature in each of these descriptions. While it will be clear where our feelings lie, our aim in this book is to take a balanced view of the potential contribution of pottery studies to archaeology, neither too optimistic nor too pessimistic. To do this, we first need to look at the history of our subject, on the grounds, familiar to archaeologists, that to understand the present we first need to study the past. It is natural for archaeologists to attempt to divide their material into chronological phases; the history of archaeology in general, and of ceramic studies in particular, is no exception. Shepard (1956, 3) saw three phases: (i) the study of whole vessels as culture-objects; (ii) the study of sherds as dating evidence for stratigraphic sequences; and (iii) the study of pottery technology as a way of relating more closely to the potter; but she did not try to put dates to them. Matson (1984, 30) applied two of Willey and Sabloff's (1974) phases – the Classificatory-Historical Period (1914–60) and the Explanatory Period (1960 onwards) – to American ceramic studies. Van der Leeuw (1984, 710–18) saw three phases: the typological (up to 1965), the 'three levels of research' (1965–80, continuing the previous tradition, with a 'micro' level below it and a 'macro' level above it) and the 'study of the cultural element' (1980 onwards).

Here we attempt to draw together these views by setting the history of ceramic studies into three broad phases: (i) the art-historical, (ii) the typological, and (iii) the contextual, admitting that the last is characterised mainly by its diversity of approach, encompassing studies of technology, ethnoarchaeology, questions of style and problems of change (or the lack of it) in ceramics, all approached from widely-differing viewpoints. These phases can be seen to move in step with changes in the scale at which pottery is studied, from whole pots (art-historical) to sherds (typological) to a whole range of scales, from the microscopic detail of fabric to the inter-comparison of whole assemblages, not just of ceramics but of all artefacts (contextual). The splendid but elusive term 'ceramic ecology' was coined (Matson 1965, 202) to describe this holistic cradle-to-grave (or dust-to-dust, see van der Leeuw 1984, 707) approach to pottery. In our view, progress since then has been uneven, with study at the broadest level (the assemblage) lagging behind progress at other levels, partly due to the lack of the necessary methodological tools; one purpose of this book is to try to redress the balance.

We do not try to impose a rigid 'Three-Age system', like a latter-day Thomsen, but see a regional pattern of development, with new ideas being adopted at different times alongside the old ones, which are rarely totally rejected but subsumed into a wider approach. Progress is often patchy, even within a single organisation. In Britain, for example, many field archaeologists seem still to be in the typological phase, demanding 'dates' and little else from their ceramicist colleagues. We are writing this book in the hope that it will be read by at least some of them.

Four related topics have provided inputs into archaeological ceramic studies at various stages of their development – ethnography, technology, archaeometry and quantification. Ethnographic pottery studies, although existing alongside archaeological studies for some time, only 'came in from the cold' when archaeologists moved away from the typological approach and began to look at pottery in a wider context (p. 16). Archaeometry, by contrast, has been able to contribute information at all stages, from technical studies of, for example, Greek figured pottery (p. 18) to the identification of the source of a particular ware (p. 19), to a wide range of scientific techniques aimed at a wide range of questions (p. 18). Quantification has been something of a poor relation in this family. While acknowledging, at least implicitly, the need to quantify assemblages before they can be properly compared (for example for seriation or for distributional studies), archaeologists have often failed to grasp the theoretical issues that lie behind the debate over the choice of a measure of ceramic quantity, preferring practical arguments – Is it easy to do? Does it give the answer I want? – and gut feeling. We shall try to make a reasoned assessment (chapter 13.4), bringing in the results of our latest research. The place of each of these topics in the history of ceramic studies is shown in table 1.1, and will be discussed in more detail later

Table 1.1. *Summary of main phases and themes in the study of archaeological
ceramics*

Phase	Art-historical	Typological	Contextual
Date	1500 +	1880 +	1960 +
Scale	whole pots	sherds	microscopic to assemblages
Parallel theme	archaeometry	archaeometry	archaeometry
	technology	quantification	ethnography
		technology	quantification
			technology

in this chapter. Our views on their potential value will be set out in chapter 2.

The art-historical phase
Written evidence of interest in excavated pottery goes back to at least the
fifteenth century. Ebendorfer (d. 1464) described prehistoric pots found at
Stockerau as man-made objects, countering the common views that they
were 'magic crocks' that had grown in the ground or had been made in
mines by gnomes (Sklenář 1983, 16). In 1587 Petrus Albinus excavated
prehistoric vessels in the Meissen area to gather evidence that they were
man-made, and published them in what has been called 'the first proper
excavation report in prehistoric archaeology' (Sklenář 1983, 38; referring to
Albinus 1589). In 1603 John Stow described pots he had acquired from the
Roman cemetery at Spitalfields, London in 1576 (Stow 1603). In the seventeenth century, attention seems to be focussed on burial urns (e.g. Browne
1658; van Mellen 1679), perhaps because of interest in attitudes towards
death at various times, rather than in the pottery in its own right. The
eighteenth century was the great age of the collector, with Etruscan, Greek
and Roman 'vases' coming to the fore. Following an early treatise by
Groevius and Gronovius (1694), there were many publications of individual
vessels or collections, of which perhaps the grandest was by Hamilton
(1766). Emphasis was on admiration of the artistry and techniques of the
pottery, and on interpretation of classical scenes.
    Interest in 'sepulchral' pottery continued through this period (see, for
example, Weber 1719; Litzel 1749; Colt Hoare 1812); towards the end of the
eighteenth century and more especially in the nineteenth century, it
broadened out into a more general interest in pottery of various periods and
sources. Local pride seems to have stimulated an early interest in the history
of Italian maiolica (Passeri 1752) and in 'gallo-Roman' pottery in France,
starting with Grignon (1774) and Grivaux de la Vincelle (1807). In Britain,
finds of Roman pottery from London were published in 1787 (Combe and
Jackson 1787; see fig. 1.1) and 1832 (Kempe 1832) and from other major

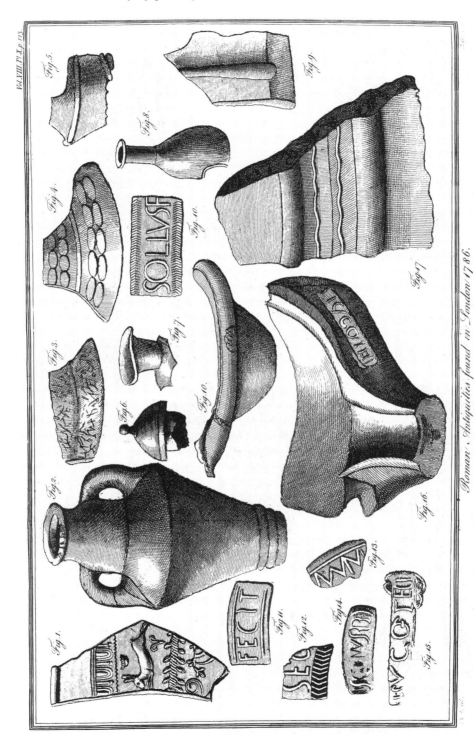

Fig. 1.1. Examples of early illustrations of excavated pottery (from Combe and Jackson 1787)

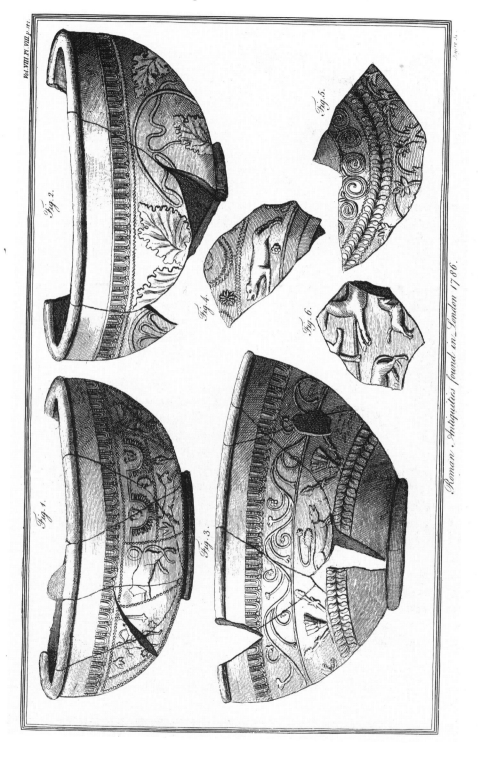

towns from the 1840s onwards (e.g. Shortt 1841) and the same can be said of Germany (Lauchert 1845).

The emphasis was still very much on the 'fine' wares rather than the 'coarse' wares, but as evidence accumulated through the nineteenth century, attempts were made to draw developments together and produce coherent histories (e.g. Birch 1858; Garnier 1880) and popular handbooks (e.g. Binns 1898).

The study of post-classical European domestic ceramics was slower to develop. At first, only decorated medieval floor tiles were thought worthy of attention, for example in England (Hennicker 1796) and France (de Caumont 1850), and as late as 1910 the pottery of the period was thought to have little to offer: 'to the ceramic historian they [the decorative tiles] supplied enlightening evidence that could tell us more about the capabilities of the early potter than any earthen vessel of the same period' (Solon 1910, 602). Early studies of tiles generally referred to a single building, but general histories started to appear in the second half of the nineteenth century (e.g. Amé 1859). Except for German stoneware (see von Hefner and Wolf 1850 for the first illustrations and Dornbusch 1873 for the first serious study), European medieval pottery received relatively little attention until the twentieth century, from the archaeologist Dunning in the 1930s (Hurst 1982) and the art-historian Rackham (1948). Before them, 'early English' pottery usually referred to material suitable for collecting from the seventeenth and eighteenth centuries (see Church 1870), and it was usually regarded as rather quaint in comparison with the dominant position of porcelain (Hobson 1903, xv).

Outside Europe and the Mediterranean, attention was directed to 'Oriental' wares, mainly Chinese and Japanese. After an era of collecting, attempts at historical accounts were provided for China by Julien (1856) and Japan by Noritané (1876–9). An interesting approach to the question of trade in Chinese ceramics was provided by Hirth (1888), who by studying the historical records of Chinese trade dispelled various myths, for example about the origins of Celadon ware.

Study of the early pottery of the United States began in the late eighteenth to mid nineteenth century, often as part of surveys of the monuments and antiquities of particular regions, for example by Squier and Davis (1848), but also in their own right (e.g. Schoolcraft 1847). An advance was marked by the foundation of the Bureau of American Ethnology in 1879 and some particularly valuable work by Holmes (1886). Work in the rest of the Americas progressed in parallel and alongside exploration, for example in Central America (de Waldek 1838) and South America (Falbe 1843).

The typological phase

As excavations in France, Germany and Britain produced ever-increasing amounts of pottery, especially samian wares, pressure for classification must have grown, if only as a means of coping with the sheer quantities involved. A very early example is Smith's 'embryonic samian form and figure type-series' (Rhodes 1979, 89, referring to Smith 1854). Coarse wares were also considered at this early date: Cochet (1860) attempted to classify pottery in order to date burials: his work was dismissed because 'the terra-cotta pot ... remains stationary' (Solon 1910, 83). Pottier (1867) made a simple classification of Norman pottery of the thirteenth to fifteenth centuries.

The typological phase can really be said to start in the 1880s, at the same time as Pitt-Rivers was developing his typological approach to other classes of artefact (Pitt-Rivers 1906, based on a lecture of 1874). To come to grips with vast amounts of material from Lezoux, Plique (1887) devised a classificatory system for the pottery, setting a trend for the corpus of samian ware type-series (e.g. Dragendorff 1895; Déchelette 1904; Ludowici 1904; Knorr 1906; Walters 1908) which continues to this day. The other side of the coin – the relationship of pottery to stratigraphic sequences – seems to start at about the same time, for example in Flinders Petrie's work at Lachish, Palestine (Petrie 1891), where he observed Phoenician, Jewish, Greek, Seleucid and Roman pottery in successive strata. The first distribution map of a class of pottery finds appears to be by Abercromby (1904), although a more general map showing find spots of Roman pottery in London had been produced as early as 1841 (Craik, in Knight 1841).

In the United States, this phase can be said to start with Kidder's excavations at Pecos (1915–29) and his integration of stratigraphy, regional survey and ceramics (Kidder 1924; 1931). This work was a model for much that was to follow, through to the 1960s (e.g. Colton 1953; Griffin 1950–4; and many others).

The emphasis in this phase was on vertical (chronological) and regional spatial distributions, with pots (or, more usually, sherds) being treated as type-fossils in a thoroughly geological manner that harked right back to Smith (1816). The vertical emphasis was inevitable, given that pottery was one of the main, and certainly the most abundant, sources of dating evidence, at a time when archaeological attention was focussed on cultural history and development (see for example Wheeler 1954, 40–61; fig. 1.2). The 'horizontal' studies served two purposes:

(i) to tie together sequences found at related sites in a region to form a master chronological sequence. This would enable any absolute dates determined from one site (for example through inscriptions, documentary evidence, and so on) to be transferred to other sites in the master sequence ('cross-dating', first used by Petrie in the 1880s (Petrie 1904, 141–5)).

(ii) to help define cultural areas, using the sort of definition provided by Childe ('We find certain types of remains – pots, implements, ornaments, burial rites, house forms – constantly recurring

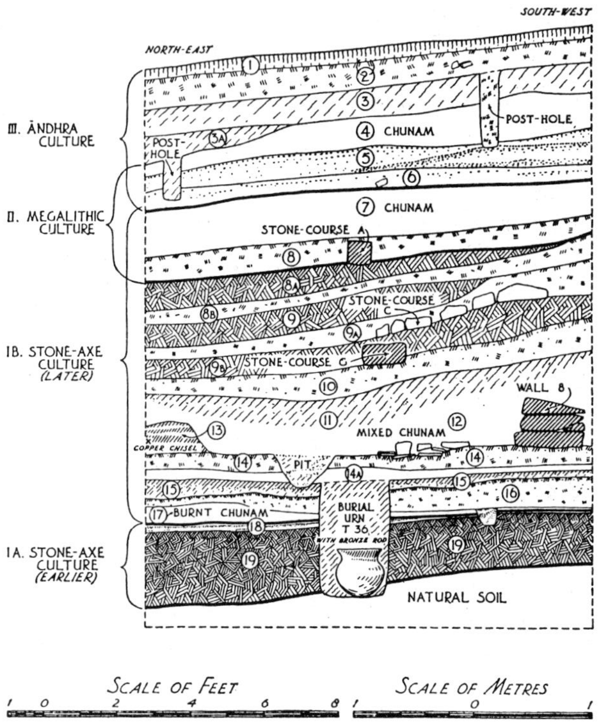

LAYER	I. STONE AXE	II. MEGALITHIC	III. ANDHRA
1	..	..	52, including 1 yellow-painted sherd
2	..	..	384, including 10 yellow-painted sherds
3	..	..	480, including 68 yellow-painted and 1 rouletted sherd
3a	..	..	67
4	..	36	269, including 51 yellow-painted sherds
5	..	68	219, including 10 yellow-painted sherds[1]
6	26	115	405, including 7 yellow-painted sherds
7	63	407	
8	150	199[2]	
8a	36	..	
8b	89	..	
9	76	..	
9a	196	..	
10	46	..	
11	33	..	
12	23	..	
13	26	..	
14	48	..	
14a	15	..	
15	198	..	
16	7	..	
17	45	..	
18	25	..	
19	321[3]	..	

Fig. 1.2. The vertical emphasis of the typological phase. Deep stratification (left) combined with counts of sherds of different types from successive layers. (Wheeler 1954, figs. 9 and 10)

together. Such a complex of regularly associated traits we shall term a 'cultural group. or just a 'culture'.' (Childe 1929, vi)). In Childe's view, many other classes of artefact had to be taken into account, but in practice pottery often had a dominant rôle.

The main methodological tool for the chronological task was seriation (see p. 189). It was created as a way of ordering grave-groups from cemeteries with little or no stratigraphy, using the presence or absence of artefact types in each group (Petrie 1899). The idea that this approach could be applied to surface collections of sherds was suggested by Kroeber (1916) and implemented by Spier (1917). At about the same time (Nelson 1916), it was observed that the proportions of types in successive layers of a stratigraphic sequence tended to follow regular patterns ('percentage stratigraphy'). The idea that such patterns had a cultural interpretation seems to have come later (e.g. Ford and Quimby 1945), and the use of seriation as a formal tool for recreating cultural chronologies from percentage data (usually sherds) in the partial or total absence of stratigraphy followed (e.g. Ritchie and MacNeish 1949, 118), culminating in Ford's manual on the subject (Ford 1962). At this stage, proportions were based on sherd counts; this reflects partly the nature of the collections but partly the lack of serious consideration of the alternatives. Ford (1962, 38) defended the use of sherd counts, dismissing other possible approaches as 'purist'. We shall return to this point when we look at the theme of quantification (p. 21). In Europe, the main use of seriation seems to have continued to be to order grave-groups or other 'closed' groups (e.g. Doran 1971; Goldmann 1972). Theoretical inputs came from Brainerd (1951) and Robinson (1951), followed by Dempsey and Baumhoff (1963), and the theory was integrated by a return to Petrie's work and a mathematical study which showed the equivalence of the two main approaches then in use (Kendall 1971). In the 1970s, attention turned to the appropriateness of the theory for real archaeological problems (Dunnell 1970; Cowgill 1972; McNutt 1973) and the topic was thoroughly reviewed by Marquardt (1978). Both the mathematical aspects (e.g. Laxton 1987; 1993) and the archaeological aspects (e.g. Carver 1985) continued to develop.

But above all, this was the age of the 'type', although the term was given subtly different meanings on each side of the Atlantic. Common to both was a belief that types were more than just a convenient way of sub-dividing material. Once created they could be ordered, according to ideas of 'development', and used to demonstrate chronological sequences. Such arguments could easily become circular, and were gradually replaced as more direct (for example, stratigraphic) evidence became available. In the Americas, the idea that sherds could, and indeed should, be sorted into types, goes back to before 1920 (Kidder and Kidder 1917) and was well-established by the 1930s (Colton and Hargraves 1937). The definition of a type was usually as later formalised, for example by Gifford (1960, 341), 'a specific kind of pottery embodying a unique combination of recognizably distinct attributes'. As more work was done and more and more types were defined, it became apparent that, although resulting in much economy of thought and presentation (Krieger 1944, 284), a single-tier classificatory system was inadequate (Ford 1954). A two-tier system of 'type' and 'variety' was proposed and widely adopted (Krieger 1944; Gifford 1960), although sometimes with a different nomenclature (Phillips 1958). Above these levels, more theoretical cross-cutting groupings of types (for example sequence, series, ceramic type cluster and ceramic system – see Wheat et al. 1958) were proposed, but were generally more contentious. An alternative approach based on 'modes' was put forward by Rouse (1939; 1960); they were defined as 'either (1) concepts of material, shape or decoration to which the artisan conformed or (2) customary procedures followed in making and using the artefacts' (Rouse 1960, 315). He suggested that an 'analytic' classification, to extract modes from attributes, should precede a 'taxonomic' classification which would define types in terms of modes, not of attributes (pp. 315–16).

In Europe, by contrast, the term 'type' was often used implicitly to mean a form type, and commonly defined in terms of the shape of a 'typical' pot. In other words, types were often defined in terms of their centres rather than their boundaries. This can be linked to the development of modern conventions for drawing pottery (Dragendorff 1895; Günther 1901). A tradition grew up of using an excavator's drawing numbers as 'types', even if the author never claimed them as such. One very widely-used series was Gillam's one of Roman pots from northern Britain (Gillam 1957), which became abused as dating evidence for pots from all over Britain. More recently, a structured approach to types has returned (e.g. Fulford 1975; Lyne and Jefferies 1979).

Despite an early start to the objective description of pottery fabrics (Brongniart 1844) and some early applications (Tite 1848; de la Beche and Reeks 1855), fabric types or wares were generally named by reference to their source (real or supposed), and descriptions were often based on little more than colour, with perhaps a one-word characterisation such as 'coarse', 'fine', 'shelly' or 'vesicular'. The realisation that a single source could produce several different fabrics, possibly differing in date, led to renewed interest in the detail of fabrics, spurred on by Peacock's (1977) guide to characterisation and identification of inclusions using only a low-powered ($20 \times$) binocular microscope and simple tools (see Rhodes 1979, 84–7). A further twist to the meaning of 'type' was given by the use of the term '... type ware' to designate a sort of penumbra or fuzzy area of uncertain fabrics grouped around a known ware (for example Whitby-type ware, see Blake and Davey, 1983, 40).

A working typology based at least partly on fabric requires comprehensive descriptive systems. A surprisingly modern one was given by March (1934).

Some aspects gave more trouble than others, especially texture (Guthe 1927; Hargraves and Smith 1936; Byers 1937), which has not been entirely resolved to this day, and temper (see Shepard 1964). Coding systems have been put forward from time to time (e.g. Gillin 1938; Gardin 1958; Ericson and Stickel 1973), including ways of coding the drawings of pots (Smith 1970); perhaps not surprisingly none has gained widespread acceptance. The problems of comparability between different workers, even when using a standardised system, were highlighted by Robinson (1979).

The contextual phase

The work of Shepard (1956) can be seen as a nodal point in ceramic studies. She drew together strands then current – chronology, trade/distribution and technological development – and identified the aspects of excavated ceramics which should be studied to shed light on each of these areas (pp. 102): identification of types for chronology, identification of materials and their sources for trade, and the physical characteristics of vessels to show their place in technological development. In doing so she laid the foundation for many future studies. Much subsequent general work relies heavily on her synthesis of approaches; indeed, one of the challenges of writing this book is to avoid producing a rehash of her work.

Her book also made considerable contributions to ceramic studies in its own right, both practical and theoretical. At a practical level, there were comprehensive attempts at shape classification, based on 'characteristic point' (Shepard 1956, 227–45), drawing on the work of Birkhoff (1933) and Meyer (1888, but see Meyer 1957), and of descriptive systems for 'design' (decoration) (Shepard 1956, 255–305). The latter, drawing on work by Douglas and Reynolds (1941) and Beals et al. (1945), analysed design in terms of elements and motifs, symmetry, and motion and rhythm. On a theoretical level, she gave a detailed discussion of the uses and limitations of the concept of 'type' (Shepard 1956, 307–18). Reacting against the almost Linnaean view of typology that characterised much work from the 1920s onwards, she proposed a view of typology that is tentative rather than fixed, relies on technological features and accepts the limitations inherent in trying to classify pots on the basis of (mainly) sherds. She also repeated the warning about identifying ceramic traditions with cultural entities.

After Shepard's formative work, ceramic studies 'rode off in all directions', and it becomes increasingly difficult to take an overview of a fast-expanding subject. Attempts to maintain such a view were made by the holding of international conferences at Burg Wartenstein (Austria) in 1961 (Matson 1965) and Lhee (Holland) in 1982 (van der Leeuw and Pritchard 1984). The first was held 'to evaluate the contribution of ceramic studies to archaeological and ethnological research' (Matson 1965, vii), but also partly 'to convince many anthropologists that ceramic studies extend beyond simple description and classification' (Rouse 1965, 284). The second, intended as a follow-up twenty years after the first, had the more difficult task of holding together a subject that was expanding so fast that it was in danger of flying apart.

What were the directions in which ceramic studies were being pulled in this period? Firstly, there was the task of mopping-up resistance to progress beyond the 'sherds as culture type-fossils' attitude of the Typological Period. Typical of this approach are points made by DeVore (1968) that sherds do not actually breed, evolve, and so on, nor do they invade, and Adams' (1979) demonstration of a failure of ceramic tradition to follow known historical events. Nevertheless, pockets of the old view still persist, particularly amongst field staff in teams whose responsibility is split between fieldwork and finds work.

Secondly, a continuation of the trend towards ever-smaller physical units of study is apparent, opening out into a whole spectrum of scientific techniques. At one end we have relatively simple techniques, relying on nothing more than a low-powered binocular microscope and perhaps an algorithm for identifying inclusions (e.g. Peacock, 1977); at the other end are very intensive techniques requiring scientific and statistical expertise to exploit them fully (see scientific methods theme, p. 18).

Another important development was the realisation that the links between 'life' assemblages (pots in use) and 'death' assemblages (sherds as found or excavated) were far from simple, and could be distorted by processes of discard, site maintenance, and subsequent activity on site. Such concerns were subsumed into a wider concern for 'site formation processes' in general (Schiffer 1987), since many of the problems are common to a wide range of material.

This phase also saw serious attempts to integrate ethnographic studies (p. 15), scientific techniques (p. 18) and aspects of technology (p. 17) into mainstream pottery studies. In fact, the apparent diversity of this phase can mask a growing unity, as the way in which all these themes hang together and can support each other is gradually realised. An excellent example of a way in which these approaches can be brought together is Buko's (1981) study of early medieval pottery from Sandomierz (see fig. 1.3).

Finally, the need for standardisation has come to the fore as the need to compare sites, not just to report on each individually, has been felt more keenly. In Britain, this need has been met by semi-official reports (Young 1980; Blake and Davey 1983); in the United States, by manuals devoted entirely (e.g. Rice 1987) or partly (e.g. Joukowsky 1980, 332–401) to pottery. The French approach has been more formal (Balfet et al. 1989), following the tradition of Brongniart and Franchet.

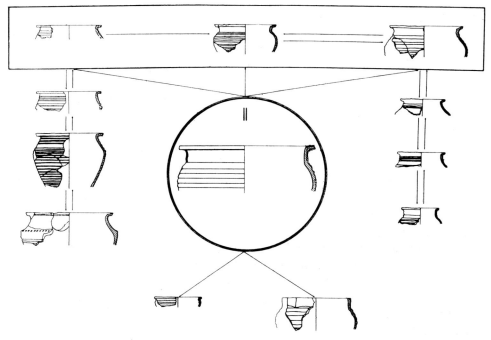

Fig. 1.3. An alternative approach to typology in the contextual phase. The *Vessel Shape Family*, which embraces an assemblage of diverse forms linked by a common set of morphological, technological and ornamental attributes. This association is repeated in the pots, no matter what their function. (Buko 1981, fig. 48 and p. 274)

Parallel themes – ethnography

A major trend is the recognition of the value of ethnographic studies in archaeological interpretation or model-building. A very early interest in the uses of pottery in historic times, chiefly as eating or drinking vessels, was provided by Le Grand d'Aussy (1782). Systematic ethnographic studies of American Indian pottery began in the 1880s (e.g. Cushing 1886); by the 1920s it had developed into a comprehensive study of the pottery production process (Guthe 1925; Linné 1925; Bunzel 1929). An early attempt to link ethnography with archaeology was made by Franchet (1911; see p. 18). Throughout the twentieth century studies were made of potting techniques in many parts of the world; it would be invidious to select from them for this brief survey. The relevance of such work to archaeology was emphasised from the 1950s onwards (Tschopik 1950; Foster 1959; Balfet 1965). In Europe, studies of kilns (as in Hampe and Winter 1962; 1965) seem to have been most taken to heart by archaeologists. Often the function of ethnographic accounts seems to be as a 'cautionary tale', either pointing out situations where pottery does not mirror broader events (Tschopik 1950; Adams 1979) or in describing a specific situation and almost challenging the archaeologist to say whether

Fig. 1.4. Pottery in art. This painting, *Peasants playing Gallet outside an inn* by Adriaen van Ostade, helped archaeologists to discover the function of some enigmatic pots from London. They were used as bird nesting boxes (inset). (Stevenson 1991). (Photo: British Museum)

and how he could detect it in the archaeological record. A good example is Papousek's (1984) account of potting strategy in a situation of debt-bondage in Los Pueblos, Mexico.

In the contextual phase, ethnoarchaeology developed as a way of using ethnographic evidence to help archaeologists examine the processes that lay between their excavated finds and the societies that produced and used them. A typical problem is the relationship between 'life' and 'death' assemblages, and how it is affected by differential breakage rates of different types (David 1972; DeBoer and Lathrap 1979). Conventional views on the archaeological study of pottery were challenged, as by David and Hennig (1972) who suggested that archaeological classification might be more detailed than the material warranted. This phase was excellently described by Arnold (1985).

Although not usually regarded as ethnographic evidence, the large amounts of contemporary written evidence for potting in historic periods has contributed to questions ranging from the organisation and methods of pottery production (Le Patourel 1968; Peacock 1982) to the ultimate uses of the pots (Moorhouse 1978). The representation of pottery in art (fig. 1.4) was also seen as giving useful evidence, both of date (one of the earliest studies of British medieval pottery concerned its date as suggested by illustrations in dated manuscripts, see Jewitt 1878) and of function (Jacobs and Peremans 1976).

Parallel themes – technology

As well as the artistic side of ceramics, evidence for its manufacture created interest from the seventeenth century onwards. Conyers observed Roman pottery kilns during the preparatory work for the building of the new St Paul's Cathedral in London (Conyers 1675; 1677) and produced a remarkably accurate account and drawings (Marsh 1978, 195). Pottery kilns in the Nene valley of eastern England were published early in the nineteenth century (Artis 1823), and the vast fineware- (especially samian-) producing sites of France and Germany began to be excavated and published in the nineteenth century – Montans (Rossignol 1862), Westendorf (von Hefner 1862), Lezoux (Plique 1887), La Graufesenque (Hermet 1934) and Rheinzabern (Ludowici 1904). At the end of the century a gazetteer of seventy Roman potters' kilns in France could be produced (Blanchet 1899). The study of kilns continued to be developed and systematised right through to the 1970s (Musty 1974; Swan 1984), although by this date the importance of studying related structures and functions (which had been badly neglected) was being stressed (Musty 1974, 57). Study of kilns as structures led to interest in the firing process (e.g. Colton 1939) and to series of experimental firings of both pottery kilns (Mayes 1961; 1962; Coleman-Smith 1971; Bryant 1977) and tile kilns (Greene and Johnson 1978).

Early interest in the technology of the pots themselves concentrated on the 'high-tech' questions of how certain very fine wares were made. Brongniart (1844) analysed the material of Greek black gloss pottery, but unfortunately made an error which was not put right for nearly a century (Binns and Frazer 1929). The study of such approaches has continued with an ever-increasing range of scientific techniques (Bimson 1956; Matson 1981). It developed in two other directions:

(i) an interest in technology in its own right as an indicator of social progress (in which pottery played a relatively minor part), represented by Scott (1954), Richter (1956) and Jope (1956),

(ii) after a sporadic early interest (e.g. Greenwell 1877), a broadening-out into the technology of all types of pottery, under the influence of ethnographic work (p. 15), starting perhaps with Franchet (1911). This remarkable set of collected lectures foreshadowed much of what was to be presented by Shepard (1956). He studied the 'primitive' (that is pre-industrial) production processes from the selection of clay to the firing of pots, using both chemical and physical analyses to answer questions that had been a matter of speculation. Although to some extent a product of its time (a strong belief in unilinear evolution and 'progress' shows through in places), this is in many ways a very modern book, and one wonders what its influence would have been if it had been published in English. This approach accelerated from the 1950s (Matson 1951; Weaver 1963; Matson 1966; van der Leeuw 1976; Howard and Morris 1980; Moorhouse 1981), including the work of professional potters (Rye 1981) and the study of ceramic building materials (Drury 1981). As technology was seen more and more in its social setting, the processes which bring about or hinder change came under focus (Nicklin 1971; Blake 1980; Orton 1985b).

Scientific methods have played an increasing role in the study of the manufacture of archaeological pottery. Thin-sectioning was shown to be able to indicate technical differences (for example hand- versus wheel-throwing) (Hodges 1962), and later X-ray methods were used for the same purpose (Rye 1977). Thermal expansion was used to estimate firing temperature (Roberts 1963) and experiments with the scanning electron microscope (SEM) (Tite and Maniatis 1975) have shown that it can help to answer a wide range of technological questions.

Parallel themes – scientific methods

Scientific techniques have been of especial use in three areas of ceramic studies – dating, sourcing (provenance studies) and the study of function. They have also made contributions to the study of site formation processes and in the study of ceramic technology and manufacture (p. 17). The extent to which they have permeated at least the thinking, if not always the practice, of mainstream pottery studies, is shown by the extensive list of techniques given by Blake and Davey (1983, 13–22).

Dating

Ceramics were only marginally involved in the 'radiocarbon revolution' of the 1950s and 1960s, rarely having an organic content that could form a basis for ^{14}C dating. However, the potential for extracting remains of organic inclusions (such as crushed charcoal) from low-fired pottery was recognised by Evans and Meggers (1962); this approach has continued to be very useful within its limited circumstances (for example rice husks yielding dates for Thai pottery, Glover 1990, 155).

For a scientific technique suited for dating a wide range of ceramic material we have to wait until the arrival of thermoluminescence (TL) in the late 1950s (Kennedy and Knopff 1960; Tite and Waine 1961). The development of the application of the TL method to ceramics at Oxford was a story of attempts to overcome a series of problems (Fleming 1966; 1970; 1979). Further problems arose from the demands it made on excavation techniques. A more recent technique, optically-stimulated luminescence (OSL) (Huntley et al. 1985) may well replace it in time. An excellent description of both techniques is given by Aitken (1990). The use of remanent magnetism for dating was suggested by Folgheraiter in 1899 but its application requires too many assumptions to be generally useful (Aitken 1958).

Provenance studies

The idea that one could obtain information on the source of pottery by studying the physical or chemical properties of the clay or temper goes back at least a century, but underwent a long period of gestation before emerging as a useful group of techniques in the 1960s. This was probably because of the prevailing belief that coarse wares were not traded over any distance, and therefore had to be locally made, while the sources of fine wares were best determined by other methods, such as stylistic analysis.

The first techniques to be used were petrographic ones, looking at the filler rather than the clay – thin-sectioning (Bamps 1883), gravimetric methods (Jenkins 1908) and heavy mineral analysis (Oakley 1933). Although successful in their aims, the last two failed to become popular, because they were very time-consuming. However, Peacock (1967) recommended heavy mineral analysis for answering very specific questions. The breakthrough came in the 1930s with Shepard's large-scale application of thin-sectioning to discover the origins of Rio Grande glaze-paint pottery (Shepard 1942), which showed the long distances across which coarse wares could be traded. Thin-sectioning started to become popular in the 1930s in America (e.g. Gladwin 1937), Britain (e.g. Liddell 1932, 175) and continental Europe (Obenauer 1936).

Compositional techniques were later to arrive, and have proved especially useful for discrimination problems (assigning 'new' ceramics to one of two or more 'known' groups). X-ray diffraction spectroscopy (XRD) was used inconclusively by Drier (1939), and apparently successfully by Young and Whitmore (1957), who also suggested the use of X-ray fluorescence spectroscopy (XRF). With the successful use of XRF on Mycenaean and Minoan pottery (Catling et al. 1961), it gained an ascendance over XRD, which was however recommended for high-fired pottery such as porcelain and stoneware (Bimson 1969). Neutron activation analysis (NAA) was another product of this fruitful period, and was also first used on Mediterranean pottery (Sayre and Dobson 1957) and later on mesoamerican pottery (Sayre et al. 1958) and samian ware (Emeleus 1960). Other techniques of this group are optical emission spectroscopy (OES), used first on Roman mortaria (Richards 1959) and later on Mycenaean and Minoan pottery (Catling et al. 1963) and atomic absorption spectroscopy (AAS) (Hughes et al. 1976). The latest technique in this family is inductively coupled plasma emission spectroscopy (ICP) (Hart and Adams 1983). The uses of compositional techniques have been regularly reviewed (e.g. Millett and Catling 1967; Peacock 1970; Wilson 1978; Bishop et al. 1982; Bishop et al. 1990). Early reviews concentrated on presenting and explaining the new techniques, while later ones have concentrated on the problems of a maturing discipline, such as comparability between differing sources of data.

Functional studies

The earliest approach to the study of function was the assumption that it was in some way linked to the original name for a form. The first attempt we have traced (Baif 1536) was in error, but a tradition persisted for centuries of using such terms, especially for classical pottery, for example *olla*, *lagena*, but also for post-medieval British pottery (for example *tyg*; see Celoria and Kelly 1973, 15). Ethnographic parallels seemed for a time to be a way out (p. 15), but doubt has been thrown by studies showing how very similar forms can have different functions (e.g. Miller 1985). Four ways to make progress have been suggested:

(i)   to examine the associations of pottery types with the stratigraphic features in which they were found (Millett 1979a); we shall return to this topic in chapter 13.

(ii)   to examine the residues of original contents or surface treatments. An early example is by van Bastelaar (1877), who found sixty quotations from Latin writers about organic coatings – pitch, oil, wax, and so on – on ceramics and attempted to verify them experimentally. A recent review of the study of visible residues is given by Moorhouse (1986, 110–1). A new development is the use of gas chromatography to identify residues extracted from the fabric itself (Evans 1983–4).

(iii)   to examine the physical properties of pottery fabrics to assess their suitability for various functions, such as cooking (Steponaitis 1984; Bronitsky and Hamer 1986).

(iv)   to examine wear marks on pots (Griffiths 1978; Hally 1983), and of sooting on both exterior and interior (Moorhouse 1986, 108–10).

Parallel themes – quantification

We here use the term 'quantification' in a precise and restricted sense, to mean the measuring of the amount of each type of pottery in an assemblage, with a view to describing the assemblage in terms of the proportions of each type present. As a concept, it belongs firmly to the 'typological' phase, being a *sine qua non* of all attempts to seriate pottery assemblages (except those based on the presence or absence of types, but this approach is usually only applied to grave groups). But equally firmly, in this phase it was not an issue, as study in this phase was at the level of the sherd, so one simply counted sherds, and based analyses such as seriation on the percentages of sherds in assemblages.

With the contextual phase comes the idea that other measures of the amount of pottery might be more appropriate. The first alternative was weight (Gifford 1951), followed by number of vessels represented (Burgh 1959), vessel-equivalents (the idea can be found in Bloice 1971 and Egloff 1973, the term was coined in Orton 1975; see below for definition), surface area (Glover 1972, 93–6; Hulthén 1974) and displacement volume (Hinton 1977). The last two are very similar to weight, and need no explanation; the term 'vessel-equivalent' may be less familiar. Starting from the idea that every sherd is a certain proportion of the whole pot of which it once formed part, we can (in theory) assign these proportions to sherds as 'scores' and add them up to find the total amount of a type. Since a whole pot has a score of 1, we can say that a group of sherds with a total score of x is equivalent to x pots (x is usually not a whole number). In practice it is not usually possible to assign a score to every sherd, and one is restricted to sherds such as rim sherds whose size in terms of the proportion of some whole (in this instance a complete rim) can be measured. Since we are sampling the measurable sherds from an assemblage, we refer to the *estimated* vessel-equivalent (abbreviated to *eve*). This concept has been misunderstood at times and will be explained in more detail in chapter 13.

Once there was more than one measure, attempts were made to compare them (Baumhoff and Heizer 1959; Solheim 1960). Glover (1972, 96), comparing sherd count, weight and surface area, concluded that 'any one would be quite accurate as a measure of frequency'. Hinton (1977) compared sherd count, rim sherd count, weight and displacement volume, concluding that weight was the fastest but sherd count probably the most accurate measure, but of what it is not clear. Millett (1979b) compared sherd count, weight, adjusted weight (an estimate of surface area) and minimum number of vessels; he concluded that they were all highly correlated but, for practical reasons, weight was probably the best. Chase (1985) examined the relationships between sherd count and vessels experimentally, but did not take into account the incompleteness of excavated assemblages. The development of our view can be traced in a series of papers (Orton 1975; Orton 1982; Orton and Tyers 1990). These studies have ruled out sherd count and number of pots as biased, and favour eves (where practicable) with weight as a respectable but less useful measure. The arguments will be presented in chapter 13.

Another point that emerged is that two measures together give more information than the two separately. It was first made, in the context of count and weight, by Solheim (1960), and developed by Bradley and Fulford (1980), Orton (1985a) and Schiffer (1987, 282). Such approaches are especially useful in the study of site formation processes (p. 14).

Finally, we can see developing interest in integrating ceramics into a wide analysis of finds assemblages. The approach depends on the nature of the other finds and the way they are recorded, whether in bulk (for example bones) or individually (such as 'small finds'). The former was tackled by Vince (1977), but the latter had to wait until the 'pie-slice' approach (Tyers and Orton 1991; see chapter 13). This must be the next step in ceramic studies: having integrated the various aspects of ceramic studies in the 'contextual' phase (1960–90 and after), we must now begin to integrate ceramic studies into the wider field of general finds assemblages.

2

THE POTENTIAL OF POTTERY AS ARCHAEOLOGICAL EVIDENCE

Aims

The aims of this chapter are to look at the archaeological uses made of pottery in the various phases of study described in chapter 1, to see which have stood the test of time, to point the reader forward to chapters that will deal with such themes in more detail (Part III) and to provide a general rationale for the practical approaches described in Part II. Clearly, not all assemblages, or even all sites, will yield evidence of all the types to be described below.

Discernment is needed to know what sort of questions can reasonably be asked of a particular group of pottery – this is best (perhaps only) learnt by experience but we hope that the theoretical discussions of Part III will help the reader to avoid the twin pitfalls of under- and over-interpretation. It is nevertheless true that when excavating and recording pottery we do not know *all* the questions that are likely to be asked of it, and that therefore some ideas of 'good standard practice' in recording and summarising pottery assemblages are very useful, although they may be augmented by special information to meet special needs. Such ideas we hope to provide in Part II, without giving the reader the claustrophobic feeling of a rigid fixed system for all times and all places. We should make it clear before starting that just because an idea belongs to an earlier phase of study, or paradigm, that does not mean it is of no use to today's worker.

The 'big three' – evidence for date, trade and function or status

If you ask archaeologists in an unguarded moment what they use pottery for (or why excavated pottery is kept and not thrown on the spoil-heap) they will probably reply 'for dating evidence'. If you give them more time, or ask someone who has worked with pottery or at least read about it, they will probably come up with three types of evidence that one could reasonably expect to obtain from excavated pottery:

(i) dating evidence.
(ii) distributional evidence, for example relating to trade.
(iii) evidence for function and/or status.

These are based on the obvious facts that every pot was (i) made or used at a certain time; (ii) made at a certain place; and (iii) used for a certain purpose or purposes. The interesting question is how much we can glean about (i) when,

(ii) where and (iii) for what, from a handful of mute sherds. We shall look at these questions in detail in chapters 14, 15 and 16 respectively. To some extent, these questions pose more basic ones about (i) how was a pot made?; (ii) of what was it made; and (iii) what shape was it?, which we shall consider in chapters 10, 11 and 12 respectively. In chapter 13 we set out the theory we need in order to be able to describe, discuss and compare assemblages rather than individual pots, and finally in chapter 17 we look at what can happen to pots after their useful life is over – the problems this can cause and the information it can give. But first a preliminary look at each of our 'big three' uses.

Pottery as dating evidence

Pots vary. Contrary to Solon (1910; see p. 9) the terra-cotta pot does *not* remain stationary. At any site, the pots in use vary over time in terms of how they were made, of what they were made, for what they were used, probably where they were made and certainly by whom they were made. Such differences will be reflected in the fabric, form, technology and decoration of the sherds excavated from different contexts.

At an empirical level, we can build up a picture of how these aspects vary by studying the co-occurrences of different types or characteristics in different contexts – this is known as seriation (p. 189) and enables us to create a sequence of relative dates. To provide absolute dates, we need to find 'fixed points' in the sequence from other sources of evidence, such as documentary (including coins, which are a special sort of document) (p. 187) or from scientific techniques, usually applied to material other than the pottery (for example ^{14}C or dendrochronology), which has to be carefully related to the pottery sequence (p. 189). Interpolation between the fixed points will probably be needed.

At a more theoretical level, we may perhaps observe developmental trends within such sequences. In the early days of the typological phase, material was sometimes ordered according to supposed trends of development, which were given chronological significance. Generally, such trends were seen in terms of 'improvement' or 'increasing complexity' and can with hindsight be linked to nineteenth- and early twentieth-century beliefs in 'progress'. Today it is clear that pottery manufacture in stable external circumstances does not automatically 'improve' (whatever that may mean). A well-known example is the history of the successive samian ware industries of Roman Gaul – South Gaulish, Central Gaulish and East Gaulish (see Johns 1977). Within each industry there is a trend of declining standards, so that 'by the beginning of the second century, South Gaulish ware had become very poor and unattractive' (Johns 1977, 23), and 'exports [of Central Gaulish ware] end at the end of the second century, but inferior samian continues to be made [in Central Gaul] in the third century' (p. 25), and again 'The standard [of East Gaulish ware] declined steadily until . . . the moulded ware had become very crude and primitive' (p. 26). Looked at in a wider perspective, the picture is of long-term decline (over at least 200 years), punctuated by bursts of improvement as a rival source area picks up the role of principal exporter.

Even if a developmental sequence can be established, there is no guarantee that it progressed at a steady rate. Recent application of catastrophe theory (Renfrew and Cooke 1979) shows that sudden changes may punctuate long periods of relative stability, triggered off by apparently minor external factors. An example of this sort of change (in this case an anastrophe, or 'good' catastrophe) is the 'explosion' of the black-burnished ware industry (BB1) of Roman Britain around the year AD 120 (see Farrar 1973; Peacock 1982, 85). Until that date, BB1 was a purely local industry of central southern England, producing hand-made pottery, fired in simple kilns, in a tradition that went back at least 100 years to the late pre-Roman Iron Age. After that date, BB1 is found in large quantities on both civil and military sites across most of Roman Britain, as far north as Hadrian's Wall (500km from the source). Despite widespread copying of its forms by potters using the wheel (the BB2 industries), BB1 remains in the hand-made tradition and in fact outlasts its more sophisticated competitors.

The possible role of the individual innovator should not be overlooked. In documented cases, such as the Andokides painter's part in the introduction of Athenian red-figure ware in the sixth century BC (Boardman 1975, 15), this role can clearly be seen; in undocumented situations it would obviously be much harder to identify. The extent to which innovators are part of their social setting and the extent to which they stand outside it is a thorny question.

Finally, there is the interesting question of how precise can we expect dates provided by pottery to be? If we could set a theoretical limit to the precision, even under ideal circumstances (by analogy with the $\pm$ attached to ^{14}C dates), we would know which chronological questions it was possible to answer from the evidence of pottery, and which it was not, and potentially avoid the angst of asking questions that can never be answered. Some work has been done on the life-spans of pottery of different types (p. 207) and to this source of uncertainty must be added the uncertainty about the date of manufacture. Bringing these two factors together for Romano-British pottery of the first to second century (considered to be among the best-dated periods) has suggested a minimum margin of error of twenty to thirty years that must be attached to any one pot; the margin attached to an assemblage decreases as the quantity of pottery increases (Orton and Orton 1975). It seemed that the better a type could be dated, the greater the life-expectancy of pots of that type, so that the overall margin of doubt remained the same – a sort of chronological analogy of the Uncertainty Principle of physics or Murphy's Law of everyday life.

Pottery as evidence of trade

Pots also move about. They may be manufactured at a production centre and traded in their own right over greater or lesser distances, they may be traded as containers for wine, foodstuffs (for example sardines; see Wheeler and Locker 1985), fuel (such as oil; see Moorhouse 1978, 115) or other material (for example mercury; see Foster 1963, 80), they may be exchanged as gifts or brought back as souvenirs from travels (Davey and Hodges 1983, 10). Documentary evidence can shed light on unexpected aspects of 'trade'; as shown by this extract from a letter from John to Margaret Paston, dated 1479: 'Please it you to know that I send you . . . 3 pots of Genoa treacle, as my apothecary sweareth to me, and moreover that they were never opened since they came from Genoa' (Davis 1971, 512). Much information is potentially contained in the geographical distribution of pots, but to gain access to it we must be able to identify the source from which particular pots come. This will usually involve study of the fabric, and especially of the inclusions in the clay (p. 138).

A whole spectrum of approaches is possible here, from simple visual observation with no more equipment than a low-powered binocular micro-scope to the latest scientific techniques for physical and chemical analysis (p. 144). There is a delicate trade-off between the two ends. Some questions (for example of sourcing clays with only sedimentary tempering) may need very sophisticated techniques, but the overall rôle of techniques that can only, because of cost, be used on a very small proportion of an assemblage, must be in doubt. The uses to which such techniques can be put are varied; apart from the obvious ones of sourcing clay or temper there are also technological questions that can be answered.

It is tempting to link particularly distinctive forms with their source, if known, but this can be misleading since at many periods forms were copied from one production centre to another. Indeed, the very success of the products of one centre may lead to the copying of particular forms by other centres. It is therefore important that those responsible for excavating pro-duction centres should be able to characterise their products so that they can readily be identified elsewhere, and equally unfortunate that the sheer quanti-ties of waster pottery often found at such sites can easily overwhelm the excavator, delaying or even preventing the dissemination of important infor-mation.

If we are able to identify the sources of most of the pottery from a site, we need to consider how different modes of distribution may affect the propor-tions of pottery from different sources at this and neighbouring sites (fig. 2.1). Sites cannot be studied in isolation for this sort of analysis. We need to build or find models for distribution by various modes (for example through local markets, by travelling pack-men, by consumers collecting pots from pro-duction centres, by centres dedicated to supplying a particular site, and so

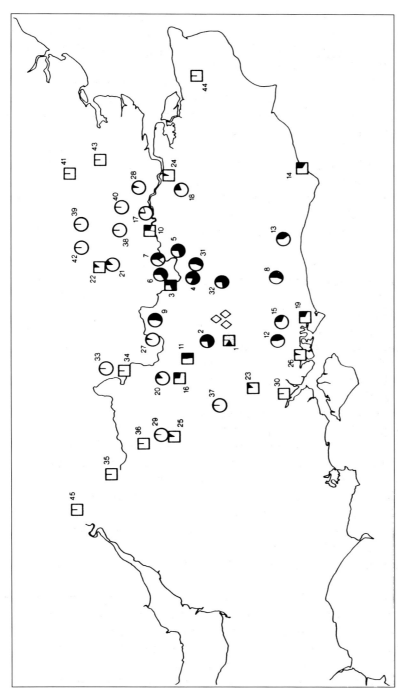

Fig. 2.1   Diagram to show proportions of pottery from the Alice Holt kilns found on different sites in south-east England in the period 270–420 AD (Lyne and Jefferies 1979, fig. 47). The shaded zones show the proportion of Alice Holt ware at each site. The kiln site is shown as lozenges.

on), and compare them with our data. This lies within the province of spatial analysis (Hodder and Orton 1976; see also Hietala 1984) which is based on geographical theory but for which archaeology generates its own peculiar problems, such as differential densities in fieldwork due to the distribution of archaeologists (Hodder and Orton 1976, 21–4).

There has been a tendency to believe that such studies are relevant only for fine wares, and that for many periods and many places the coarse wares are indeed 'stationary', geographically if not chronologically. This position began to crumble with Shepard's work on the Rio Grande pottery in the 1930s (Shepard 1942; see p. 19), which showed that coarse wares could be moved over surprisingly long distances. More and more examples of quite mundane wares being moved over long distances are coming to light (Peacock 1988; Santley et al. 1989; and many others) and it is clear that as the blinkers are removed and pottery is studied on a broader scale, more can be expected to be found.

Pottery as evidence for function or status

This is generally recognised to be the most neglected member of our 'big three' (for example by Fulford and Huddleston 1991, 6). This may be because it is more difficult to gain information on the function of a pot than on its source, and cautionary tales about very small differences in visible characteristics reflecting large variations in function abound (see Miller 1985), or because archaeologists believe such information can be gained from other sources of evidence (for example structural), or simply because they are not asking such questions. Deeper reasons are

    (i)   the relatively small proportions of pottery found in 'primary' contexts (p. 192). To ask the function of, for example, the town dump is either trivial or meaningless.

   (ii)   the need to work at the level of the assemblage rather than the individual pot, since not all pots in an assemblage can be assumed to have identical functions. Indeed, a particular function may require more than one form for its fulfilment – as a simple example, cooking pots and lids.

Nevertheless, useful information on the suitability of a pot for certain functions can be obtained from a study of its form and physical characteristics (p. 217), even if we cannot say that a pot was used for the purpose to which it was apparently most suited – sometimes technological considerations may overrule practical ones. Alternatively, a pot may possess features which are irrelevant or even detrimental to its purpose or manufacture, but are present because they were relevant to prototypes made in a different material, for example metal. Pots with such features are called skeuomorphs. A good example comes from fifteenth-century Dutch ceramics: early attempts

Fig. 2.2. Fifteenth-century bronze cauldron from the Netherlands (left) and its earthenware copy, also fifteenth-century and from the Netherlands (right). (Photos: Museum Boymans-van Beuningen, Rotterdam)

to copy bronze cauldrons imitated them down to the last detail, including the angled shape of the handle (fig. 2.2). This shape makes perfect sense in bronze, but is a source of weakness in ceramics – such handles cannot in fact bear the weight of a full pot (Ruempol and van Dongen 1991, 76).

Establishing the function of an individual pot should lead on to ideas about the function(s) of a site, or different parts of a site, although of course other sources of evidence (for example structures and other classes of find) will need to be taken into account too. In our view, this should be approached by comparing the compositions of assemblages relating to different sites or parts of sites (that is comparing the proportions of different functional types in those assemblages). Ideally, and this is now possible thanks to recent statistical advances (p. 173), assemblages of all classes of artefact (not just pottery) should be considered. We shall give a case study when we look at the quantification of assemblages (p. 178); an earlier example is provided by Ciolek-Torillo (1984), who classified rooms at the Grasshopper Pueblo into six classes, corresponding to the domestic activities of manufacturing, storage and food-processing, and their combinations, on the basis of the compositions of the finds assemblages in the various rooms.

Status is perhaps even less accessible than function. One particular problem, often overlooked, is that pottery is only one of many materials that can be used to fulfil certain functions, and that other materials may be far less apparent in the archaeological record, perhaps because they can be recycled (glass, metal) or perhaps because they degrade more readily (for example leather, wood). Thus status may be reflected more by choice of material than by variations within a material, and this may vary from one form to another. For example, Dyer (1982, 39), in a discussion of the British late medieval pottery industries, contrasts the widespread use of metal (brass) for cooking-pots with the very restricted use of metal jugs. This means that the presence of a high-quality ceramic jug does not imply a highest-status site, since at the highest level the jugs are likely to be of metal, not ceramic. On the other hand, the presence of a metal cooking-pot (in the unlikely event of one surviving) does not indicate status either. Competition from other materials may come from below as well as above: Dyer points out that the great increase in ceramic cups, plates and bowls at the end of the medieval period represents potters moving into a market previously dominated by treen (wooden vessels), and not an overall change of function in domestic utensils. It may have been brought about by a change in relative price levels (Moorhouse 1979, 54).

Manufacture and technology

Curiosity about how things are made and how they work seems almost to be an innate part of human nature, witnessed by the continual popularity of books with titles like *How it works*. But curiosity alone is not sufficient justification for the effort put by pottery workers into studying details of the manufacture of their excavated pottery. We have seen (p. 18) how the old ideas of technological progress have given way to a model of a mosaic of different techniques and details of production, so what can we still hope to learn by studying the technology of a pot?

Firstly, it can help us to characterise the products of certain sites. Often, idiosyncratic details can be more useful than broader but more readily copied characteristics. As an example we compare late medieval jugs from sources in France and southern England. Although forms and especially decoration can be quite similar (certain French styles were copied by potters in the London area and elsewhere), there are very diagnostic technical features in the ways that handles and spouts were made. Handles on the English jugs, whether of 'rod' (round) or 'strap' (flat) section were made by 'pulling' from a lump of clay or by rolling out a 'sausage' of clay. The French approach was completely different: the potter threw a cylinder of clay which was then sliced both horizontally and vertically, thus creating several handles at once. This was more efficient for the potter, but from our point of view it leaves important diagnostic traces in the form of throwing marks running vertically down the inside of the handle. It also gives a different shape (in effect, a rim) to one edge of the handle compared to the other, leading to an asymmetrical cross-section, sometimes known colloquially as the 'French roll' (Ponsford 1983, 222) (fig. 2.3). The technique was not (so far as we know) copied by English potters; some earlier English jugs have apparently wheel-thrown

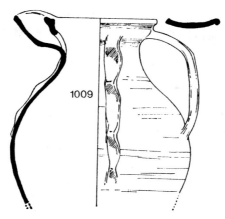

Fig. 2.3. Thirteenth-century French jug from Southampton, showing characteristic cross-section of the handle. (Platt and Coleman-Smith 1975, fig. 182, no. 1009)

handles (Pearce et al. 1985, 26), but they have a symmetrical cross-section and do not show throwing marks. A similar contrast applies to spouts: the English spout was usually formed by folding or pinching the rim of the jug itself, or by making a tube of clay. The French approach was to throw a small conical shape, and cut it vertically to produce two halves, each of which could be applied to a jug rim to form a spout, the corresponding part of the rim being cut away (Ponsford 1983, 222).

Such idiosyncrasies can sometimes be narrowed down to individual sources rather than broad regions (e.g. Pearce 1984). Some workers would go further and claim to be able to distinguish, not only between production centres, but between individual potters at a centre, by identifying personal idiosyncrasies and quirks (Moorhouse 1981, 106). This may be so as a *tour de force* in particularly favourable circumstances, but we do not believe it is possible to generalise from such experiences.

Secondly, a study of technology can help set pottery production in its social context, which is an important aspect of the contextual phase of study. We can learn about the scale of equipment needed – wheels, kilns, specialised tools, settling tanks, and so on, although it is to be hoped that structural evidence would be available for many of these. It certainly would be if excavations of kiln sites regularly covered potting areas other than just the kiln itself (a common complaint, see Moorhouse 1981, 97). These in turn may lead on to questions of the pottery 'industry' in the local or even regional economy – the degree of investment required, bearing in mind the low level of surplus above subsistence requirements for much of mankind over much of his past (Braudel 1981, 74), part-time or full-time, seasonal or year-round, individual or communal, division of labour between different tasks, and so on. Ethnographic parallels may help us to see the alternative modes of production that are possible, between the poles of domestic production for one's own use and large-scale industrial manufacture (Peacock 1982). Linked with distributional studies, we can even start to see how different areas articulated their production and trade, though we must remember that potting was almost always a relatively minor industry (Blake 1980, 5) and generally of low status (e.g. Le Patourel 1968, 106, 113), and that its very visibility may give a false impression of its importance. However, it has been argued (see Davey and Hodges 1983, 1 for both sides of the argument) that pottery acts as a marker for less visible economic and social activities, so that its visibility can be put to good effect. This is likely to be so in a positive sense – it is hard to imagine large amounts of pottery being moved from A to B without a high level of social contact of some sort – but the opposite is less clear: does the absence of pottery from A at B indicate a lack of contact?

Sherds in the soil
Talk of the high visibility of pottery brings us to the point at which discussions of the archaeological value of pottery often start – its ubiquity and apparent indestructibility. While it is true that pottery as a material is more robust than most archaeological materials (bone, leather, wood, and so on) and has the advantage of being little use once broken, it is also true that pots as objects are very breakable, and at each successive breaking of a pot we potentially lose information about its form and function. Even the basic material of fired clay is not as indestructible as we might think, and certain soils are said to 'eat' certain fabrics. Even if sherds remain undestroyed in the ground, they may not always be found in excavation. Experiments have shown that sherd colour can have an important role in the chance of a sherd being spotted by an excavator (Keighley 1973), and sieving for seeds and small bones almost invariably produces an embarrassing crop of small (and not-so-small) sherds. Even different parts of the same pots may be retrieved at different rates; for example Romano-British colour-coated beakers have thin fragile rims and thick chunky bases. The rims break into small sherds which easily evade detection, while the bases may well not break at all and be 'sitting ducks' for the trowel. This raises severe questions about the way such wares are quantified.

However, the apparently irritating way in which pottery breaks up and is moved about can be used to good effect. In the course of time, sherds from the same pot may be dispersed, sometimes over surprisingly long distances, and recovered from different contexts (and even, in urban excavation, different sites). They can tell us about the way in which deposits were moved about after the pot was broken and discarded, as they act as a sort of 'tracer' for soil movements (p. 214). The degree of breakage can, under favourable circumstances, yield parameters which can be of great value in interpreting a site (p. 178). Another aspect of this movement, the degree of abrasion, can also be very useful (Needham and Sørensen 1989). To take advantage of these possibilities, however, requires a site where the pots are sufficiently distinctive for it to be possible to sort out which sherds belong to which pots, not so abundant that this task is overwhelming (in terms of space, time or money needed), but not so sparse that the outcome cannot be interpreted reliably.

The playground of ideas

Beyond these basic uses, pottery workers are limited only by

(i) their imagination in thinking up ideas, probably dignified by the title of hypotheses.
(ii) their skill in deducing properties of excavated pottery capable of supporting or refuting their hypotheses.
(iii) the ability of a site or sites to provide enough data to either refute a hypothesis or convincingly fail to do so.

This makes pottery a happy hunting-ground (or playground) for those with ideas and aspirations about the less tangible aspects of material culture, for example the symbolic value of decorative styles and motif (p. 227). This is an enormous area, and too open-ended for us to be able to comment on more than very basic general principles. This we are glad to do, because it is very easy to overlook principles about the relationship between theory and data in the excitement of pursuing a new idea. So we make the points that

(i) it must be possible to deduce observable and recordable characteristics of pots or assemblages from our initial ideas, so that we can use data to either refute or support them.
(ii) if our ideas involve observed differences between assemblages (and it is likely that they will), differences due to hypothetical causes must not be confounded with differences due to extraneous causes, such as site formation processes. A simple example may make this point clearer: if our argument depends on different proportions of different types in two assemblages, and if our proportions are based on counts of sherds, any observed differences may simply reflect the fact that one assemblage is more broken than the other – the true proportions may be the same. Problems of this sort are examined in greater details in chapter 13.
(iii) it is not valid to use the same data to generate a hypothesis and then validate it. Validation is very important, and if it is unlikely that we will be able to obtain further data to test our ideas, we must split our original data in two, and use one half to generate ideas and the other to test them.

A classic case study is Hill's (1970) work on the pottery from Broken K Pueblo. He studied the spatial distribution of ceramic style elements to provide evidence for matrilocal residence groups. But it was later shown that the patterns he described could just as well be explained by chronological or functional variations in the pottery (Plog 1978).

Implications for practice

The possibility that their excavated pottery could, in principle, be used for any of the above purposes, places a heavy burden on excavators and primary processors or recorders of the material (for example the on-site finds assistant). This is especially true in Britain where funding arrangements may well mean that only a very basic record can be prepared, and detailed or comparative research is precluded by 'project funding' (Fulford and Huddleston 1991, 6). The worker's role may be simply to set up signposts for future research. What is needed in such circumstances?

As we have hinted above and shall argue in detail in chapter 13, the primary task of pottery research is comparison – of pot with pot and assemblage with assemblage. This means that pottery must be grouped and recorded in a way that facilitates rather than hinders comparison.

Wherever possible, this implies the use of existing form and fabric type-series. Form type-series often exist for kiln material, and should be employed on occupation sites where material from that source is found. The creation of a new type-series should be seen as a last resort, rather than a way of perpetuating one's name – it may be very gratifying to achieve immortality by calling a form a Bloggs 111, but is it useful and in the best interests of the subject? However, if the nearest type-series is based on such distant material that it is unlikely to refer to pottery from the same source(s) as ours, then we may be forced to set up our own. Advice on doing this is given in chapters 5 (fabrics) and 6 (forms).

Similar remarks can be made about drawings of pottery. Does the archaeological world really need yet another drawing of a well-known type? If not, why draw it? If it is necessary to draw a substantial number of pots (for example for a new type-series) they should be in a consistent style, even if drawn by several people: there is no room for the solo virtuoso performance. Drawings should obviously show accurately the shape and decoration of a pot, and should also carry information which it is difficult to describe in words, such as surface texture. Advice on these matters is given in chapter 7.

When it comes to creating a catalogue, or archive, one must remember that it is primarily for the use of others. What sort of questions are they likely to ask? A very basic one (at the level of the individual pot) is, 'Have you got any of these?' The 'these' will usually refer to specific fabrics or forms, often from a kiln site. Use of an established type-series will make this question easier to answer, but indexing is also important, so that researchers can easily lay hands on just those sherds they need to examine, and can be confident that none has been missed. More complex questions may be 'How much of this do

you have?' (usually in percentage terms) or even 'Do you have any assemblages like this one?' To answer such questions, we need a reliable method of
quantification. Archiving in general is discussed in chapter 8 and quantification in chapter 13.

The rapid increase in the volume of excavated material, especially in
Britain, has raised questions about disposal versus retention, and of sampling
as a way of reducing the volume of material retained. There are no easy
answers, but forewarned is forearmed. Our views are expressed in chapter 8.

Finally, there comes publication, which is only the tip of an iceberg, the
bulk of which is the archive and the retained material itself. The aims of
publications vary greatly, depending on the nature of the site and its pottery,
the amount and nature of previous work done in the area, the existence of
relevant type-series and the opportunity (or lack of it) to raise one's nose
from the grindstone and synthesise a little. But at the very least, the publication should act as a set of signposts to its archive and through it to the
objects themselves, so that readers can tell whether they need to consult the
archive and/or examine any of the artefacts.

Some archaeologists find publication psychologically difficult: it has an
awful finality not unlike that of death. Part of the dread comes from the
mistaken belief that what we say will be the last word on the subject, so it had
better be 'right'. But in archaeology there are no last words, all is provisional,
and if no-one ever improves on our work it is not because it is perfect but
more likely because it is terminally boring. Approach publication in this
spirit, and with the advice of chapter 9 in mind, and it may not seem quite
such a burden.

PART II

PRACTICALITIES: A GUIDE TO POTTERY PROCESSING AND RECORDING

3

INTEGRATION WITH RESEARCH DESIGNS

The archaeologist is in an unenviable position every time he or she plans a field project, since archaeological fieldwork destroys the subject of its study. This is true of a field survey almost as much as it is of an excavation, unless artefacts are examined where found on the ground and left in place. Almost all people working on sites previously investigated by an earlier generation of archaeologists have wished at some time that their predecessors had taken up some other profession. Those involved in an archaeological project therefore have a responsibility not only to carry out their stated aims but also to integrate their work into that of their predecessors and to ensure that their methods of recovery, analysis and recording are going to produce a usable archive for future workers. In some parts of the British Isles, for example, it is estimated that modern development, mineral extraction and agricultural practices will have brought field archaeology to an end within a few decades. If this should prove to be the case then those lucky enough to be involved in fieldwork now will be creating the only research materials available to their successors.

Nevertheless, the most important duty of any pottery researcher is to ensure that the recovery, analysis and recording of the pottery from a project is carried out smoothly and efficiently and within previously agreed limits of time and money. The practical steps should be: (i) to estimate the likely quantity of pottery which might be recovered during the project; (ii) to read and absorb previous work in the study area and, where possible, to build upon this work; (iii) to be aware of the best practice in the field and to adopt it, unless compelling arguments can be made for not doing so; and (iv) to produce and cost a strategy for allowing the estimated volume of pottery to be dealt with as part of an overall research design for the project (Fulford and Peacock 1984).

The archaeologist in charge of a project may have little practical experience of pottery work and a limited series of objectives, which if carried through might produce only a fraction of the potential information from the pottery. Where the site or area under investigation was pottery-using it is common to find that pottery, along perhaps with animal bones, forms the bulk of the finds and potentially the bulk of the expenditure on the project. In these circumstances the project manager needs good advice and the strategy which is adopted must be talked through by all concerned so that as many of the potential pitfalls as possible can be foreseen and avoided. In the end, of course, there is no substitute for experience and it is too much to expect anyone with a general training in archaeology to immediately step in and run a large pottery project.

If it is envisaged that the pottery will be eventually studied by specialists who are not going to be part of the actual field team, then these people should be consulted before the start of the project. There may be special recovery or recording requirements about which the field team should know. Furthermore, the way to get the most from a specialist is to make sure that he or she feels part of the project and believes that their ideas and knowledge have been properly used.

The standards and methods used by pottery researchers have changed so quickly during the twentieth century that there is a temptation to assume that nothing of value is to be found in previous work. This would be quite wrong. Apart from anything else, people working in the early to mid twentieth century quite often worked on a much larger scale than can be contemplated today and had first hand practical experience. If nothing else, one can sometimes spot the origin of particular ideas and evaluate their worth rather than having to accept them without question or going back to first principles and establishing every point from scratch. This is a costly, and wasteful, process.

Because of the slow speed at which archaeological work is published one may well run up against the problem that crucial work has been completed and written up but is not yet in print. There is no satisfactory solution to this problem. It might be possible to see a preprint of the paper but it can hardly be properly evaluated without the accompanying site evidence. The solution for the future is to prepare and deposit in a public archive a report, here referred to as an archive report (see p. 98), which contains a digest of the results of your work on a particular collection. Previous work was usually organised on the assumption that the finished report was the final word and that most of the paraphernalia, notes, record cards or illustrations, were ephemeral, being of value to the author but perhaps misleading in anyone else's hands.

At the very least, one should track down and examine any collections of pottery previously recovered from the vicinity of the planned fieldwork. Even without an accompanying report or stratigraphic data, such collections give you an idea of the range of forms and fabrics to be expected. If the work has not already been done, you can use these vessels as the basis for your fabric and form series (see p. 72 and p. 77).

Another task which should be done before the project starts is to look at what is known about pottery production and clay sources in the study area. Geological memoirs often include a section on economic geology which will list those beds of clay which are known to have been used for pottery, brick or tile manufacture. In some parts of the world traditional methods of manufacture continue to be carried out and it is possible to find out at first hand what resources and production methods are being used. Finally, one should know as much as possible about the main export wares of the period and area. In a region where little pottery work has been undertaken previously these wares may form your first means of producing some sort of local chronology.

The most important function of any strategy for dealing with the pottery from a project is to allow the aims of the project to be fulfilled. They will almost certainly include the dating of activity on a site and the broad period of occupation of sites and may include comparison of activity in different areas or sites, looking for evidence for or against social differentiation or specialised activities, for example.

To achieve these aims it may also be necessary to examine aspects of the archaeological record which are not of primary interest. For example, the processes by which the archaeological record came into existence must be understood before any further use can be made of the data (see p. 209).

There will almost certainly be other aspects of the pottery data which could be examined but which are neither of primary interest nor crucial to further interpretation. The temptation is therefore not to record these aspects at all. For example, there is certainly information to be found in studying pottery assemblages deposited in similar conditions and circumstances on different sites. A good example is the post-medieval cesspit assemblage. Pottery has been collected from backfilled cesspits in both Europe and the Americas and comparison of one group with another should reveal both similarities and divergences in culture on either side of the Atlantic. The work involved in examining even the material from a single pit is enormous and it is important, if any information is ever to be extracted from this data, that there is some standardisation in the way in which the contents are recorded. There is a similar interest in standardisation from those concerned with the reconstruction of marketing patterns and trade routes through the study of pottery (see p. 197). Studies, such as those of Hodder and Fulford on the distribution of Romano-British pottery used data from existing collections and managed to find some interesting patterns within them (Hodder 1974; Fulford and Hodder 1974). Further advances, however, require the study of larger collections, with some sort of stratigraphic control, and it would be wasteful, if indeed it were possible, for an individual to record or re-record all the necessary data him or herself. This type of study too requires a measure of cooperation between researchers.

On many excavations it has been the practice to treat certain classes of pottery in a different way from that of the mass of pottery. Examples are very common in the field of Romano-British pottery studies, where for many years samian ware, mortaria and amphoras have been studied by separate specialists, so that it has not been possible to study the relative frequency of these wares as a proportion of the total ceramic assemblage on a site (Fulford and Huddleston 1991, 9–11, 48).

Data therefore need to be recorded in such a way that they can be used by other workers. The most obvious area of standardisation concerns terminology and classification, although the names used for a particular class are irrelevant so long as it is possible to translate from one worker's classification to another's. Quantification is a less obvious area for standardisation and yet all examples given above require standardised methods of quantification (see p. 166).

Having emphasised the need for cooperation and standardisation, the case for ensuring some sort of continuity within a region must now be made. If there is a system of classification and recording in operation within a region then any move to abandon this system must be thought through carefully. Change for the sake of change is pointless and will have the effect of making all previous records less accessible and less useful. Such is the speed of change in pottery studies that there are excavation units in the United Kingdom which have been in existence for less than two decades but which nevertheless have three or more incompatible systems of recording amongst their records. To use computer jargon, it is important to ensure upwards compatibility when a system is modified. At Lincoln and London many data sets have been transformed from earlier systems into current formats. It is never as simple as it might appear and usually requires re-examination of the potsherds themselves. This creates problems of logistics, especially if the material is stored in a different place from that where the work will be undertaken.

Archaeology does not take place in an ivory tower and the factors which eventually lead to the choice of system to be used on a project will include time and money as much as the aims of the project, the potential uses of the data and the need to work within an evolving discipline. Potsherds can be classified and recorded in the most minute detail and some of the recording systems developed and used in England in the 1960s and 1970s recorded virtually every characteristic which could be recognised, from fabric and form, through sherd thickness and hardness to the colour of the core and surfaces of the sherd. Fashion has moved on, and it is currently in vogue to record the bare minimum as a basic record. It may seem obvious that the more one records the longer the recording will take, but there is always a temptation to record in more and more detail and a tendency to forget that while it may only take a few seconds longer to record two traits instead of one, on a single occasion a typical site pottery collection might contain tens of thousands of sherds. The more common a trait is, the greater the possibility that its study might be rewarding in terms of revealing a pattern but the more time and effort will be added to the project. By contrast, rare features, such as complete, highly decorated vessels, might be recorded in tremendous detail without adding appreciably to the length of the project, but without adding much to the sum of knowledge either. As in life in general, you don't get anything for nothing.

To summarise, in this section we have looked at the importance of project design and of making sure that the system of pottery study adopted will not hinder any of the aims of the project being fulfilled. We then looked at the need to collect data for others, in the expectation that they might do the same for you one day, and the importance of keeping some form of compatibility between the classification and recording systems adopted for the future and those used in the past. Finally, we looked at the importance of time and money in the design of pottery recording systems. From all of this we can conclude that there is no single, right method of recording pottery from an archaeological project and that every practical system will be a compromise between conflicting demands.

4

LIFE IN THE POT SHED

Introduction

In this section we look at the stages by which pottery is collected from an excavation or field project, and how it is identified, recorded and analysed before, eventually, being consigned to storage in a museum or archaeological resource centre. The first stage is to set up a base but this is quickly followed by the adoption of a retrieval strategy – to sieve or not to sieve. There are occasions where one deliberately does not collect all the pottery present in a deposit and the rules governing collection policy are discussed next. We then look at the way in which finds are processed and the initial sorting of pottery from other finds. At this stage it is common for there to be a preliminary viewing of the pottery, referred to here as *spot-dating*. There may, however, be a considerable interval after this point before 'serious' analysis of the collection begins. We start by looking at the typical flow of work, from the laying out of the collection to its identification and recording, and then look at the range of further analyses and processes which may be required for specific sherds. Then follows a digression while we look at the various exceptions to these general rules (classes of ceramic artefacts which need to be treated differently). They might, like building materials, need to be recorded in less detail than potsherds or, like, kiln waste, they may lend themselves to a series of special questions or, like crucibles, they may relate directly to non-ceramic finds. Finally, we look at the structure of the pottery records, the use of computers in data storage and analysis and the integration of pottery records with other databases.

Setting up base

The location of the finds processing for a project will depend very much on the availability of work space and resources. On a traditional rural excavation the base might be a tent or caravan whilst in an urban excavation parts of the building being demolished might be available for use. Large excavation units with several excavations running concurrently may wish to centralise finds processing so as to make economies of scale and to enable workers to move between material from one site and another as the work flow varies. In any particular case there may be no option but to take whatever is available and adapt it as one can. However, there are certain rules and requirements which can be set out and used wherever choice exists.

In hot dry climates the provision of water for washing and desalination of finds may be a problem. It is not uncommon for all the water needed by a project to have to be imported. Where salts encrust the finds they must be soaked in fresh water for a considerable time. Muslin or netting bags can be used to separate the material from several contexts in a single container. In the United Kingdom the more normal problem is not the provision of water but its disposal. Normal domestic drains, for example, will rapidly become clogged with silt and so silt traps must be added below the sink. Periodically they will require emptying and so there must be some means of disposing of quantities of wet sludge.

Adequate lighting is also important. People will be sitting down washing the edges of sherds and marking their surfaces. They need to see what they are doing. Furthermore, if the pottery is to be spot-dated on site then access to direct sunlight is an advantage. If this is impossible then a desk or a table lamp per person or some similar light source will be needed.

On a productive excavation there may be very large quantities of finds being processed. They can be washed much more quickly than they can be dried and there will come a time when every available space has been covered with trays of drying pottery, bone and so on. Racking and mesh-bottomed trays can alleviate this problem, but it is very easy to overlook it, especially if one is looking at a potential work area as being for a single person. Whenever conditions become crowded, and in particular where the pot shed is part of a general work area, or forms part of a means of access, there is the danger that someone will trip over trays of drying finds and the material from more than one context will become mixed. Another danger of making the pot shed too accessible is that people wander through, pick up sherds and put them back in the wrong tray. No amount of warning or scolding will do any good – especially if the culprit is the site director or a distinguished visitor – and it is better to make sure the problem does not arise by keeping the drying areas at some distance from the other work areas.

If the pot shed is also to be used for the post-excavation work then a large amount of bench space will be needed. The ideal work space for the material from a large excavation would be the size of an aircraft hangar. Few urban projects are able to supply suitable working areas and consequently their work tends to suffer.

It may well be possible to provide much better accommodation at a distance from the excavation but this will also bring problems. Firstly, the finds will have to be transported from the site to the pot shed. To ensure that all the finds arrive safely they should be listed at one end and checked off at the other. Secondly, the further away from the site the pot shed is physically the further away it is socially. There was an occasion where atrocious weather led to the calling-off of excavation for the day and the team headed into the nearest town in their Landrover. It was only when they arrived that someone remembered the finds supervisor, who was obliviously washing pottery in an outhouse at the local farm. This does nothing to encourage a team spirit.

Should the option of centralising finds processing be taken then these problems are exacerbated. A division into 'them' and 'us' will arise both on site and in the pot shed and this will lead to difficulties for the finds staff in monitoring site recovery and collection and the suspicion by the site staff that the money could have been better spent on more excavation. Wherever possible it is much better to have a finds specialist at hand on site. They can give instant advice and identification and be able to adapt recovery and processing to the needs of the site.

Collection policy and practice

Much of the information potential of your pottery will depend on the methods used to collect it and the rigour with which they are applied. Experiments using different methods of recovery and excavation have emphasised that recovery methods not only control how much of the total pottery in a deposit you recover but can lead to biases in the data.

To take the most brutal form of excavation, using a pick and shovel, as an example, only the largest sherds will be seen by the digger and this is bound to create a bias against the recovery of sherds from vessels which were either not very big when complete or tend to fragment into smaller pieces, perhaps because of the thinness of their walls or their brittleness. Hand recovery using a trowel or similar tool can be very thorough, depending on the speed with which it is carried out, the contrast in colour between potsherds and the soil matrix and the consistency of that matrix. Clayey soils may break up into large lumps which might contain potsherds whereas sandy soils disintegrate entirely into their constituent grains, making it much easier to see finds. There are various ways in which these biases can be corrected and, indeed, it may well be that having recognised that the bias exists there is no need to correct it. One method of correction might be to excavate a sample of a deposit using a trowel and then remove the rest by pick and shovel. One can make a case for saying that if one is interested in the relative proportions of different types and the range of types present in an assemblage of pottery then it is much better to have a medium-sized, unbiased sample than to have a large but biased one.

The use of sieves to screen the soil is essential for the standardised recovery of objects whose maximum dimension is less than *c.* 30mm. This is not to say that smaller objects will not be retrieved by hand, only that they will be found less frequently than they should be. Different methods of sieving have been developed, depending on the objectives of the exercise and the consistency of the soil. On clayey, silty or organic deposits it is essential to use water to break down the lumps. Chemicals such as hydrogen peroxide will make this process more efficient, but these are expensive to use on a large scale. It is important, when sieving for pottery, to make sure that the mesh size is not too small. Sherds less than 10mm across take a long time to process and identify and in most quantification methods will make little difference to the overall statistics of an assemblage. Sherds less than 20mm across might, on the other hand, be vital if one were trying to reconstruct a decorated fine ware vessel but would be irrelevant if they came from a storage jar. A different approach is needed when sieving to recover all the pieces of a vessel than when one is merely ensuring that all sherds over a certain size have been recovered.

In order to assess the results of sieving you will need to keep sherds from sieving separate from those recovered by hand. On the excavations at Billingsgate in the City of London, five numbers were assigned to every deposit, distinguishing: (1) finds recovered during excavation; (2) finds recovered during metal detecting; (3) finds from coarse water sieving (20mm mesh); (4) finds from fine water sieving (2mm mesh); and (5) finds from environmental samples. Ironically, analysis of the pottery from these different recovery methods showed that (1) and (2) were the most productive in terms of sample size and range of types present. This is because the sub-sample which was water sieved was much smaller than those excavated or metal detected and because the original vessels were rarely smaller than 100mm tall and 150mm wide. Finally, the method of analysis adopted involved the measurement of rim-eves (see p. 173) and more of the rim sherds were found by hand. Should you intend to use sieving to produce a correction factor remember that you will need to know the total assemblage recovered from a given sample of soil. If you are also interested in working out recovery rates you will need to record the potsherds as three groups: (a) found by hand in the sample; (b) found in the sieve; and (c) found by hand in the rest of the deposit. There are occasions where the quantity of pottery per unit volume of deposit may be significant. This is best examined by the sieving of samples of the same size, *c*. 30kg for example.

A closely related issue is the use of sampling. What collection policy is adopted will again depend very much on the use to which the data are to be put. Whereas a localised sub-sample might well provide an adequate estimate of the composition of the total assemblage, it will be useless if the main value of the pottery is to be found in the spatial distribution of pottery on the site. In the latter case it is better to assume that bias is going to be similar over the whole site and to record the finds by grid or by 3-D coordinates. The use of either of these systems will involve the staff in considerable paperwork but there is no problem in analysing such data by computer. It is always possible to combine the records from appropriate grid squares to produce a total for a deposit. The reverse is not true, so it is important to recognise the need for detailed recording before too much of a deposit has been excavated.

It is often possible to predict which parts of a site are likely to contain the most useful pottery assemblages and it may be necessary to adapt the excavation strategy to include them. For example, medieval towns in Britain usually had buildings fronting onto the streets and pits and wells behind them. The building levels will probably produce little pottery and the excavation of them alone cannot provide information on the ceramic history of the site, its earliest occupation and so on. Sampling is also necessary in regional surveys. For example, one may want to test the hypothesis that imported pottery was used only at the upper levels of the settlement hierarchy, or by particular social classes. If this can be demonstrated, then the position of a site in the settlement or social hierarchy can be estimated from its pottery. Since hierarchies have fewer sites the higher one rises, to maintain an adequate sample size it is necessary to investigate a higher proportion of the less common type of site.

Initial processing

By the time the excavation or survey begins you should therefore have chosen a base, ensured that it is equipped with light, water and space and have determined which methods of retrieval and recording are to be adopted. Next you have to sit down and wait for some finds. Excavations do not produce a regular flow of finds. There will be an initial slack period while overburden (concrete in towns, topsoil in the countryside) is being removed. Even once the excavation has begun in earnest finds will arrive in fits and starts. Unless the site is very unproductive, or there are many staff in the pot shed, there will be a delay of a couple of days or more between excavation and processing. Processing will almost certainly continue well after the excavation itself has finished. It might therefore be more sensible to do the minimum of processing on site and then to deal with the finds once the total size of the collection is known. This has the advantage that you ought to be able to estimate the work load more accurately once the finds are actually out of the ground. However, this approach has in the past been responsible for the loss of information. Finds which are stored damp will rot their packaging, and labels will become unreadable. Plastic labels can be used, although you also need special ball point pens to go with them. A perfectly preserved label is of no value if the writing on it has become illegible. Embossed tape can also be used to form a heavy duty label but do not trust the adhesive on the back of the tape. Put it inside the plastic bag. A delay in processing also leads to the loss of opportunities to follow up particular discoveries, for example by taking a bulk sample of a particular deposit or extending the excavation to recover the whole of a particularly interesting assemblage. Lastly, there is no means of checking that the finds have been correctly recorded.

Finds processing can be used as a means of redeploying diggers when bad weather or photography hold up excavation, but only if there is enough equipment, enough space and adequate supervision. The pot shed is also useful as a place for employing those who for one reason or another are temporarily unable to dig. Beware, however, that the pot shed is not seen as a convenient dumping ground for people who have proved themselves incapable of useful work on site. Work in the pot shed may be less strenuous than on site but it requires just as precise and conscientious an approach.

Equipment

If your project has easy access to a modern town you can probably find most of the equipment needed for the pot shed without too much difficulty. Hardware stores can supply most goods whilst large towns may have a supplier who can make up plastic bags to your requirements. The range of materials needed and their quantities can be decided in the first few days of the dig, or supplies can be topped up as they run low. Large units will have a central supply of equipment on hand. In developing countries it is both ethically and socially preferable to purchase as much equipment locally as possible. It is probably just as easy to spend time in the local bazaar as it is trying to find out what happened to your supplies at the airport. If you do not know what will be available locally try to find out before you get there from someone who knows. If there is a preliminary expedition to the site try to get on it or give a checklist to someone who is going.

There will be occasions where most of the equipment has to be imported to the site. With small items, like tooth brushes, mapping pens or Indian ink it is much better to be over-supplied than to run out. The space required in your transport to pack bulky items will probably form a limiting factor to the scale of your operation. If you can envisage something breaking then try to pack a spare.

Once the dig starts, the first thing you will need is a suitable type of container to collect finds on site. For hand recovery wooden or plastic seed trays are good. They should have some means of attaching a label to them, although most supervisors find it sufficient to weigh the labels down with a heavy stone or potsherd. Don't write the context on the tray itself because someone could reuse the tray without noticing the marking. The supervisor should provide two labels per tray, marked with the site code, the context number and perhaps his or her name and the date. The second label will be needed during washing so that one can go with the washed finds and one can stay with the unwashed, cutting out a potential source of error. If it is necessary to write out extra labels, for example if a group of finds do not all fit into one drying tray, they should have all the information listed above, plus the name (or initials) of the person writing them.

Bulk samples for sieving will need heavy duty containers, such as dustbins. Very productive deposits, such as those containing pottery waste or vast quantities of building materials, may require very large trays. Large plastic crates are suitable, if you can get hold of them. Tea chests, on the other hand, are too heavy when full and have no handles or grips. If nothing else is available then wheelbarrows can be commandeered but can obviously only be used as a temporary measure.

Retrieval procedures

The advantage of using trays and crates as on-site finds containers is that the finds can be spread out in them for immediate scanning. Although the practice should not be encouraged, it is also easy to toss finds into a tray. There is nothing wrong with using plastic bags, except that it is a bit more wasteful or involves the pot shed staff in washing the bags to recycle them. It is certainly not acceptable to have finds loose on the side of the trench. They cannot be labelled properly, they might get stepped on or they might fall back into the trench and get incorporated into the wrong deposit. If finds are being carried off site for processing they will certainly need to be put into sealed containers. The self-sealing strip on plastic bags seems to only work when the bag contains two or three sherds. The most secure method is to fold over the mouth of the bag, with the labels inside but visible, and staple it shut. If the bags are made from plastic of adequate gauge then they can be opened by pulling the opening sharply apart, forcing the staple out without recourse to a staple-removing tool. Plastic-covered wire ties can be used but are more difficult to open than staples. Labels tied onto bags with wire tend to rip, unless plastic ones are used.

The practice on some excavations of marking the bags containing finds, as an alternative to using labels, should be discouraged. Only rarely will the bag into which the finds were placed at the moment of excavation be the same as that in which they will be stored, both before and after study, and recycling marked bags is a potential source of error.

Some excavations make it a rule that finds are passed on to the pot shed at the end of every day, whilst others retain finds trays until the whole of the deposit has been excavated. Unless the site is very secure the finds should never be left in the trench over night. But if they can be left it does make administration simpler if all the finds from a context arrive in the pot shed at the same time, although this may make the work flow more irregular.

Pots are sometimes found in a complete but fragile condition. Anglo-Saxon cremation urns, for example, were typically buried in shallow graves so that the top of the urn may have been damaged by the plough and the whole vessel will have been subject to the forces of weathering. Even if the vessel looks to be in good condition it may be traversed by hairline cracks. In addition, the emptying of these vessels can benefit from the existence of radiographs, giving prior knowledge of the presence of grave goods. For these reasons you should get advice about the lifting of these vessels from a trained conservator, and if it is likely that this sort of find will be made on a site where no conservation advice is on hand then make sure you know the procedure yourself and have the correct equipment. If a group of sherds from one vessel is found together on site it should be dealt with separately and you should use your judgement as to whether they should be lifted as a block or merely excavated as normal.

It is a good precaution to list the finds being sent off site so that they can be checked in as they arrive in the pot shed. Most supervisors know of cases where they know finds were recovered from a deposit and yet the pot shed has no record of them. Although the primary use of these lists is to enable recrimination to take place there is also the possibility that the missing finds might be discovered. On some excavations finds are assigned bag numbers as they leave the site. This is, on the face of it, a good idea since it makes the process of listing and checking easier. Context numbers will be assigned to deposits or cuts which produce no finds and a single context can produce more than one bag of finds or be dug over several days. You can't therefore just sort the bags into context number order and check them as easily as you can when you know firstly that any one bag number is allocated once only and secondly that you have been sent a block of finds bags running consecutively from one number to another.

Bag numbers have a poor reputation amongst pottery specialists because the system was commonly used in the past as a substitute for writing the details of the site context onto the bag or label. When the site was published the concordance of bag to context would be discarded or, much the same thing, deposited with the finds in the museum. Despite this, the system has a lot to recommend it. For example, if a group of finds is incorrectly assigned to a particular context, perhaps by transposing the numbers or by an incorrect identification of a deposit on site, then only the particular group of finds is affected whereas without a bag number system all the finds from the deposit would be contaminated by this mistake. Another way to deal with this problem is to be liberal when assigning context numbers on site. The finds can always be amalgamated during post-excavation analysis.

Cleaning and drying

Pot-washing uses ordinary domestic washing-up bowls, scrubbing brushes and tooth brushes. Although pot-washers are told to make sure that all the soil is removed from the finds they must also be made aware that finds can be encrusted with deposits which may be of archaeological interest (see p. 224). Sooting, burnt food debris, some type of decoration (for example painted) and traces of pot contents should all be treated carefully. If it seems that they might flake off then the sherd should be packed in a separate plastic bag or box once it is dry. Mortar, cess and salt incrustations are of less interest, since they probably reflect the post-depositional history of the sherds, but their presence should be recorded before any attempt is made to remove them. Cess incrustations are probably composed of calcium phosphate which is insoluble in water. They can be picked off the sherds by hand or by using a small dental pick or similar tool. However, since there is a real danger that glaze or surface coatings will be removed with the cess it is better to leave this to a conservator. Salt incrustation can be removed by soaking for a long period in fresh water. If sherds are not treated they will disintegrate as the salts dry out and crystallise. Water tanks and net bags will be needed for this.

Sieves can be used with a strong water supply to wash the worst of the dirt off finds before finishing by hand. In certain circumstances, for example when dealing with production waste where the fabric is known and no reconstruction of vessels is to be attempted, there may be no need to wash all the finds manually. Use of a hose on this scale will, however, create a problem of water disposal.

Drying can take place in plastic or wooden trays but will be quicker if the sherds are placed on mesh-bottomed trays which can be stacked in racks. The mesh should ideally be smaller than the smallest finds, although this system can be used with sheets of newspaper lining the trays. Animal bone should be dried slowly and evenly so as to minimise stresses in the bone which may lead to warping or cracking. This may well determine the way in which your finds are dried but potsherds can be dried much more quickly without any apparent ill effects. You may therefore find it expedient to separate animal bone from other finds at this stage and have an area set aside for them to dry at their own rate while you place the potsherds and other finds in the warmest areas you can find. Thick sherds contain a large amount of moisture, especially if they have a porous texture. Organic-tempered sherds must be dried thoroughly or they will grow moulds. If placed in paper bags or cardboard boxes in this condition they can cause rot. At the very least they will need to be re-washed once post-excavation work gets under way. At worst they may cause the whole collection to have to be repacked.

Initial recording and processing
At this stage it is common practice to separate the finds by type and to undertake some preliminary recording. If the study of building materials is well enough advanced it may be possible to use a reference collection to identify materials, count or weigh the fragments, or both, and then discard them. However, hearth-lining and kiln fragments are easily mistaken for daub or mud brick and it is preferable to keep all materials until the post-excavation stage, so that they can be examined in the light of the site stratigraphy. Examining the whole collection at the same time may also make evident trends and patterns which would otherwise be overlooked. Certainly, no finds should be discarded until the specialist who is to publish them has had a chance to examine them.

In some circumstances the range of materials likely to be found in a deposit is well enough known for a pre-printed sheet to be produced on which you merely have to tick the presence of a particular type of find and note the quantity present in rough terms. These 'bulk records' can be used as the basis for costing and planning post-excavation and publication work and can be made even more useful by including a reference to the storage location of the finds, for example a box number. In the long run it is better to plan this in conjunction with the museum or resource centre where the finds will ultimately be stored, but in practice there are many reasons why this may not be possible. To give just two: (i) you may be boxing classes of finds which will eventually be discarded, leaving gaps in the number sequence; and (ii) there may be good reasons why you want to have a different type of storage during post-excavation work (when finds may well be moved over long distances several times) and their eventual storage, where they may only be moved within the building. If the finds are stored in separate boxes for each material it will be simpler later on to extract a class of finds for study. The 'bulk record' will act as an index to which boxes are required. It is also easier to estimate the length of time needed for analysis if finds are always stored in standard-sized boxes.

Once the finds are separated into their materials and classes, the pottery and other ceramics can be marked in Indian ink using a mapping pen. Never use a technical drawing pen to mark pot, and always get new pot markers to practice on bits of discarded tile before setting them loose on important finds. Marking is absolutely essential if there is any chance that finds from more than one context will be laid out for study together. Everyone has momentary lapses when they find it impossible to remember where they picked up a sherd. If it is clear that all the sherds in a deposit are from the same vessel it is tempting not to mark any of them, or to mark them only on the edges. In this way the vessel can be reconstructed for display without having unsightly markings all over it. However, do beware of sending vessels in this state to conservation laboratories. You may end up with a displayable but archaeologically worthless pot. The answer to this problem is to think ahead and make sure that the underside of the base of the vessel is marked, since this will probably be unobtrusive when the vessel is restored. If the vessel is a hollow form it is possible to mark the inside of the sherds in such a way that the marking can be seen if necessary but will be invisible once the pot is on display. Quite often you will find parts of what seem to be the same vessel in more than one deposit. The fact that you are actually dealing with two or more vessels may only become apparent during conservation. You will also find odd sherds from other vessels with the sherds of a shattered cremation urn. This emphasises the need to mark every sherd with both site code and context number except in very unusual circumstances.

Over the years, many people have thought of ways in which you could take the effort and boredom out of marking pottery. Indeed, the very nature of the task leads you quickly to that line of thought. Rubber stamps have been tried and, surprisingly considering the rough surfaces of most potsherds, the impression quite often comes out successfully. However, the ink supplied with these stamps fades whereas the Indian ink used for pot marking does not. If the pottery being marked is mainly black it is useful to have a supply of white ink. Amazingly, you will actually need to point out to your pot markers that putting black ink onto a black pot is not a good idea. However, it is usually possible to see the marking if you hold the sherd up to a glancing light source. Also, ensure that the marking is not too close to the edge of the sherd since this is the area most likely to chip off in storage. There is a hidden force in some people which makes them feel that sherd marking is not neat unless it is along the edge of the sherd. Porcelain is difficult to mark, since the sherds are often small and the marking can easily be rubbed off the shiny surface. Attempts to seal the marking with a plastic emulsion might work but have been known to lead to all the marking just peeling off the sherd. Finally, always have a spot check to make sure that the right marking is on the sherds. It is very easy to drift off while marking pot and wake up with a start to realise that you have been marking the previous number on several hundred sherds of pottery. Pot marking is not a suitable activity for dyslexics but almost everybody suffers from the occasional lapse, hence the need to check at frequent intervals. If mistakes have been made the two options are to scrape off the erroneous marking with a scalpel blade or to cross it out in Indian ink and write the correct version alongside it. Trying to alter one number to another by overwriting almost always creates doubt about the intended marking and is not a good solution.

Initial viewing and spot-dating
Archaeologists have always wanted to look at their finds as soon as possible but as we have seen there are dangers in allowing people to handle the finds until they have been marked. It is after this stage, therefore, that pottery first becomes available for study. A cursory glance at an assemblage can be enough for a specialist to be able to assess the rough date of the potsherds and to recognise extraordinary material. The sooner one knows the date of the pottery in a deposit the better, especially when the excavation is being carried out under rescue conditions. On large, multi-site projects it is useful for someone to look through the finds formally with the site supervisor in order to ensure that there have been no errors of marking, transcription or excavation. If this is not formalised it can be forgotten. On the Winchester Research Unit excavations this event was one of the high points of the digging week. Assistants would bring in the trays of pottery, the director would look at them, call for the supervisors to account for themselves and then pronounce. All decisions made would be recorded. In essence, this same ritual takes place in many archaeological projects. The important point is that although the pronouncements are provisional, they will probably be used as a basis for site publicity, interim reports and lectures.

In London in the early 1980s this process was known as spot-dating and the results were recorded on record cards, which would be called upon by the site directors when writing their site narratives. The cards recorded not just the date of the group but the number of sherds, or a rough estimate, and sometimes notes on the types present. As part of the computerisation policy these records were formalised so that they included a list of all types present in the assemblage. The value of this record was realised once study of the Roman, Saxon and medieval pottery began in earnest. One could retrieve a list of all sites on which a particular type occurred and the provisional dates assigned to the groups in which they were found. Because there was never any attempt to quantify the assemblages the recording could be very quick, especially if carried out by two people, one to call out the codes and the other to write them down and check whether certain types had already been noted. Simple, pronounceable, codes were used which speeded up the recording, for example: LOND (London-type ware), SPAM (Spanish red micaceous ware) and KING (Kingston ware) are all single syllables. Codes which cannot be pronounced but must be spelt out were less successful, such as SWSG (Staffordshire white salt-glazed stoneware) and LCGR (Low Countries grey ware). Using this system, most of the pottery excavated in the City of London since 1974 was indexed.

Other advantages of the spot-dating index were that the records from individual contexts grouped together on the basis of stratigraphy or interpretation could be amalgamated on computer. Whereas individual assemblages might be small and therefore only datable within broad limits the combined list of types provided a more reliable method of determining the deposition date of the pottery. The importance of 'feed-back' between the finds and site records was thus emphasised, to their mutual benefit.

If, however, it is planned to analyse all the pottery in detail immediately after the excavation then there is no advantage in making the spot-dating record first and one can revert to making a quick overview or quantify the pottery as it is excavated. On most sites, however, there will be parts of the sequence where it is clear that there is little further information to be gained by quantification. In those cases the spot-dating record, or an equivalent, can form the final record of the assemblage.

Sorting

Before starting to record an assemblage, it is advisable to lay out as much of the collection as possible, preferably in stratigraphic order. This is by far the simplest way of determining which of the various site-specific aspects of the collection need to be recorded. It may well be that a qualitative statement covering sherd size and condition is all that is needed or it may be that more rigorous analysis is necessary. At this stage it is quite likely that sherds from different contexts will be recognised as part of the same vessel. What one does with this information and, indeed, what one does with the sherds themselves, is subject to considerable variation from worker to worker. We consider this topic in more detail on p. 209. Where numerous cross-fits or sherd-links are found it may be necessary to give each sherd family a number. Where they are rare it may be satisfactory simply to cross-index the records of the contexts concerned. Finding cross-fits becomes more and more difficult the larger the assemblage being studied. In the most extreme cases it may be necessary to separate sherds by fabric and lay them out one fabric at a time. Even then, not all cross-joins will be found, although it can be useful to have a newcomer look at the collection after you have found all the links you can. Colour may be deceptive as a guide, since some sherds may have been burnt after breakage, but there will be some vessels which stand out from the majority and which can easily be spotted.

Physical reconstruction
Having established that a group of sherds form a sherd family, in other words that they all came from the same vessel, there is a temptation to reconstruct the vessel. Reconstruction may be necessary if a photograph is required of the vessel and it may be impossible to draw the pot without at least partial reconstruction, although masking tape can be used to hold small numbers of sherds together as a temporary measure. Masking tape should not be used on vessels with poorly adhering slips or glazes as they will tend to be pulled away from the surface by the tape, and if left for a long time the glue may dry out and leave marks on the sherds. If a vessel is required for museum display then it is likely that the museum will supply its own conservators to restore it. Make sure that you record every item you might want about the vessel before it leaves your care. In particular, it may be easier to draw the vessel before complete restoration. If plaster is to be used then you will probably find traces of it all over the surface of the restored pot in an attempt to make the restored area blend into the original. Try to keep a small sherd separate as a potential fabric and organic residue sample. Last but not least place a proxy card into the collection to inform future workers that the vessel has been removed.

If you wish to stick sherds then be careful to ensure that the glue you use is soluble as you need to be able to remove the glue and start again should you make a mistake, or find an extra piece to fit. Glues based on cellulose nitrate or polyvinyl acetate are recommended since they can be softened and dissolved in acetone, which is relatively inexpensive and readily obtainable. Most adhesives (and solvents such as acetone) are volatile and highly inflammable and the manufacturers' recommendations concerning their conditions of storage and use, in particular the ventilation of the working area, should be carefully followed. If the excavation is overseas then remember that such highly inflammable materials cannot be carried in ordinary airline baggage.

To keep the sherds together while drying use a sand tray and masking tape. use the minimum of glue and keep it away from the sand, or you will get

Fig. 4.1. Life in the pot shed. Painting by Janis Mitchell, from *The hamster history of Britain*, published by Thames and Hudson Ltd., © Thames and Hudson 1991

quartz grains adhering to the pot. Remember that the join being stuck will stretch during drying unless the two sherds are secure. With small sherds you can use gravity to ensure a good join but larger ones must be arranged in the sand so that there is no stress upon the join. If you are sticking several sherds together then plan ahead, otherwise you will find that you have stuck the sherds in the wrong order and cannot insert the next one. You may need to wash or brush the sherd edges again before sticking them.

Cataloguing

We assume that you have made some sort of preliminary record of the pottery and have determined what parts of the collection will be subject to a fuller study (fig. 4.1). There are no hard and fast rules as to what should be recorded although for the benefit of other scholars there might be two minimum requirements:

1) The presence of a type of pottery in the collection should be recorded. Urban excavations often produce large quantities of pottery redeposited in modern deposits or for which no archaeo-

logical context can be assigned (such as from boreholes or cleaning the surface of an excavation following the use of mechanical excavators). There is little point in making detailed records of such pottery, since most of it will have been derived from deposits, parts of which survive to be excavated. Quite often, missing pieces of stratified vessels can be found in the unstratified collection. However, it is possible that the whole of an earlier deposit will have been removed and that this unstratified pottery is the only evidence for activity of a certain date or kind.

2) A full list of pottery types found in a stratified context should be recorded. The associations of pottery types become more and more informative as the number of instances when they occur increases. It may be possible to use this type of data to show which pottery types occur together and were therefore in contemporary use. Even assemblages of two or three sherds may eventually yield information.

There are several decisions to be made about recording a pottery assemblage. The first is to establish the basic unit of record, that is the smallest amount of pottery that will be recorded separately. Pottery from different contexts should not be recorded together (although it should be cross-referenced if part of the same vessel), but even within a context there are several possibilities:

(a) individual sherds
(b) groups of sherds from the same vessel (sherd families)
(c) groups of sherds from vessels of the same fabric type and form type (see pp. 72 and 77 for discussions of fabric types and form types)
(d) as (c) but at the level of vessel class (for example cooking pot, jar)
(e) groups of sherds of the same fabric but of unspecified form
(f) groups of sherds of the same Common Name (see p. 74) and of unspecified form
(g) groups of sherds of the same Ware – form unspecified

If your project is operating in isolation from any other archaeological work then you are free to choose any of these options. There is little to be gained from the recording of individual sherds instead of combining the information from all sherds of the same vessel, unless the sherds have separate recorded grid coordinates, in which case each separately recorded location can be treated as a context. Option (b) is therefore preferable to option (a) but you may be losing potential information on sherd size or weight or on breakage patterns (for example, the frequency of occurrence of spouts attached to handles, handles complete from rim-handle to body-handle join, number of examples of sherds broken at the neck and so on).

If you choose option (c) over option (b) then you may lose the ability to measure completeness and brokenness (see p. 178). This information may prove to be vital when considering site formation and interpretation (p. 179).

If you choose option (d) over option (c) you then rule out the possibility of studying details of typology, such as rim forms, handle-types and decoration.

By opting for option (e) you will cut yourself off from the study of form and, therefore, from studying variations in site function or activity within a site. At option (f) you will be unable to use changes in fabric to date the output of a production centre and at option (g) you lose the opportunity to study the source of supply of the pottery.

These seven options are not the only possibilities, since you could decide to record fabric at a low level and form at a high level of detail but it should be clear already that the less detailed the recording, the less time and effort will be involved. Somewhere upon this sliding scale will be a level which satisfies your intended use of the data, provides other specialists with a means of comparing your results with previous and subsequent ones and will allow your results to be incorporated into wider studies. Examples of at least five of these options could be given from current practice in British archaeological units. Option (a) was popular in the early days of computing, when advice from non-archaeological data processing specialists would normally lead to the creation of a very detailed sherd-by-sherd record. For the sake of simplicity, and because it is probably the ideal maximum level of recording, we will assume that you are pursuing option (b), and that each record consists of the data associated with a group of sherds from the same vessel from the same context.

You also need to decide exactly what you will record for each of these basic units that you have chosen. As a minimum, you need to record the context, information about the fabric and about the form and any decoration, some idea of how much pottery is involved, a reference to any illustrations, and any additional information that may throw light on the use of a vessel or its post-depositional history.

The practicalities of recording form and fabric are described on p. 77 and p. 72 respectively. A key decision is whether this information is to be recorded in the form of descriptions or as references (often coded) to existing type-series (fig. 4.2). While forms are generally recorded according to the class of vessel and (if enough is present), its type, it has been quite common practice to record much descriptive detail about the fabric. In our view it is better to refer to each sherd family as an example for a particular fabric type (an abbreviated mnemonic is a particularly good way of doing this) and to keep the description of that type elsewhere in the records. This is equivalent to the 'relational' as opposed to the 'flat-file' approach to computer data-bases, and can save much space, time and effort while still allowing properly detailed descriptions to be made (see below, p. 62).

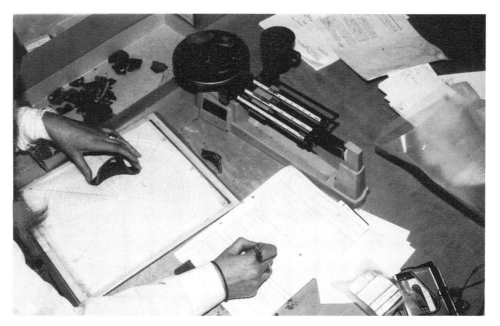

Fig. 4.2. Pottery cataloguing using pre-printed recording sheets, scales and a rim-chart

The recording of the amount of pottery present (the 'quantification problem') has caused much controversy and is still not fully resolved. Our views are set out in chapter 13 (p. 166), but it should be noted here that in choosing a 'measure' of quantity it must be kept in mind that important information, especially on site formation processes (p. 178) can be obtained by comparing different measures.

Illustration is another topic that merits a separate chapter (p. 87), but it is important to note that it must be possible subsequently to identify unambiguously any vessels that have been drawn or photographed. Similarly, sherds or vessels which have been removed from the collection for any reason need to be separately recorded.

There are two ways in which this can be done. Firstly, you can place a note in the box or bag from which the sherd has been removed. Museums quite often have a system of placing pre-printed proxy cards in lieu of artefacts which have been removed from their normal storage or display location. This system works well with archaeological collections. The other place where such information should be recorded is in your written record. It is quite possible to be able to record information about a collection without any means of identifying the individual sherds. To make an alteration to that record, based on further study of the collection, you need to be able to link particular records with sherds, or groups of sherds. The obvious way to achieve this is to assign every sherd a unique number or code. Such a solution can work well for small collections, in the order of tens or hundreds of sherds. Individual sherd numbering for collections with thousands or tens of thousands of sherds has been tried in the past and failed. A disproportionate amount of time is spend in recording and checking the numbering system and in most cases the individual number is never needed. It may well be that computer technology will in the future enable individual numbers to be assigned and recorded with more ease, for example by the use of bar codes or other machine-readable marking. In the meantime you will probably be faced with the problem of how to identify a minority of the sherds in a collection. One solution is to have a separate number series for every category of information which you wish to record, for example a slide number series, a black and white photograph series, a thin-section number series, a loan number series (for sherds sent to specialists) and so on. The advantages of a separate number series are that one knows immediately how big a series is (through knowing the last number used) and one knows if any information is lacking, since there should be as many slides or thin-sections as there are numbers in the series. The disadvantages are that you may end up with several numbers referring to a single sherd, and the number series will need to be distinguished one from another in order to avoid confusion. As a guide, whenever a type of record is not automatically linked one-to-one with a sherd then you will probably need a separate number series. For example, you can have several slides each showing different aspects of the same vessel, or containing more than one vessel, whereas a loan will always be for the whole sherd or vessel, or multiples thereof.

The next aspect of a collection to be considered is the evidence for use and re-use of the vessels. This comes most often in the form of sooting or of deposits on the interior of the vessel. It can also come from wear on the base or feet, chipping at the rim or base, arising from rough handling or scratches on the inside of glazed vessels which show the use of a rough scourer to clean them. Much can be done using this type of data from complete or near complete vessels and it is probable that more could be done on sherds than merely recording presence or absence of traces of use (see p. 222).

Evidence for the post-depositional history of sherds can come from comparisons of various measures of quantity (see p. 178), but more direct evidence can also be employed. The degree of abrasion of both surfaces and broken edges can be assessed on a simple ordinal scale, bearing in mind that freshly-broken edges may be the outcome of excavation technique. Particular contexts may have particular effects on sherds, either leaching or depositing material (see p. 215). The comparison of various measures of quantity, particularly relating to different parts of vessels, for example rims, handles and bases, can give evidence for bias in recovery (see p. 179).

Computers in pottery research

The use of computers during the pottery processing cycle has already been referred to several times above. The widespread availability of relatively inexpensive yet powerful computers and reasonably friendly software packages has impinged as much upon ceramics study as on many other aspects of archaeology (see Richards and Ryan 1985 for a general account of the role of computers in archaeology and an explanation of technical terms). Many projects consider the role of computers from a very early state in their planning, while for others computerisation seems an afterthought, and considerable ingenuity may be required to shoe-horn poorly structured data into an unforgiving computer.

Two thoughts should be borne in mind when approaching the computerisation of records of archaeological ceramics. Firstly, many of the basic ground rules are equally applicable to the organisation and manipulation of paper records as they are to their computerised counterparts; and secondly, it is essential that the records of pottery can be co-ordinated both with the records of other classes of artefact and structural or contextual data. When presented with a pre-existing recording and computerisation system it is generally advisable to co-operate with it, unless there are very cogent arguments for doing otherwise.

The practicalities of computerised recording systems for ceramics can be considered in two parts: (i) what to computerise; and (ii) how to organise the records. Many of the answers will be guided to a great extent by factors such as the sophistication of the available equipment, your access to it and the work flow, working conditions and so on, but there are some general rules-of-thumb.

What to computerise

Some ceramics data could benefit from very early computerisation. Spot-dates, incorporating lists of pottery types and dates of contexts, will prove of immense value both during and immediately after the excavation of a site. Such data are particularly suitable for computer manipulation, and within the abilities of even the simplest of packages. For most day-to-day purposes retrieval, sorting and simple mathematical operations will be those most widely used. A request from one's colleagues of the 'What date is context 100?' variety could be answered simply by finding the list of pottery types recorded from that context on a recording form or card, which could themselves be stored in context order. But once the question moves on to 'Give me a list of all sixth-century contexts' or 'Give me a list of all contexts containing pottery type *X*', then computerised records become essential. The ability of the computer to retrieve such data both swiftly and accurately eliminates much of the tedium associated with such searches, and indeed encourages both ceramic specialists and others to approach a site with broader questions in mind.

Fig. 4.3. A type-series of Roman pottery types stored on cards

Spot-dates can be usefully entered directly onto computer, completely eliminating the paper record. The compact breeds of lap-top or hand-held computers now available are very suitable for the direct input of this type of data and they are rugged enough to withstand the conditions regularly encountered on archaeological sites. Of course it is only common sense to copy the data off these machines onto something more secure at an early opportunity.

There is often a tendency to attempt to computerise rather too much information. Experience has shown that large amounts of free-text (prose) description is often of rather limited value and is poorly handled by many of the simpler types of software package which will be most often encountered. Inconsistencies in punctuation and spelling often make this type of data very difficult to retrieve efficiently and short keywords or mnemonics are preferable where they can be applied.

It will usually not be possible to record images, in particular pot drawings and photographs, at an early stage in the project (if at all). A properly indexed set of drawings on cards will suffice for most purposes and will be easier to use in most field situations (fig. 4.3).

How to organise the records
We can now consider the structure of the computer record. On a practical level it should mirror the organisation of any paper records as much as possible, with a smooth transition from one to another. This will make it

easier both for those working with them on a day-to-day basis, and also for anyone who comes afterwards to try and work out what happened.

Most database packages allow data to be stored and manipulated in what is called a 'relational' structure. The theory of relational databases is complex and it is not necessary to describe the details here. In practice there are two rules to bear in mind:

(i)   You should view some of the data in one file as in some sense 'signposts' to data held elsewhere.

(ii) You should try and arrange matters so that information is only recorded once, and then referred to from elsewhere.

A practical example will clarify this. A simple record describing the quantity and type of pottery in a context might look something like this:

Context	Fabric	Form	Diam	Eve	Weight	Drawing number
191	PRW1	DISH	10.5	32	230	4112

This records the details about a sherd family of a particular fabric (PRW1) and form (DISH) from a single context (191). To gain further information about any of these elements we can treat them as signposts to data held in other files. Thus for the description of PRW1 we may look in the fabric code file and find:

Code	Description
PRW1	Pompeian-red ware fabric 1

We could add other data to this file which records, perhaps, the date or origin or the ware, or the function of the vessels (cooking ware, table ware and so on).

Code	Description	Source	Date	Function
PRW1	Pompeian-red ware fabric 1	Italy	15BC–AD80?	Cooking

The important point is that this information is not recorded alongside every occurrence of PRW1 in the quantified data file, but once only in a separate location. The relations of the context field can be even more complex. Each context may belong to a feature, such as a ditch, floor, wall and so on, and these in turn may be grouped into large structural units, such as buildings, or organised into phases or periods. A simple structural record may look something like:

Context	Feature
191	Pit 6

and this structural record may in turn relate to broader groups:

Feature	Phase
Pit 6	IIIa

Phase	Date
IIIa	AD50–70

The query languages built into most relational database systems are designed to allow selections to take place by specifying criteria which span from one file to another. Thus it would be possible to select all contexts which contain, for instance, cooking wares in Phase IIIa, by following the links from one file to another and back to the main ceramic data file. The benefits of such an arrangement are also clear when the time comes to make changes to the data. If Phase IIIa is no longer considered to be AD 50–70 but AD 70–100, then only one change is necessary rather than many hundreds or even thousands – all cross-references are automatically up-dated. Similarly the movement of groups of contexts from one phase to another, which invariably happens many times during the record-preparation process, is accomplished by adjusting only one or two links.

Finally, it is important to maintain adequate documentation on the procedures that you have used in creating and maintaining any database (and indeed any other type of recording system). This should routinely include all expansions of all keywords or codes used and explanations of the relationships between the records and files. Using an undocumented computer system is akin to keeping your records on the backs of old envelopes, and many of the long-term hopes of building up reusable archives of data will never be realised.

To keep or not to keep

Sooner or later you will face the problem of establishing or operating a retention policy. If you work as part of a museum or large excavation unit then it should already exist but if not you may have to consider some difficult problems. Museums have always existed to manage collections, whatever their other objectives. It is therefore contrary to normal museum practice to discard material; yet it is neither possible nor desirable to collect material regardless of its potential information content. In some parts of the world, North Africa or the Middle East for example, the quantity of pottery produced through excavation may be too great to consider the total retention of all material, although this attitude in the past has led to a situation where few if any complete stratified assemblages are available from many such regions. Where pottery is scarce, or archaeology is well-funded one can consider keeping all material. The essential value of excavated collections is the stratigraphic context of the finds. If finds, for one reason or another, have no stratigraphic context then there is a case for making a minimal record and retaining only selected sherds. If the finds are stratified there is almost always some further analysis which could be undertaken which for one reason or another you have not carried out.

Archaeological deposits are unique so that it is not possible to think of an excavation in any detailed way as a scientific experiment, a repeatable event. Obviously human behaviour was and is limited by culture. Otherwise archaeology would only be able to reveal the particular events which took place on a certain site rather than reveal patterns of behaviour. We should consider excavations as producing the source material for future study. No historian would consider ripping out the pages of a manuscript once having read and transcribed them, but there again very few historians would refuse to throw out yesterday's papers on the grounds that they form the source material for tomorrow's history. In short, there are strong reasons to retain as much as possible of your collection for future study and you, the pottery researcher, are probably the best person to decide upon the importance or potential of assemblages in a collection. If you do decide that you must discard stratified pottery then this will have to be reflected in the way in which you record that pottery. In particular you will have to develop systems for describing factors such as the traces of use or reuse on vessels, sherd rounding and redeposition – topics upon which relatively little work has been carried out to date.

5

FABRIC ANALYSIS

Introduction

Fabric analysis is the study and classification of pottery using the characteristics of the clay body from which the pottery is made. These characteristics can be divided into three classes: (i) those which are a function of the firing temperature and conditions; (ii) those which are a function of inclusions; and (iii) those which are a function of the clay matrix. Pottery analysts consider pottery fabrics to consist of two elements: a 'matrix' composed of clay minerals less than 0.002mm across and 'inclusions' which are larger. Roughly speaking 'inclusions' can be seen with the naked eye or a binocular microscope whereas individual constituents cannot be seen in the matrix except using high-powered microscopes and thin-sections or a Scanning Electron Microscope (SEM). The term 'fabric' is used by pottery researchers to mean all three characteristics whereas geologists use the same term to describe the spatial relationship of minerals in a rock. The term 'paste' is sometimes used by pottery researchers synonymously with 'fabric'. The two basic components (matrix and inclusions) are governed mainly by the choice of raw materials used by the potters and by any preparation which the potters carried out. However, both are modified, to a greater or lesser extent, by firing conditions (see p. 133).

Equipment

A magnifying glass, hand lens or binocular microscope is an essential part of the equipment used in ceramic analysis. The three main uses are to examine the fabric of a vessel, to look in detail at the way in which the vessel was made or decorated and to look at evidence of use. The first use is by far the most common and will determine the type of microscope or lens which you need. Depending on the nature of the fabrics present in the collection you may need to use a lens to examine every sherd or it may be possible to identify all the pottery by eye. In cases where the identity of inclusions has proved to be of no diagnostic value it will probably be the texture of the fabric which is used in classification. Where the majority of grains are less than 1mm across a magnifying glass will be useful. Where the identity of inclusions is a vital part of a fabric classification it may be necessary to examine the sherds at magnifications up to $\times 25$. For this you will probably need a binocular microscope, although a hand lens could be used. The main advantage in using

67

a hand lens is that it can be carried on the person. It is useful to examine sand or clay sources in the field and can be used to aid identification in the field or in museum stores. Natural light or strong light with a daylight bulb is needed with a magnifying glass or hand lens. It is possible to obtain magnifying glasses with a built-in circular neon tube and hand lenses with a built-in light source can also be obtained. They are probably less easy to use than a simple hand lens. Most binocular microscopes have a built-in light source.

Before purchasing a microscope it is important to test it to see if the light source can be adjusted. It may be better to purchase one with a fibre optic light source. Many of the optional extras on a binocular microscope have no archaeological use and the important points are: (1) can a complete vessel be examined, by swinging the eyepiece around so that the vessel can be held with part of its body below the level of your bench; (2) how many different magnifications can be obtained, and how difficult is it to obtain them (in some instruments you need to change eye-pieces whilst in others there is a built-in rotating eye-piece) and (3) is it possible to use the microscope in photography. Never take a salesman's assurance that this is possible without seeing a demonstration. The quality of most binocular microscope lenses is not good enough for photography since there is too much distortion around the edge of the field of view. In some cases you need to purchase a complete camera body and attachments whereas others allow you to use standard camera equipment.

Firing characteristics

The effect of firing upon pottery has been studied using a variety of techniques. First and foremost is the use of visual examination and the recording of colour, hardness and fracture.

Colour

Colour is usually recorded using a standard chart, such as that produced by Munsell (see p. 136). If asked to describe the colour of a potsherd a student would probably either use terms such as 'red', 'white', 'grey' or 'brown' or would qualify these terms using adjectives whose precise meaning is not clear, such as 'brick red', 'off-white', 'metallic grey', or 'light brown'. Even if there is broad agreement over the meaning of these terms in English, such idioms would not translate well into, say, French, Italian or German. The Munsell colours, however, have a standard notation which enables anyone with a Munsell chart to look at a colour description and see what is meant; although there will still be differences between the way in which individuals record colours, a further advantage of the Munsell system is that it provides a means of measuring the similarity of different colours.

Experience has shown that it is useful to describe a pot's colour in five zones. First is the core. This is the part of the fabric least exposed to the kiln atmosphere and protected to some extent against extreme temperature. Pots whose cores are black or dark grey probably contain carbon derived from the incomplete burning of organic material in the fabric. As this carbon is burnt it will take oxygen and this can lead to local reduction of the fabric and hence a grey colour. As firing continues, however, oxygen in the kiln atmosphere may oxidise the core leading to the development of brown and red colours. Next one describes the margins of the pot, that is the zones between the core and the surfaces, if there are any differences between them and the core. No difference between core and margins may indicate either that firing conditions were held long enough for the fired vessel to reach an equilibrium, or (with some grey and black fabrics) may indicate a very short firing. If the inner and outer margins are of different colour, this may suggest that the mouth of the pot was closed in some way, perhaps by being fired inverted on the kiln floor or as part of a stack of vessels. Finally, the colour of the surfaces of the pot are described, if different from the margins. A difference between surface and margin colour suggests a short-lived change in firing conditions; perhaps the kiln was opened up whilst the pottery was still hot, allowing oxygen to rush in. This would produce a browner or redder surface. Deliberate reduction can be achieved by throwing green timber onto the fire at the end of the firing, giving rise to vessels which might have oxidised margins and cores but reduced, and therefore greyer, surfaces.

For any one pottery fabric the colour range will be dependent on firing conditions, the iron content of the clay and the way in which the iron is distributed within the clay (that is, does it occur as discrete inclusions or is it bound to clay minerals and is it already in an oxidised state?). Therefore, if one knows that the fabric is from the same clay source then changes in colour must be directly related to changes in firing. For fully oxidised wares a rough estimate of firing temperature can be obtained by refiring samples at known temperatures for a standard time. Conversely, if samples of different fabrics are refired at the same temperature and conditions then their resulting colour will be related directly to difference in iron content between the fabrics.

Hardness

The hardness of materials can be measured in a variety of means but in pottery studies the most commonly used means is Mohs' hardness scale, or a simplification of it (see p. 138). A pot's hardness is determined by attempting to scratch the pot surface with progressively harder materials, starting with talc and ending with diamond. The hardness is defined by the number of the material which just failed to scratch the surface. Hardness provides a rough indication of firing temperature and may be of value in the classification of high-fired wares, such as stonewares and porcelains, but it is rarely a determining feature in the classification of fabric groups.

Fracture

The way in which a potsherd fractures provides a further indication of firing temperature, and the amount and size range of inclusions. Porcelains and other high-fired fabrics with few inclusions have fractures similar to those found on flint, obsidian or glass. These are termed 'conchoidal'. For the fracture to be conchoidal, ripple marks must be present. If they are not, the fracture is termed 'smooth'. At lower temperatures or with more inclusions a rough fractured surface is produced, termed a 'hackly' fracture because it is similar in appearance to the hackles on a dog's back (to those with a lively imagination). Sometimes the pot can be seen to fracture in layers; this is termed a 'laminated' fracture. When recording fracture it is worthwhile looking to see whether the pot has fractured through the inclusions or around them.

Feel

Some pottery researchers find it useful to describe the feel of a pottery fabric when rubbed with the thumb. This characteristic is merely a function of a combination of hardness, inclusions and surface treatment. Descriptive terms include 'harsh', 'rough', 'smooth', 'soapy' and 'powdery'.

Slip and glaze

Slips and glazes are included by some pottery researchers as part of fabric analysis and certainly slip should be described if possible using the same terminology and procedures used for the main fabric. Glaze can be described in terms of the cover (patchy, internal, external or whatever), the thickness, the surface appearance (smooth, pitted) and the colour. The use of colourants should be distinguished from the accidental colouring resulting from impurities taken up from the clay body. With experience this can often be done visually, but sometimes more advanced techniques are needed (see p. 145).

Inclusions

Before describing the way in which inclusions are studied by pottery researchers we must be clear about terminology. Inclusions can be taken to include any large features in a pottery fabric, even voids. It is often impossible to decide whether the inclusions in a fabric are there as a result of natural processes or because the potter has deliberately added them. Terms such as 'filler' and 'temper', however, imply that the inclusions are artificial additions although the terms are used in cases where it is most unlikely that this is the case (as with some 'shell-tempered' pottery). For this reason, if using the term 'temper' to mean deliberately added inclusions this meaning probably ought to be made explicit.

The study of pottery inclusions owes a great deal to sedimentary petrology, a subject too vast and complex to be included in detail here. Two aspects which must be mentioned, however, are the identification of inclusions and the recording of their contribution to the texture of a fabric.

Identification of inclusions

A very wide range of materials can be and have been used as pottery temper, ranging from donkey dung to powdered slag. Since 1977 they have been identified in the United Kingdom mainly by using the key published by Peacock (1977) and reproduced in the appendix (p. 238, table A.2). This key enables inclusions to be identified using a binocular microscope, a steel needle or blade, a pipette with a bottle of 10% dilute hydrochloric acid, and a magnet.

Some inclusions may be very distinctive, and enable a fabric to be located to a particular geological outcrop (see p. 140). On the other hand, the more common inclusions, such as quartz sand, and shell, are frequently very non-specific and force the pottery analyst to study less 'objective' characteristics.

Textural parameters

When dealing with pottery from known sources, pottery analysts often find that the best way to discriminate between them is via a clutch of rather ill-defined characteristics which collectively might be called 'texture'. Although they include the nature of the fracture (see p. 135), they are mainly characteristic of the inclusions, and can be broken down into their frequency, size, sorting and rounding. Briefly, frequency refers to the proportion of the fabric which consists of inclusions, sorting to the range of sizes of inclusions around their average, and roundness to the smoothness/roundness of the individual grains. The simplest way to record them is by reference to standard charts (see appendix, p. 241), although more sophisticated techniques are also used (see p. 141).

The matrix

The clay matrix may contain minute fragments of rocks and minerals or it may consist solely of clay minerals and glassy ceramic. This difference can be useful in classification but cannot be reliably described by eye. In thin-section, one must be aware that slight differences in the thickness of the section might have a large effect on the apparent frequency of silt-sized and smaller inclusions, since if they are smaller than 0.03mm across they will be masked by further matrix. It can be difficult, if not impossible, to identify these inclusions even in thin-section but there are cases where their identity is an important factor in the characterisation of a fabric. For example, some fine-grained pottery can be seen to contain minute fragments of rocks and minerals of volcanic origin. Around the Mediterranean a common raw material for pottery was (and is) calcareous marl. This has been used extensively for tin-glazed pottery because it adsorbs the liquid from the glaze and paint so quickly. In thin-section this marl can be identified by the occasional presence of microfossils, *foraminifera*.

The clay matrix is affected by firing. In the calcareous marls described above firing in certain conditions leads to the creation of a non-calcareous ceramic and quite often one can see in thin-section that part of a vessel has been affected whilst another part remains unchanged. In those parts of the matrix not fired at a high temperature the clay minerals produce interference colours in crossed polars. The intensity of these colours declines as more and more of the matrix is transformed into ceramic until finally no colours are visible at all. It is therefore useful to record whether the matrix is anisotropic (shows these interference colours) or isotropic (shows no interference colours).

Creating and using a fabric type-series

If there is already a fabric type-series for the area in which you are working, you should use it in preference to setting up a new one (fig. 5.1). This does not mean that you will not have to define new fabric types, or expand the definition of existing ones, but at least you will have a basis from which to start. If the existing series covers only part of your area, or part of your chronology, or is located at some distance from your base, you may find it more convenient to set up a 'satellite' type-series and add to it yourself. You may even prefer to use codes that are different from those of the original type-series, but if so make sure that the definitions are compatible, and prepare a 'translation table' so that other workers may move smoothly from one system to another.

You should first attempt to define coherent groups within your own material, before linking it to an existing series or setting out to define your own. The work you have done on assembling sherd families will be useful here; the definition of a fabric should be broad enough to encompass all sherds from the same vessel. Few things are more embarrassing than defining two (or more) fabrics and then discovering that they come from the same vessel. This work should always be done on the actual pottery, not from written descriptions or a computer database, since subtle differences which at first elude verbal description may prove vital in distinguishing between fabrics. Written descriptions are valuable as a means of indexing and guiding you towards possible matches with type-examples, but the basis of assignment to a type should be, if at all possible, a sherd-to-sherd visual matching.

It is important to note that different sorts of matches produce different levels of reliability. The groups which can be defined are therefore of two types: those which are based on general similarity. As a good example of the former one can take Neolithic pottery produced in Cornwall and containing fragments of Lizard Gabbro. This rock has a very limited outcrop and either

Fig. 5.1. A ceramic type-series. The individual sherds are stored in individual slots in large metal drawers. Fabrics with similar inclusions are stored together and coded using a system such as that described on p. 242

the pots or the inclusions must have been obtained close to the Lizard, no matter how far from the Lizard the pots are found. As an example of the latter one might take pottery tempered with dung or chaff – chaff-tempered ware. Objectively, two sherds of chaff-tempered ware might have just as many characteristics in common as a pair of Gabbroic-tempered sherds but this is no indication at all that the former sherds shared the same source.

The question inevitably arises as to whether two sherds (which do not belong to the same vessel) belong to the same fabric type, or alternatively whether a new sherd belongs to an existing type. The answer often seems to depend as much on the psychology of the worker as on the nature of the pottery. As in many other fields, workers can be divided into 'lumpers' and 'splitters': the former tend to assume that all fabrics are the same unless they can be demonstrated to be different, while the latter assume that all fabrics are different unless they can be demonstrated to be the same. These assumptions are often deep-seated and not verbalised, yet strongly held. The former may appeal to some logical proposition such as Occam's razor for support, while the latter will point out that two fabric types, once defined, can always be merged later, but if one discovers later that one fabric type is really two, one has no option but to re-examine all the material of this type. Frequently what seems to happen is that the worker defines two apparently distinct types from examples seen in early stages of the work, but finds to his (her) dismay that the space between them is gradually filled by a chain of intermediate types until it is difficult to sustain the original distinctions. This implies that it is important to examine all the material before starting to create definitions, and that you should be as aware as possible of your own tendency to 'lump' or 'split'.

The lowest level of definition is the fabric type, which may encompass no more than the variation seen in sherds from the same vessel. It may well be useful to keep more than one reference specimen of a type, representing (for example) oxidised/reduced parts of clamp-fired pottery, or glazed/unglazed parts of partially-glazed vessels. An exception may have to be made if different parts of a vessel have fabrics which are different by intent – for example, a handle may contain more filler if it is thicker than the body of a pot. Of course, sherds from different vessels may be indistinguishable and they should be included in the same fabric type.

The next level of integration is more arbitrary: groups of vessels whose fabrics conform to a single description with defined limits of variation. The intention of this level of classification is to include all vessels made in a particular centre to the same basic recipe. Craft potters will tell you that they alter the quantity of added temper in their clays to produce a mixture which is workable on the day. Water content and the degree of bacterial breakdown of the clay can be allowed for by adding more or less temper. If pottery from a single firing was being studied then the recognition of separate batches of clay might both be possible and have an appreciable information content. In practice, even waster dumps contain the rejects from numerous firings and batches of clay. On the other hand, the choice of tempering material within a single centre may be both worthy and capable of study and it is this level of detail which individual fabric classification attempts to reach. A fabric reference series is extremely useful in dividing pottery to this level, since it both ensures consistency on the part of the specialist and provides an initial source of information for those wishing to learn about the contents of the collection.

There may be cases where a range of fabric types, as defined above, were produced in a single centre, but where previous study has either shown that the differences between them were random, or where the potential infor-mation yield from recording the data is not worth the effort involved in recording it. In the Department of Urban Archaeology of the Museum of London this distinction was marked by the use of fabric type numbers for the lower level and 'Common Name' codes for the second level.

The next level would lump together all the codes from a single production centre, for example everything made in the London area. The occasions where one might want to make this level of amalgamation at the initial recording stage are very rare, but it is quite possible to imagine cases where you might want to rework the pottery from earlier projects at this level, for example if the aim of your study is to record variations in supply through time or space in assemblages whose date and formation details are already known or can safely be ignored. At the very least one would probably want to be able to split the assemblage into major ware types, such as oxidised earthenwares, reduced earthenwares, tin-glazed earthenwares or stonewares.

Finally, the question of coding or naming fabric types and higher-level groupings can give rise to conflict, both within and between organisations. It is probably best to give individual fabric types distinct reference numbers, although some sort of mnemonic indexing (see appendix, p. 242) may be very useful for retrieving information and deciding just which reference specimen(s) may match your problem sherd. A long-established reference collection may contain thousands of types, and you want to avoid having to compare with each in turn.

The creation of higher-level groupings may cause more trouble. What do you call them? 'Ware' is probably the most common generic term, but seems to have almost as many meanings as there are archaeologists. We prefer the more neutral term 'Common Name' to mean a grouping as defined above. The giving of names to such groupings should follow a rational procedure, which may depend on whether you are dealing with traded pottery or domestic production. For the former, source names should be used if the production centre is known, or can reasonably be inferred from the geographical distribution of examples. Otherwise, a memorable descriptive term is probably the best temporary measure until the source can be located. Names based on the first chance find of a distinctive type (such as the notorious 'Malling' ware; see Hume 1977, 2) are best avoided; they seem to lead only to fruitless wrangling about the suitability of the name.

Ultimately, though, a name is only a label, and what matters most is the internal homogeneity and consistency of what is inside the 'box' of your type-definition, not the aesthetic appeal of the label on the outside.

6

CLASSIFICATION OF FORM AND DECORATION

Introduction

Until quite recently the archaeological study of pottery was the study of pottery forms and typology. The analysis of pottery forms and decoration has a long history and has been in the vanguard of the development of the discipline. There are, however, many difficulties encountered in studying forms, especially if one is trying to extract information from small sherds or trying to make a quantitative study.

There are many different ways of classifying forms. The choice depends partly on the existing conventions within your area of study and partly on the aims of your study. It also depends on the use to which others may wish to put your date and on the character of the collection under study.

Uses of form data

Certain aspects of a vessel's form are determined by its intended function. Thus, if you were making a storage jar you would have to think about the capacity, the stability of the vessel, its strength when full, means of sealing the contents and perhaps means of moving the full vessel. You would arrive at a completely different set of criteria if you were making a drinking vessel or one for use in cooking. It is therefore reasonable to divide an assemblage into basic functional classes which might then lead to knowledge of the activities carried out on the site. Of course, not every vessel was used entirely for its originally-intended purpose and there were and are many types of vessel which were reused having fulfilled their original purpose. Amphorae and oil jars are good examples. Roman amphoras were used as ovens, as containers for all sorts of goods and even for burials. Italian oil jars of eighteenth- and nineteenth-century date were widely used in Jamaica as water containers. There are therefore dangers in assuming that the presence of vessels of a particular functional class on a site implies that a certain activity took place there.

Pottery can also be a medium for expressing social position or wealth. The large collections of Oriental porcelain amassed by the European aristocracy in the seventeenth and eighteenth centuries and the collections of Spanish and Italian maiolica made by their predecessors are an extreme example of the way in which the possession of pottery could reflect status. At different times in different places pottery played a similar role. To extract information about status from a pottery collection you have to look at the suitability of vessels for display, for example the presence and type of decoration. The function to which vessels were put could vary with their rarity, which in turn would depend to a large degree on the distance from their source. In these circumstances it is difficult to make decisions when one is recording an assemblage as to the social significance of the sherds. Nevertheless, in both Roman Britain and seventeenth-century England it is important to distinguish undecorated bowls which must have served some utilitarian purpose and bowls which could have been used as a medium for display. The distinction survives into modern times with the existence in many families of the best dinner service, which may actually never be used but passed on from generation to generation, whilst cheap and cheerful wares are actually used around the house.

Forms are also worth recording because they may have been sensitive to passing fashion and therefore capable of being dated. In some instances it may be that the pottery reflects some other element of changing fashion, such as the growth in popularity of tea and coffee drinking in the seventeenth and eighteenth centuries, whereas in others it may be that more subtle changes were responsible. Indeed, there are undoubted chronological progressions in such features as the size of cooking vessels, the shape of their rims or even, in the case of Romano-British black burnished ware, the angle of the burnished lattice decoration. The meaning of these trends, and indeed the question of whether they ever had any meaning, is irrelevant to the fact that they provide a means of dating pottery and, therefore, of providing archaeological chronologies.

Creating and using a form type-series

The recording of forms has several separate problems attached to it. Firstly there is the same classificatory problem as we have just seen in the study of fabric. Each vessel is unique in form, unless produced in a mould, and these individual forms must be grouped together to form a classification. Secondly, there is the problem of missing data. It may be possible to unerringly assign a complete form to a class, based, for example on the ratio of width to height, the base diameter or the number of handles. If only a fragment of that form is present then the classification must be able to allow multiple options. Since potters work by combining standard elements – bases, bodies, rims, handles and so on – it is not always possible to infer the complete form from the fragments present in a deposit. There is a difference in approach between recording the objective facts about the vessel from which a sherd came and making an educated guess based on the knowledge of the pottery of the period. It is sometimes possible to test the accuracy of this guesswork when a single sherd is identified and subsequently more of the same vessel is found. Even those who spend their working lives studying the pottery of a period can make mistakes. Nevertheless, an educated guess may well be perfectly acceptable, so long as the potsherds are retained for further study.

A traditional way of presenting the variation in pottery forms is as a form type-series, in which each type-example represents a group of vessels which are considered to be more-or-less 'the same' in shape. It is best to work from the more complete to the less complete, basing your type-definitions on the most complete vessels available (which may well come from museum collections rather than excavations) and then matching less complete examples to them, or using them to 'fill gaps'. A type-series should be capable of expansion, as we cannot expect to have found examples of all possible types.

Form type-series can be divided into two classes, the unstructured and the structured. The unstructured way to proceed is to start with the first example and call it Type One. The next is compared with it and if different is made into Type Two. This method continues until the whole collection has been studied. It has the advantage of extreme simplicity, and you can start with a small amount of material and increase the size of your type-series as more pottery comes to hand, perhaps from ongoing excavations. The disadvantage is that as the type-series becomes larger you will find it more and more difficult to retrieve information from it – to find out, for example, whether there is a type that matches the pot in your hand. You will probably find yourself searching many irrelevant drawings looking for the 'right' one.

This problem suggests that a more structured method might be more useful in the long run, although requiring more initial input. A common approach (for example as at Southwark, see Marsh and Tyers 1978) would be to divide the pottery first into broad functional classes (p. 217) (for example I = flagons, II = jars, III = bowls, and so on). You can then subdivide each class into broad groupings based on shape, style or whatever attributes you think appropriate (for example II.A = ..., II.B = ..., and so on). Finally you can number individual types within a group sequentially (for example II.A.1, II.B.2, and so on). This keeps the system open-ended, but you only have to search the parts that are relevant to the new pot in your hand. The disadvantages are that you will have to start with a large collection of material in order to form classes that will be reasonably stable as fresh material comes to light. Otherwise you will find that you have put a group in the 'wrong' class because the early examples were not representative, and you will have to revise the whole structure. Also, sooner or later, you will encounter the 'continuum' problem that we saw with fabric type-series – the gap between two apparently distinct types will become filled with a continuum of intermediate types, and it will be not at all clear where you should draw the boundary. One solution is to abandon the hierarchical nature of your structure, and allow one type to belong to two groups, or one group to two classes. You may feel this is anathema to your feelings of tidiness and organisation, but it is perfectly sound and may reflect the complexity of the series better than a rigid hierarchical system, as well as making it less likely that you will miss matches in your searching. If you follow the structured route, you may need a formal way of assigning pots to types, types to groups, and so on. Various mathematical techniques that you may find useful are mentioned below, and are described on pp. 155–163.

A problem common to both approaches is that experience and experiment have shown that there is considerable disagreement between typologies developed subjectively by different workers. Sometimes a typology is accompanied by a written description to make it clear to the user what the differences between types is meant to be. However, in the end most of these descriptions come down to stating that a type is like a previous one only with more of a particular characteristic – more rounded, more everted, more angular or whatever. One solution to this problem is to determine experimentally where boundaries exist which can be recognised repeatedly by the majority of students. However, this may well mean that the real differences between types, and the information which they contain, is lost.

Just as for fabrics, the psychological differences between 'lumpers' and 'splitters' are likely to become apparent. As we have seen, variations are inevitable in a hand-made product. Some may represent chronological or other trends, while others may be just a potter's attempt to relieve the tedium of throwing so many pots each day. Studies from production sites may help you tell which is which. Practically, there is no reason not to record to a high level of detail, provided that, with a little training, the classification can be committed to memory. Even apparently illogical systems can be learnt if they are used regularly and it's easier to move from splitting to lumping than in the opposite direction.

Describing shapes

It appears that less work has been put into the problem of describing the shape of vessels than into the parallel problem of describing their fabrics. This is probably because: (i) a drawing can represent well the shape of a type, but a visual representation of a fabric is much more difficult; and (ii) form types are best based on complete vessels, which are relatively rare, whereas every sherd has a fabric (if nothing else).

Nevertheless, various mathematical methods of describing and comparing the shapes of pots can be devised. One can measure dimensions – height, maximum width, rim and base diameter and so on – and by plotting certain combinations work out whether there are any clusters within the data or whether every measurement and ratio has a unimodal distribution.

By looking at ratios one can study the overall shape of a vessel irrespective of its absolute size (see p. 155). However, in many cases a potter will have made the same basic form in a variety of sizes to suit different intended purposes. It has also been demonstrated that there are subtle changes in form

with size. These are brought about because of the influence of the manufacturing process on the form so that rims or bases of similar size and
shape might actually have come from vessels of differing size and shape.
Another approach is to digitise the drawing of the vessel or rim under
study and to use mathematical curve-fitting routines to describe the shape.
The values obtained will be objective and can then be compared using
clustering and other classificatory programs. Such methods are as yet
beyond the resources of most archaeological projects, but means of auto-
mating recording and refining the processing of the results are being developed so that this approach will become more common in the future.
Another, related, approach is the use of 'envelopes', shapes which enclose
vessels of one type only (see p. 158). Like the mathematical approach, the
'envelope' method has the advantage that it is repeatable and independent
of the worker.

Vessels and sherds
It is almost always possible to say something about the shape of a vessel from
which a sherd came. One basic classification is into hollow or closed wares on
the one hand and flat or open wares on the other. Not only will there be a
different curvature to most hollow ware sherds to that found on flat wares but
the inner surface of a hollow ware will have no traces of finishing whereas the
inner surface of a sherd of exactly the same size and shape from a flat ware
will probably be finished in some way. Larger sherds may well be classifiable
into the broad geometric shape of their parent vessels – spheres, cones,
cylinders and combinations. There are classification systems which use these
basic shapes as their starting points.

   Determining form from part of a vessel is limited by the fact that potters
made vessels for different purposes starting with a few basic shapes. Cauldrons could be made by adding three feet and two handles to a vessel of basic
jar form. Skillets were formed by adding three feet and a horizontal handle to
a conical bowl, whilst a variety of vessel forms in tenth- and eleventh-century
England could have tubular spouts or handles added to their rims (fig. 6.1).
The possibility that a sherd comes from a jar rather than a cauldron or a
skillet rather than a bowl will vary depending on the size of the vessel
fragment present. At a certain critical size it will be possible to say for certain
that the vessel did not have two handles or that it had no feet whereas below
that size the possibility exists. If one is trying to study pottery forms using
only sherd material then the definite absence of certain features may become
as important a point to record as their presence.

   The analysis of decoration is another area where much work has taken
place. With small sherds it can be impossible to say anything about the
overall design but even in those cases it is possible to describe the decorative
technique used, which may be sufficient to help classify the sherd. The range

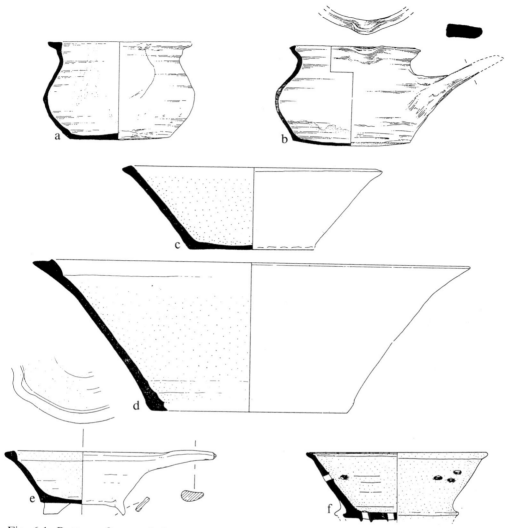

Fig. 6.1. Potters often used the same basic form as a starting point for vessels of widely differing function. Medieval Surrey Whiteware cooking pots (a) could be turned into pipkins (b) simply by adding a horizontal handle and a pulled lip. Sixteenth-century Malvern Chase bowls were made in a range of sizes, (c) and (d) whilst the same basic shape could be turned into a skillet by the addition of a handle, three feet and a pulled lip (e), or a chafing dish by piercing the sides and base and luting the bowl onto a separate base (f). In each ware featureless body sherds of these forms are, naturally enough, indistinguishable. Scale: 1/4

of possible materials and techniques is so great that many powerful classifications have been based solely on this type of data.

The basic decorative methods can be divided into those in which material was applied to the surface of the pot and those in which the surface of the

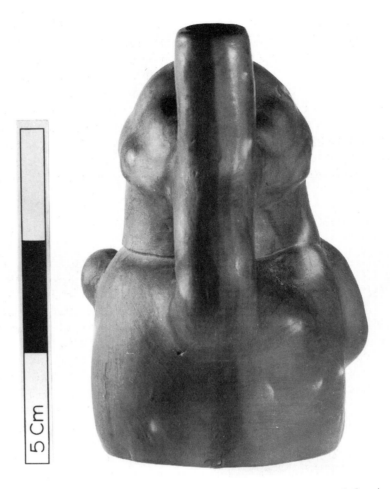

Fig. 6.2. Moulds were used in the classical world to make lamps and figurines and in Mesoamerica were used to produce elaborate anthropomorphic figures. (Photo: University College London, Institute of Archaeology)

vessel was modified in some way. There are a range of materials which have been used to decorate vessels. The most common, undoubtedly, is clay. Clay was applied in a variety of consistencies, each of which produces a distinctive appearance. Slips were made by adding water to clay until it formed a liquid. They could be applied as a wash, leaving an even coating over the vessel, or could be used to form a design. Clay could be applied in a plastic state and modelled on the surface of the pot. At its simplest this method could be used to apply strips of clay, whilst at its most complex the vessel becomes a sculpture (fig. 6.2). It is also possible to apply dry clay or crushed flint to the surface of a newly formed pot. This method was used to produce 'roughcast' beakers in the Roman empire and was used again in early seventeenth-century England to produce mugs.

A variety of colours could be achieved through the use of different clays and by manipulating firing conditions. These colours are derived from the different states of iron present in the clay. In oxidising conditions, colours varying from white, then yellow through light and dark browns to brick red can be obtained, whilst reducing conditions can produce blue-greys, greys and purples. It was, of course, extremely difficult to produce reduced and oxidised conditions on the same vessel. This was the basis of the decoration of some Egyptian wares and may have been intentionally achieved on Romano-British colour-coated wares which were fired stacked one inside another so that the lower parts of the vessels were reduced, through lack of oxygen.

In addition to clays, other materials could be added to the surface of a pot, providing they could withstand the firing temperature. Examples include mica, which was applied to some vessels in the Roman empire as a slip, and grains of quartz or other rock fragments. The latter technique was used in the Iberian peninsula in the sixteenth and seventeenth centuries AD.

Glazes, coatings of glass, have had periods of almost universal use interspersed with periods when the techniques either fell out of favour or were forgotten. Four basic types of glaze have been used in the past. Alkaline glazes are composed of compounds of sodium, potassium and silica. Soda-potash glasses form at quite high temperatures but will melt at lower ones. They are therefore prepared by previously forming the glass, then crushing it to a powder which is mixed with a small amount of clay to bind it together. The body of an alkaline-glazed vessel can consist of a very high proportion of crushed quartz.

Lead glass is formed mainly from a mixture of lead and silica. It fluxes at a lower temperature than soda-potash glass and can therefore be applied to a pot in its raw state: as the metal itself, as an oxide or as some other compound, such as the sulphide, galena (Rice 1987, 98–102).

Salt glaze is the name given to an alkaline glaze which is formed on stoneware vessels in the kiln, using salt as a catalyst. It forms at temperatures in excess of 1100°C and differs in appearance to other alkaline glazes in that the glaze is usually very thin and quite often has a distinctive textured surface; when combined with an iron-rich slip this produces the 'tiger skin' appearance characteristic of seventeenth-century stonewares. Lastly, porcelain glazes are formed from compounds rich in feldspar.

Paints coloured by iron, manganese, copper and cobalt have been used on pottery vessels, the latter three usually in conjunction with a glaze. The colours depend on the type of glaze. Manganese on a salt glaze produces a purple colour whilst iron on a salt glaze can be colourless or brown. Cobalt appears blue on salt glazes, alkaline glazes and lead-based glazes, while

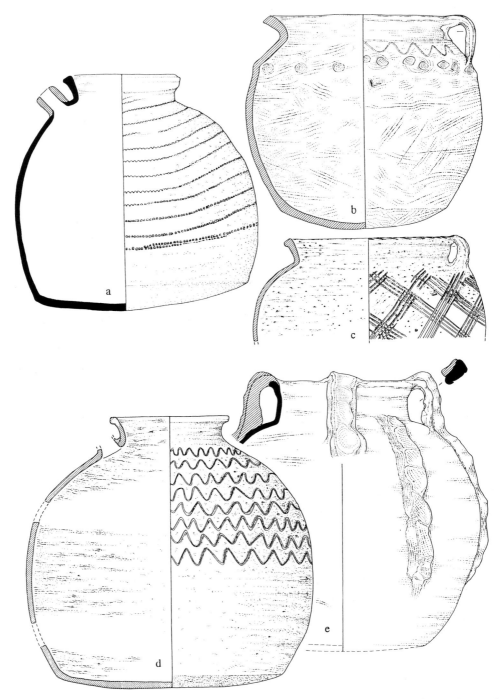

Fig. 6.3. Decorative techniques used on a range of eleventh- and twelfth-century jars and pitchers found in London: (a) roller-stamping, (b) raised bosses pinched between thumb and forefinger, (c) Lattice formed with a four-toothed comb, (d) horizontal wavy lines incised with a round-tipped implement, (e) applied strips thumbed on one side only. Scale: 1/4

copper appears turquoise on alkaline glazes and green to ox-blood red on lead-based glazes, depending on its state.

Organic paints or coatings can sometimes be distinguished on the surface of a pot. For example, some Iron Age pottery produced in Sussex was decorated around the neck with a single band of material which in some cases has started to peel off the pot. It has not been analysed but was very probably an organic compound.

Vessels could also be painted after firing, either as part of the initial manufacturing process or at some later stage. In these cases the decoration is often very fragile.

Enamels, powdered coloured glasses, were used to decorate some stone-wares and porcelains. Unlike other paints they were applied after a first glazing.

A final applied technique which must be mentioned is the addition of metal foil to the surface. Examples are known from the Roman period and from eighth- to ninth-century Europe (Tating ware). In many cases the foil, tin in the case of Tating ware, will have decayed leaving a stained area comprising the remains of the foil and/or its adhesive.

The many techniques used to scratch, cut or impress decoration into the surface of a pot can be difficult to classify. The main methods are listed below and illustrated in fig. 6.3:

Combing	a very simple technique could be applied with a snapped lath of wood.
Grooving	decoration scratched into the surface of the vessel with a tool of some sort. Variations in the shape and size of the tool will affect the appearance of the decoration.
Incision	in which the surface of the vessel is actually cut away. One of the best known examples of this method is samian ware with cut glass decoration.
Fretwork	in which the wall of the vessel is pierced through to make the decoration. This technique was used extensively with puzzle jugs from the seventeenth century onwards, since it immediately made the user wonder how the vessel could still hold liquid.
Impressed finger-tipping	one of the simplest methods of decoration. Used, for example, on British Neolithic pottery (Peterborough ware).
Burnishing	another very common and very old technique. The effect of polishing the leather-hard surface

of a pot was to align the clay mineral platelets parallel with the surface of the pot, giving it a sheen. In some cases this technique was combined with the addition of a slip, finer in texture than the body of the vessel.

Knife-trimming
a knife was often used to pare away the surface of a pot and the surface effect produced was sometimes used decoratively, for example to produce facets around the vessel.

Roller-stamping
a cylinder-shaped roller with an incised pattern is rolled over the surface of the vessel while it is leather-hard. A repeating pattern of the design on the roller is produced 'in negative'. This technique is occasionally referred to as roasting (see below).

Rouletting
a pleasing and complex pattern can be produced with a flexible blade bent over at one end and held up against the surface of the pot as it is turned round on the wheel. With some adjustment, and a little practice, the blade will judder up and down rhythmically, producing bands of fine lines on the surface of the pot. The method was used extensively in the first and second centuries AD to decorate Roman fine wares. The alternative term, chattering, is occasionally used for this technique.

Depending on the extent to which your pottery is decorated, you will probably need a decoration type-series as well as a form one, although if there is a close correlation between form and decoration, one overall series will probably suffice. It should describe technique as well as design, because: (i) particular idiosyncrasies of technique may be diagnostic of particular sources; and (ii) for many small sherds technique is all that can be observed. The description and classification of decorative patterns is a difficult and contentious area, especially if attempts are made to understand the symbolic content of the pattern.

7

ILLUSTRATION

Introduction

Pottery is normally drawn in a highly stylised manner, although archaeologists soon become so used to the system that they find it remarkable that
given a sherd of pottery an illustrator unfamiliar with the conventions will
actually draw what he or she sees. Wheel-thrown or other vessels with a
central symmetry are conventionally shown with a central vertical line. On
one side of this line the cross-section of the vessel wall and the interior surface
of the pot is shown while on the other the exterior surface of the pot is shown.
The convention most widely followed is to show the interior view on the left
and the exterior on the right, but in some publications, in particular those
from eastern Europe, this is reversed.

As a means of producing a simple record of a vessel, for use by a pottery
researcher or as part of an archive for example, pottery drawing can be quick,
cheap and effective. Once a decision is made to make drawings to a publication standard, showing texture and surface treatment, illustration can
become very slow and expensive. It can become one of the most costly
elements in pottery research. It is therefore important to consider at an early
stage what exactly you will be using pottery illustrations for and what
implications this will have on your project design.

The purpose of illustrations

Pottery illustrations are intended to make comparison of vessels simpler by
reconstructing on paper as much as possible of the complete form, even if
only sherds of it have been found. Information and detail which would hinder
this comparison, such as the condition of the sherds, concretions adhering to
them or sherd edges (unless needed to show the extent of decoration), is
omitted.

At their simplest, illustrations can serve as a record of the contents of an
assemblage and be made as a matter of course as part of the recording of the
collection. Such a record is almost certain to contain redundant data which
will never be of use to anyone, but there may be cases where this approach is
justified. In particular, if it is not possible to retain the collection for some
reason and no typology is available then, as a poor second, the rims, bases
and other featured sherds can be drawn and a certain amount of information
extracted from the drawings at a later stage. The mindless illustration of

pottery 'because it's there' is frowned upon in Britain, for the reasons given above. Ironically, it is often the illustrations which enable early archaeological pottery collections to be re-examined and new analyses to take place.

Another strategy is to illustrate a type-series, so that only representative examples of particular types (however they are defined) are illustrated. The logic of this approach is that it provides some form of evidence for the presence of a type on a particular site and ultimately forms a reference series which can be used in the analysis of subsequent collections. The problem here is that as one moves away from illustration as a record towards illustration to make a particular point so it becomes less and less clear that the illustrated material should be drawn from examples within the collection under study.

A type-series, logically, should be constructed using the most complete example of each type, no matter where that example has been found. Thus, it is extremely difficult to construct a type-series without undertaking a large amount of background research. An example of this was the London Medieval Pottery Corpus, which was constructed as part of the analysis of medieval pottery stratified in large dated assemblages excavated in the City of London, but where only a small fraction of the vessels used as type examples actually came from archaeological contexts (Pearce and Vince 1988) – many came instead from older museum collections.

As one moves from illustration of a site assemblage as a record through to the construction of a multi-site or regional type-series, so the character of the illustration itself may change. At the one end of the spectrum one needs a simple record of the form, which may perhaps be of use in subsequent typological analysis, while at the other one wants to convey information about the original appearance of the vessel, as an aid to identification and study, and the method of manufacture, since this may itself be a means of identification, as well as being a subject of interest in its own right.

A basic decision that has to be made is whether to illustrate by means of drawings or photographs (or both, as the two are not mutually exclusive). It has been found that drawings give a better representation of shape and can show both inside and outside simultaneously, which photography cannot do. Photographs are better at showing texture, some classes of decoration and technical details such as the means of attaching handles. They can also give attractive 'wedding portrait'-style illustrations of large assemblages, such as pit- and grave-groups. It used to be said that line drawings were preferable to photographs for purposes of publication because of the difference in the cost of reproduction. This has narrowed in recent years, but still holds in the case of colour photography, which should be used sparingly and in very special circumstances (for example highly-decorated polychrome pottery). Overall we may say that drawings are better for a permanent record and for conveying basic information, while photography is better at creating impressions and conveying subtle information.

Drawing pottery

There are several works describing the method used to draw pottery reconstructions (especially Griffiths et al. 1990). The traditional method is to mark
in pencil on paper or drawing film two perpendicular base lines, one of which
represents the vertical axis of the vessel while the other represents the top or
bottom (depending on whether the rim or base is present). The illustrator
then establishes the diameter of the rim or base, using a rim chart or direct
measurement if a complete pot. This is then marked onto the drawing. The
depth/height and diameter of other significant features on the pot are then
determined and marked on the drawing. This can be done by placing the
rim/base at the correct position on the rim chart and then using a set square
to find the correct height/diameter of each point.

Once the major features of the vessel have been accurately located on the
drawing one can either use the same method at intervals to help determine the
intermediate points or use some form of mechanical aid, such as a profile
gauge (as used by builders and DIY enthusiasts to cut floor covering to shape
around curved surfaces). With experience it will become clear that a discrep-
ancy of even a few millimetres on any measurement can make the profile look
wrong and that it is often better to use fewer measurements but more
observation when drawing the profile of a pot. A common problem with
mechanical aids such as the profile gauge, particularly in the hands of
inexperienced illustrators, is that rather more attention is paid to drawing the
device than the vessel.

The next stage is to measure the thickness of the vessel and the interior
shape of the rim or base. These are drawn on the left-hand side of the central
line. Next, sharp changes of profile can be shown as a line on the appropriate
view. The basic shape of the vessel has now been completed. If there are no
additional elements then one can start to tidy up the drawing and ink it in.

Handles are conventionally shown on the right-hand (exterior) view of the
pot. A cross-section is shown perpendicular to the handle profile with two
short lines showing the position of the section (fig. 7.1 (a)). There may be
cases where a vertical section through the handle would be informative, for
example to show the means of handle attachment. If used, this section would
be drawn alongside the handle profile. If the vessel has two opposed handles
then one can be drawn in profile and the other in vertical section. Three
handles would be indicated by drawing one in profile and extending the
exterior view to the left of the centre line to show the second handle in
three-quarters view (fig. 7.1 (b)). Lug handles are usually shown on the
central line.

Spouts are usually shown on the left-hand, interior, side of the drawing.
Where formed as a deformation of the rim it is usual to show two cross-
sections superimposed, one is the normal section and the other the section
across the lip. Some medieval jugs had very elaborately constructed spouts

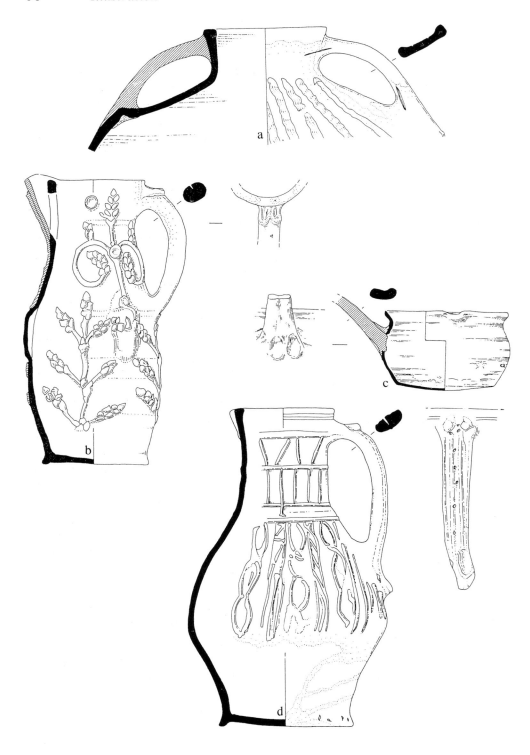

which can require both a sectional view and a frontal view, which is usually shown to the left of the drawing (fig. 7.1 (c)).

Decoration is difficult to illustrate satisfactorily. For some purposes it can be important to show the plan view, especially where the vessel is an internally decorated bowl or plate. Whenever one is trying to show the decoration on a spherical surface there will be some distortion. One way of lessening this distortion is to 'unwrap' the decoration (fig. 7.2). This shows each element without too much distortion but makes it impossible to see how the decoration fits the shape of the pot.

You may need to use conventions to show the use of different colour slips, paints and lustres. The rule seems to be not to try to fit every drawing into the same conventions but to show stippling or hatching which makes the pattern clear and to provide a key alongside the drawing.

The use of drawings to show surface texture is not universally accepted, one suspects because few archaeologists have the necessary illustrative skills. Cost is also an important factor, but many drawings are carefully shaded to show the curvature of the pot (redundant since we know the pot is round, and if it were not then special attention would be drawn to the fact). Even worse is the painstaking stippling which achieves nothing except to make the pot appear to be made of expanded polystyrene. If the time devoted to such ritualistic exercises were spent on a realistic representation of surface texture, the standard of illustration would be raised enormously. Similarly, drawings can be used to show constructional features, such as the coils of hand-built vessels, and surface treatment such as paddle-and-anvil and knife-trimming, all of which help the reader to understand the pot (fig. 7.3).

Another difficult question is whether and how to reconstruct in a drawing the missing parts of a vessel. Some authorities say that you should only draw what is present, no more (Blake and Davey 1983, 42), but this seems unnecessarily purist provided you make it clear what you have done. There are in fact two distinct problems, which one might call 'vertical' and 'horizontal' interpolation/extrapolation. The vertical sort, usually extrapolation, is needed when the profile of the drawn vessel is incomplete. It may be reasonable, using knowledge of similar vessels, to extend the drawn profile beyond the limits of the actual pot, to give an estimate of the shape of the whole thing.

Fig. 7.1. Illustrating handles. These four vessels are all examples of thirteenth- or fourteenth-century Surrey Whiteware found in London. The standard convention of drawing the handle in profile on the right hand side of the drawing has been adapted to best portray the manufacturing details and decoration. (a) Two-handled storage jar in which the body has been pushed into the handle and the resulting depression inside the pot filled with an extra wad of clay. (b) Jug on which the rod handle is decorated with stabbed holes and two 'ears' of clay best portrayed by a vertical view. (c) A pipkin whose handle has been inserted through the body and the resulting hole sealed by an extra wad of clay. (d) Jug similar to (c) but whose furrowed and stabbed handle is best illustrated by a horizontal view. Scale: 1/4

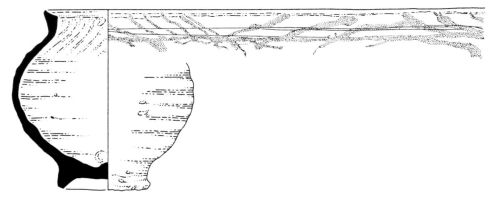

Fig. 7.2. The decoration on the surface of a vessel 'unwrapped'

To be honest, you must show which parts are 'real' and which are extrapolation; this can be done, for example, by not blacking-in the extrapolated section, using broken lines, or by the use of discrete marks beside the drawn profile (Gillam 1957).

The horizontal problem arises when, at any depth below the rim, not all of the horizontal circumference of the pot is present. Strictly speaking, the problem is one of interpolation because the circuit of the pot is closed (that is if you go round far enough you return to your starting point). The problem does not really exist for undecorated pots since they can be assumed to be 'the same' all the way round and drawn accordingly. Decoration which is 'horizontal' in nature, such as burnished zones, cordons, horizontal lines (applied, grooved, and so on) present few problems, since radial symmetry can again be assumed. But how far can you go with more complex decoration? This depends on the regularity of the pattern and the extent of one's knowledge about the class of pottery concerned. Once again, the golden rule is to make it clear to your readers how much exists and how much has been 'made up', leaving them to judge how reasonable the attempt was. Similar considerations apply in the addition of features which you can reasonably assume to have been present on more complete examples of certain classes of vessel, such as handles, feet and spouts.

Since pottery illustrations can be both laborious and repetitive there have been several attempts to partially or completely mechanise the method. By and large these attempts have not been successful, or at least have not superseded manual methods to any great extent. One which may have a certain appeal, but is not to be recommended for use with museum accessions, is the use of a large circular saw to slice through every rim. One half is then placed onto paper or film and the outline drawn around (Holladay 1976). There are a number of published descriptions of simple gadgets which some practitioners have found valuable aids to pottery drawing (e.g. Terrell and Osborne 1971; Trump 1972; Edwards 1974). With the wider availability

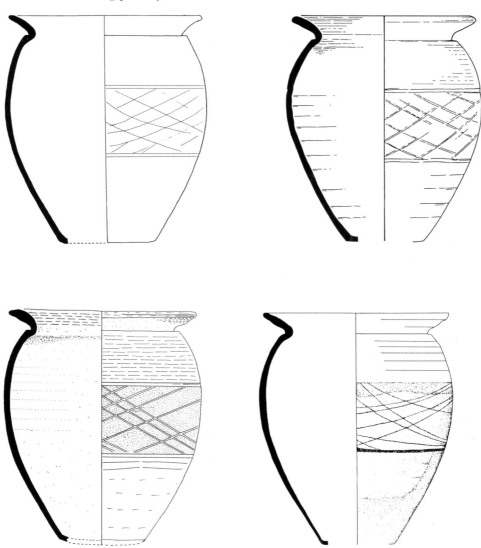

Fig. 7.3. The limits of objective recording. The same vessel drawn by four different illustrators. (Drawn by John Newton, Paul Tyers, Clive Orton and Sunil Nandha)

of computers others have sought to eliminate paper and pencil altogether. Turner et al. (1990) describe a system based on a modified 'mouse' with attached probes to input profile data directly onto the computer. Such a system may be a quick and efficient method of converting profiles into a computer-readable form for some form of shape analysis (see p. 157), but the trend in publication drawings should be away from the 'machine-made' look and towards more realistic renderings.

Photography

Photography can be very useful in recording pottery. Photographs of vessels *in situ* may aid interpretation and can form the most vivid means of demonstrating the function of a vessel. Individual sherds can be recorded by photography as a source of reference in research or as a means of illustrating lectures or workshops. Photographs should be taken of sherd families before restoration as a final record of their size and shape. Complete vessels should also be photographed as a matter of course. If they have any monetary value then the photograph will act as a means of registering their identity and there will always be calls for photographs to illustrate articles and leaflets as well as to form elements in museum displays.

Close-up photography is very useful for recording surface treatment and details of manufacture as well as providing an aid to identification if the broken sherd edges are photographed. Micro-photography is used as an adjunct to fabric analysis while Scanning Electron Microscope images can also be preserved as photographs and, again, form a graphic means of presentation of evidence (fig. 7.4).

The use of a scale in photography is important. Full-size, two-metre, ranging rods will be too large for most site shots and a one-metre or half-metre rule is better. For studio shots a ten-centimetre scale may be suitable whilst a common coin will act as an instantly recognisable scale for shots destined to be used in lectures. Here too, scales are frowned upon by non-specialist publications, and even by some specialist ones. You may therefore have to augment your photographic record with the height or other maximum dimension of one of the vessels in the shot. The distortion in size in group shots is so great that no scale is going to be of value in taking precise measurements from such a photograph. For close-up work you may want to have the photograph produced at a set scale: life-size, twice life-size, half scale or whatever. This is best achieved either by photographing the sherd on top of a grid or with a scale rule laid along one edge of the shot. In the former case you would have to crop the photograph for publication whilst in the latter the scale can be kept outside the printing area. It is difficult to supply a scale in close-up photography. For use in lectures and other publicity a common object, such as the human hand, can be very effective but for record work it is better to have a small rule, perhaps part of an etched metal ruler, which you photograph before starting on the objects themselves. This will be perfectly acceptable if the camera and stage are fixed in position. The same method can be used for micro-photography and you can purchase microscope slides incorporating minute graticules. There is no easy way of putting a scale into a micro-photograph without a two-stage process of taking a photograph, determining the scale and marking it on a print and then re-photographing it. SEM photographs have the scale superimposed on them automatically.

On-site photography is notoriously difficult to get right, since the subject

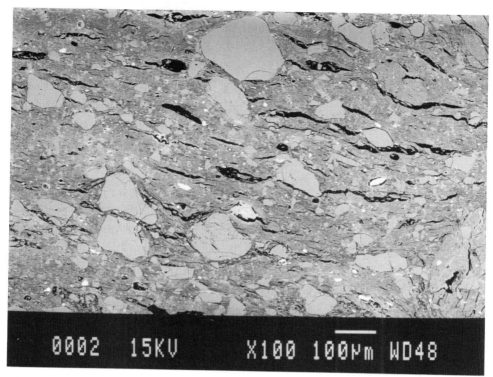

Fig. 7.4. SEM photomicrograph of Stamford ware crucible. Fabric S1 (BMRL sample 25835). Poorly sorted grains of quartz (light grey) are embedded in a fired clay matrix showing elongate cracks (black). The small white grains are iron oxides. All the photomicrographs are orientated with their long axes parallel to the surfaces of the sherds and all were taken at the same magnification, the long axis representing 1mm. (Courtesy of the British Museum Department of Scientific Research)

and angle of the shot are predetermined, no matter what the natural lighting. It is also not always possible to wait for suitable conditions, since photography holds up further work on that part of the site. Studio photography can use lamps but if necessary sherds and vessels can be photographed in natural light, preferably out of strong sunlight so as to minimise shadows.

Various types of background are used in studio shots. Whatever background is chosen, it should have a matt surface, so as not to cause reflections and glare, and not be distracting from the subject of the shot. This is not to say that it must be a plain white background. Coloured backgrounds and textured backgrounds can be used to great effect, especially in presenting pottery vessels for the general public. One problem with most backings is that the need to use two lamps can create double shadows which are distracting and slightly confusing. Sherds can be photographed on a sheet of glass so that the shadows are out of the field of view. As mentioned above, it is also possible to use a gridded background, for example a sheet of graph paper, which will make reproduction to scale easy. The result is, however, hardly photogenic.

Most camera lenses cannot be focussed closer than *c*. 0.5m and at that distance it is often possible to include several sherds on the one exposure. This can be useful, for example when making record shots or black and white prints which can be cropped for publication. For slides, however, it is best to think carefully about the inclusion of more than one sherd or, at least, of more than one type of vessel, in a shot. You may spend valuable lecturing time explaining that the audience should ignore particular sherds and even then it is quite often the irrelevant points which are picked up for later discussion of your presentation. You will find the photographing of fragmentary vessels very frustrating. On the one hand they cannot just be laid flat on the backing and photographed straight on whilst on the other they cannot easily be photographed so as to show their form. Rims and body sherds are more difficult than those with bases, which can be photographed upright. It is sometimes possible to support rims by arranging blocks of wood under a sheet until the rim is horizontal.

Complete vessels should ideally be photographed so as to show in one shot the general form of the vessel, the handle and the spout. This will normally mean that the vessel is positioned so that the rim is just visible as an ellipse. The handle will be at 45° towards the camera and one will be able to see the inside of the spout. On vessels where the spout is decorated, or where the decorative scheme is based around the spout, this arrangement will have to be reversed and if both the spout and the handle are significantly decorated you may need two shots to record the vessel. Vessels decorated with figurative scenes or other complex designs may need a series of shots to record the design or it may be that you can use a combination of photography and line drawing to portray the vessel. An ideal method of recording such vessels would be using a video camera. The pot could be slowly rotated on a turntable so that every aspect of the vessel is recorded. The main disadvantage of video recording at present is the difficulty in obtaining a hard copy of the image and its poor quality when compared with still photography.

Photographing groups of vessels produces another set of problems, similar in many ways to those encountered by photographers at weddings. Tall vessels should be positioned at the back and you may have to build up a stage so that these vessels are not completely masked by those in front. With a sizable assemblage you will find it difficult to get both the front and back rows of vessels in focus at the same time and the positioning of vessels is so critical that you need two people to take the photograph, one of whom is looking down the view-finder calling out instructions to the other, who will be making the final adjustments to the layout. The same strictures over the positioning and angle of the individual vessels still hold true. There are dangers involved in allowing professional photographers free rein in photographing pottery assemblages, since they will be primarily concerned with the aesthetics of the image rather than its information content. On the other hand, professional assistance can make all the difference to a photograph and, despite the difficulty of getting the composition right, a single group shot can be an extremely powerful means of presenting a large amount of information at one time. One photograph of Late Saxon Shelly ware vessels from the City of London has been reproduced in print five or six times in six years.

Having taken your photographs you must make sure that they are adequately indexed, especially if the photographic collection is large, otherwise you will end up wasting effort by photographing a vessel or subject for which a suitable print or slide already exists. The important data are: a unique reference to the slide; a cross-index to the existence of a black and white print; the negative number of the black and white print; details of the site and context and the ware and form of vessel. Other data may also be worth indexing, especially in the case of decorated vessels where the subject matter of the decoration may be of interest.

8

POTTERY ARCHIVES

Introduction
An ideal pottery archive would preserve both the total collection and all of the data relating to the pottery from an excavation or field project in such a way that it was physically stable, secure and allowed an instant response to any query concerning its contents. The reality has been, and often still is, far from this. Until recently it was common practice for an archaeologist to regard a pottery collection as having fulfilled its purpose once a publication was produced. It would at that stage be passed across to the care of a museum whose storage and retention policies would govern its fate. There is now, however, a joint realisation by the archaeological and museum professions that they have a duty together to produce a usable archive. After all, a vast amount of money and time will often have been spent on the pottery collection up to that point and it is wasteful of a potential resource not to curate it properly and make it accessible for use. There is a further development in that the specialised needs of archaeological archives and collections have led in the United Kingdom to the foundation of archaeological resource centres such as the Archaeological Research Centre in York.

Uses of archives
When designing a pottery archive one really wants to know how it is to be used in the future. However, with a permanent archive the sorts of questions which might be asked of it may not even have been formulated at the time the archive was created and all one can really do is to look at the ways in which you yourself might want to use someone else's archive.

Whatever is decided, the organisation must be simple and clear to grasp. After all, it will probably be curated by a staff whose concerns are much wider than simply ceramics. Furthermore, potential users will probably wish to come to the store and immediately start to use the data. They will not want to read a substantial 'User's Guide' for a simple request, nor will they be too pleased at having to use archives organised in radically different ways, although a certain amount of acclimatisation to your system is inevitable.

Another basic principle is that loose sherds which belong in the archive must be capable of being restored to it with as little difficulty as possible. Otherwise, human nature being what it is, the stray sherd will be placed in the nearest empty space or box. One must also assume no special knowledge of your pottery or its classification in the person who is to curate the collection. For example, there is a lot to be said in principle for storing vessels by ware, fabric or form. However, one cannot expect the curator to know the ware, fabric or form of the stray sherd. The correct location of any sherd must be capable of being deduced from information marked on the sherd, or on its container, and this usually means the context.

Lastly, while access to the actual pottery collection should be open to all serious users, it is preferable for the long-term curation of the collection if simple requests can be answered without having to retrieve the sherds themselves. For example, if one is interested in the decorative methods used on a particular type of pot then it will save the researcher a lot of time and effort if your archive contains information on whether sherds are decorated or not.

Practical issues

The basic principles of archive design described above have to be tempered by practical considerations concerning storage conditions, display and the location of collections.

Storage of pottery

For the museum curator, pottery is extremely inconvenient material. It can be bulky, a single assemblage might contain several hundred sherds with a total weight of tens of kilogrammes, and yet at the same time archaeological pottery can be fragile, for example Romano-British fine wares were extremely thinly potted and sherds will easily shatter. Unless enclosed in a cupboard or container (such as a wooden, plastic or cardboard box) it also attracts dust and grime. The unit size also varies considerably, from a complete storage jar or amphora which might have to sit in its own packing case on the floor of a store at one extreme to minute sherds which need to be enclosed in a box or bag simply so that they do not get lost. Attempts to impose order and uniformity in the storage of pottery will always run up against this problem.

Standard methods of storage include:

(i) *Paper bags.* The use of paper bags to contain potsherds is common. This is partly a hangover from the pre-plastic days, partly a matter of cost and partly the fact that strong paper bags will sit neatly in order in a box, making retrieval easier than with plastic bags. They can be folded-over to keep in the contents and can be labelled directly. The two big disadvantages of paper over plastic are that paper is not so strong; jagged sherd edges will rip even thick paper bags; and paper is prone to damp. This leads to mould attack and infestation and, at worst, loss of the collection. Even if damp is spotted quickly the collection will need to be re-boxed, so adding to the expense of curation.

(ii)   *Plastic bags.* Pottery is often stored in heavy-duty plastic bags on which there is a means of marking the contents. This can be by the inclusion of a separate label (made out of untearable plastic, preferably) or a matt white panel on the bag itself. In either case care should be taken to use a pen approved for archive use. Certain ball-point pen inks will fade whilst others are attractive to bacteria. Some plastic bags are sold as 'self-sealing'. They rarely work. Attempts to re-open the bag may result in the bag ripping and will certainly involve fiddling about. Large bags of sherds can be closed with plastic-coated metal ties. Folding the bag end over and using a paper clip usually fails either in the short term, when the paper clip flies off, or in the long term, when it rusts away. The combination of metal staples (copper-coated) and indestructible plastic labels, is as good a method as any.

(iii)   *Cardboard boxes* of sufficient strength to allow several to be stacked one upon the other. There is no standard size in current use in Britain. Most museums have their own internal standard and may insist on material being presented to the museum in standard containers. Boxes in a series of sizes which can be nested like Russian dolls are particularly flexible. Boxes can be marked with a pen, or can have a label pasted or stapled to their side. Care must be taken to make sure that if boxes are re-used the new contents are clear. Never rely on a box label as the sole means of identifying its contents. If the label is attached to the lid of the box then it is very easy for lids to be switched during use. In cases where the vessel itself cannot be marked then it should be enclosed in a labelled plastic bag.

(iv)   *Specialised storage units.* Some museums have racks of wooden or metal drawers which are used for pottery collections. This type of storage unit is well-suited to collections where the total quantity of sherds is low and where no complete or semi-complete vessels are present but is more suited to the storage of 'small finds'. An advantage of having one's collection stored in drawers is that it can be very quick to search through it. This type of storage also solves the problem of sherds breaking through being packed too close together (fig. 8.1).

(v)   *Cupboards and display cases.* Collections consisting of complete or near-complete vessels are best stored on shelves in glass-fronted cases. They can be viewed quickly without having to open the case and the enclosed nature of the cupboard protects the vessels from dust and grime which would eventually affect open shelving.

Fig. 8.1. Storage of individual pottery sherds. British Museum (Photo: British Museum)

The museum world has adopted various means of maximising the density of artefacts in a store, in at least one case using the technology of the computerised warehouse, so that finds are packed into crates which sit on pallets on large racks. The finds can be retrieved by the use of a fork-lift truck. Such a solution, even if one has the resources to achieve it, is only really suitable for material which might be retrieved from store only at rare intervals. It would be ideal, for example, for the storage of finds awaiting processing where the interval between excavation and post-excavation might be measured in months or years. It would also be suitable for the storage of material from kiln sites, once a type of fabric series has been extracted for the use of students. A more common system is the use of roller-racking so that the whole of a store, with the exception of a single gap wide enough for a researcher to walk down, can be filled with racking. Roller-racking is available with power assistance but it is quite easy to move by hand (fig. 8.2)

Fig. 8.2. Bulk storage of pottery using roller-racking. (Photo: University College London, Institute of Archaeology)

Dispersal of collection

Although most finds leave site boxed in groups according to the excavated context, during the post-excavation analysis they will normally be sorted into groups according to type of material. Undoubtedly there are some advantages in keeping the whole of an excavated assemblage together, for example that of being able to see the relative proportions of different materials and their condition. Such advantages are outweighed by the advantages of keeping all material of one type in close proximity. Whether all of the pottery from an assemblage should be kept together or not is more open to question. On multi-period sites a single assemblage can contain material of more than one date. One would probably analyse the different dated groups separately and therefore they will arrive back for final storage in that form. On the other hand, it can be very misleading to see an assemblage from which all but the 'contemporary' sherds have been removed.

Storage versus display

Museums have a role in education and presentation of archaeological evidence and results to the public. Pottery will probably feature prominently in this role (fig. 8.3). Most museums have teaching collections for use in workshops, school visits and similar events. There are cases of artefacts of great academic importance being rescued from such collections and it is probably wise to have the needs of teaching in mind when deciding the fate of your collection, and particularly any unstratified material within it. It is also natural that some material, whether permanently or temporarily, will be required for display to the public. Since at that stage the vessels will be divorced from any packaging it is imperative that they are individually, but discreetly, marked. The archive records should be able to record changes in the location of vessels but it is also advisable to have 'proxy cards' which can be placed with the remainder of the assemblage to indicate that one or more sherds have been extracted.

Indexing by computer

Your original site records will probably include a computer database with details of sherds by fabric, form and context. Ideally, a copy of this database would be transferred to the museum and used as the basis of future records. It is at this stage that the compatibility of your records with those of other projects becomes important. Researchers and museum staff will need to search through your collection along with all others in the museum. They may be looking for material to illustrate a theme, such as 'trade', 'cooking' or 'local industries', or they may be interested in particular vessel forms or fabrics, or in material from deposits of a particular date. Few institutions in Britain have faced up to this problem, which would be best solved by having an input from the museum into the initial project design so as to lay down minimum standards for compatibility.

Particular attention should be given to the potential problems of the long-term storage of computer data. It should not be imagined that the media upon which data are recorded today (the disks, tapes and so on) will remain

Fig. 8.3. Pottery on display. A reconstructed Roman house interior at Corinium Museum. Cirencester. (Photo: Corinium Museum, Cirencester)

readable even ten years hence – the media themselves deteriorate, tape and disk readers go out of production and standards change. Those responsible for the curation of this information should be made aware that it should be copied onto new storage media as they become available.

Disposal of pottery

At regular intervals, the problem of the permanent storage of archaeological finds, including pottery, is raised. The main motive is normally that the institution has run out of storage space, or soon will. It is undoubtedly true that the majority of sherds in an archaeological pottery collection will be unremarkable, having features of fabric and form which are typical of their period of use. The rise in interest over the years in deposition and in post-depositional transformations makes it probable that there will be attributes on even these sherds which will be of value for future researchers. As a matter of principle, therefore, we do not recommend that any discard policy should allow for the discard of material from stratified contexts. If storage is a problem then it might be solved by 'deep storage', that is the material is placed in a remote store from where, with a lot of effort, it could be retrieved.

9

PUBLICATION

Introduction

The work of an archaeological pottery specialist can give rise to several different types of publication, all of which are perfectly valid uses of pottery evidence. First is the straightforward pottery report, published as part of the general publication of an excavation or fieldwork project. The audience for this report will be composed mainly of other archaeologists, although your general conclusions may well be read by a wider audience, who may also be interested in the methods which you used and the theory and assumptions behind your work. Next, it is possible to write something about the history of pottery production and use in the study area, information which should be of interest to historical geographers, economic and social historians as well as to archaeologists. Thirdly, you may wish to write about the manufacturing methods and technology used by the potters whose products you have been studying. The audience for this type of work will consist mainly of potters, materials scientists and historians of technology. Fourthly, you should make your findings known to the lay public. The latter is the most difficult audience to satisfy since by this time you will be so deeply immersed in the subject matter that you no longer know what you need to explain in detail and what is obvious.

Here we are only concerned about the publication of primary data, the first two of the four options described above. In all cases, however, the best way to gauge the appropriate level for your work is to meet the consumer and talk to him/her about your work. Formal and informal presentation of your work is a very good way of making sure you know what your study has shown and that you can put this information across coherently.

Purpose of report

An archaeological pottery report is written with the intention of informing the reader about the character of the pottery collection, what you did with it and the conclusions which you draw from your analysis. A major use of your data will almost certainly be to aid the establishment of a site chronology. The data which provide this chronology may be qualitative, for example the presence of a particular ware in a deposit, or quantitative, such as the proportion of a particular fabric within an assemblage. More difficult to convey is the type of argument which depends on assessing the significance of

105

the absence of a type within an assemblage. Arguments of this type are always less convincing than qualitative or quantitative ones, as indeed they should be. It is important, therefore, to present enough of the evidence in each case to convey the character of the evidence and its strength.

Another major use will be to examine the cultural associations of the inhabitants of the site or area. In broad terms this means establishing the similarity of the collection, or assemblages within it on a multi-period site, to contemporary collections found on other sites or areas. The amount of effort you must put in to this will vary depending in part on the overall aims of the project. Again, you need to give enough of the basic finds to make the strength of your evidence clear while not overloading the report with undigested data.

It may also be the case that, far from giving information to the rest of the project, your work actually depends on other aspects of it. For example, there may be independent evidence from the site which enables you to date the pottery. Here you must make clear exactly how the pottery you are dating relates to the independent dating evidence. Time and again vital links in the chain of logic get overlooked at this point, planting the seeds of future confusion.

Having established a ceramic sequence and, perhaps, arrived at an absolute chronology, there will be numerous conclusions which can be drawn from the data. These may include inferences from changes in pottery forms and typology, and conclusions about the development of pottery industries within a region. Such conclusions may be inappropriate within a report on an excavation or fieldwork. If they confirm previously-held views then there is little justification for rehearsing the arguments, whereas if they are of national or regional significance they may well not fit in with the more detailed, local nature of the rest of the report. Such material would often be more suited to a separate publication but is hidden away in an excavation report because it requires less effort on the part of the author or because it is a condition of funding.

Layout of report

Most pottery reports have two tasks to perform, having first of all outlined the method of study and given a brief summary of the character of the collection. The first task is to describe the pottery by type (that is form and fabric) and the second task is to describe the occurrence of the pottery on site. In visual terms the difference is shown by the extreme cases. At one extreme the pottery is described and illustrated in form/fabric groups and information on context is relegated to tables or appendices, while at the other extreme the pottery is described and illustrated in assemblages, so that an overall impression of pottery from a single source or form can only be obtained by flicking back and forth through the whole report. One option, the belt and braces approach, is to publish both a type-series and assemblages. Variations on this approach consist of publishing the type-series as smaller scale profiles or alternatively showing assemblages in the form of three-dimensional reconstructions or in diagrammatic form.

Indexing and correlation

Whichever means of presentation suits the needs of your report best, the alternative needs of your readers will have to be catered for in some way. For example, if pottery is published by archaeological assemblages then a cross-index by fabric and form would be useful, whereas if it is published by type-series a list or appendix by context is required. The more variables one has, the more possibilities for permutations in cross-indices exist. As a rule of thumb, the longer the report and the more complex the data the more different means of exploring it should be provided.

Minimum standards of publication

In the 1980s in Britain there was a move away from the presentation of actual data within archaeological reports. The logic behind this development was that the actual data would only be of use to a handful of other specialists and that therefore it was more economical for these specialists to use the archive itself and for publications to be a synthesis of specialist work. The immediate results of this development were felt by specialists themselves. If one is not going to publish the results of a study, only summarise them, then it makes sense, if costs must be cut, to cut or pare down the costs of the study itself. The knock-on effect of this was to reduce the number of pottery specialists in work whilst the ultimate effect would be to stultify the whole discipline. It therefore seems sensible to lay down minimum requirements for the publication of pottery from archaeological fieldwork.

Amongst the data which should be published as a matter of course are the approximate size of the total collection, the means of retrieval and the present condition and location of the collection. Armed with this information one could form a judgement about whether it was worthwhile making the effort of examining the archive. There are probably very few instances where these data alone would be considered sufficient. An example might be where inconclusive excavations took place which might be intelligible if further work took place, at which time the pottery might repay analysis.

The next level of detail concerns the date-range, the forms and fabrics represented and a measure of their frequency. Unlike the previous data, such information should only be provided by a specialist, otherwise it is impossible to trust the results. There are many occasions when this is probably the only significant information that need be published about a collection. It assumes that there is no internal structure to the collection. Either it is unstratified and randomly distributed across the site or, though stratified, no significant patterning can be found within it. The final level would be a full report, as described above. This should be the aim for any site where sizable stratified assemblages are present, since there is almost certain to be patterning within such collections. Any cataloguing and quantification systems employed should be routinely described.

Microfiche and microtype, computer media
In an effort to bridge the gulf between synthetic publication and the archaeological archive, two novel means of dissemination have come into use. The first is microfiche and the second microtype. Microfiche are rectangular stiff plastic cards on which A4 pages of text and illustrations are reproduced photographically at a very small scale. Using a microfiche reader it is possible to scan the whole fiche, 96 images, quickly. They can also be read using a binocular microscope (luckily for pottery specialists). Microfiche are extremely inconvenient to use. They tend to fall out of the pockets provided for them in the back of a report and after only a few months begin to show signs of wear, especially if used in a dusty environment, such as that in which pottery is typically studied. It is not possible to flip back and forth between images as one can with a book nor can one hold a potsherd up against a microfiche image for comparison. They are impossible to use on public transport or in bed, the only places where archaeologists can find the time to read.

Microtype is produced as normal printed pages but the point size used is such that it can barely be read with the naked eye but can be read using a magnifying glass. It has been used with success to reduce multi-volume dictionaries to a manageable (though hardly portable) size and would suit the publication of data which could be hierarchically organised, as in a dictionary, and where one would only need to look at a small amount of print at a time.

A very recent development is the inclusion of computer floppy disks in archaeological reports. These could be used in the dissemination of pottery reports by making the actual archive data accessible. They depend on compatibility of operating system and the data should be in a portable format, such as ASCII. Neither of these is as difficult as it was in the 1980s although computer technology has still not reached the point where one could rely on being able to use the medium for more than a few years, if that.

Pottery specialists do it on their own
Another trend in British pottery studies has been the estrangement of pottery reports, and other specialist studies, from 'mainstream' archaeology. This is partly a result of the phase in which pottery specialists found themselves in the 1970s and 1980s. There was an explosion of archaeological excavation and fieldwork following the growth of rescue archaeology resulting in the need to publish lengthy reports dominated by the presentation of classifi-

cations. As these become established it will be possible for pottery reports to become smaller and therefore more easy to integrate into the format of an excavation report. Pottery specialists have, however, found the need to communicate within their disciplines and journals, such as *Medieval Ceramics* and the *Journal of Roman Pottery Studies*, are now well-established.

Summary

This overview of trends and principles of publication shows that there is no one right way of publishing pottery from archaeological fieldwork, although there are several ways which are wrong. It also demonstrates that there is as yet no substitute for the printed page as a means of dissemination of data and ideas.

PART III

THEMES IN CERAMIC STUDIES

10

MAKING POTTERY

Understanding the process whereby the raw materials of ceramics are transformed into finished ceramic products is a necessary precursor to the examination of both the products themselves and the remains of the manufacturing sites.

To set up any system of ceramic classification requires a knowledge of the underlying physical characteristics of the raw materials, an understanding of how they are affected by all stages of the manufacturing process and the ability to recognise and correctly identify the traces of these actions.

Our knowledge of the pottery manufacturing process comes from a variety of sources. Materials science provides detailed information on the behaviour of clay and other materials under a wide range of conditions, in particular when mixed with water or heated to a high temperature. Basic textbooks on ceramic materials (e.g. Worrall 1975; Kingery, Bowen and Uhlmann 1976; Grimshaw 1980) or briefer descriptions written from an archaeological standpoint (Shepard 1956, 6–48; Rice 1987, 31–110) may be consulted to provide the physical and chemical background to the pottery manufacturing process. The investigative techniques of materials science have been applied to particular aspects of pre-industrial pottery (Bronitsky 1986).

Descriptions of traditional pottery manufacturing by ethnographers are a rich source of information on all aspects of the production system. Earlier work of this type tended to be largely descriptive, but often overlooked or failed to record adequately aspects of the materials or process which would be of value to archaeologists considering material recovered from excavations. There are now increasing numbers of studies of traditional pottery production by archaeological ceramicists who realise the importance of recording as much as possible of a fast-disappearing craft in most (if not all) parts of the world – as much for its own sake as an aid to the interpretation of archaeological material (Arnold 1978; Nicholson and Patterson 1985; Vossen 1988; Desbat 1989; review of 'ceramic ethnoarchaeology' in Kramer 1985).

The experimental duplication of the styles and techniques of ancient pottery can also contribute to our understanding of the material from archaeological contexts. The majority of the interest in this field has been in experimental kiln-firings (Bryant 1978–9; Lucke 1988), collecting data on topics such as firing times, fuel usage and waster rates. It is not always clear,

113

Table 10.1. *Principal stages in pottery manufacture*

1	Procurement of raw materials
2	Preparation of raw materials
3	Forming the vessel
4	Pre-firing treatments
5	Drying
6	Firing
7	Post-firing treatments

however, what advantages this type of experimental work has over the observation of traditional pottery production systems.

A further source of valuable information on pottery manufacturing techniques, particularly forming and firing, are those texts written for modern craft potters, of which *A potter's book* by Bernard Leach (1940) has been perhaps the most influential.

The principal steps in pottery manufacturing described below are summarised in table 10.1. There are many complex interrelationships between the different steps – due, on the one hand to the character of the raw materials and tools, the skills of the potter and the pot-making environment, and on the other, the character of the desired product.

Raw materials for pottery manufacture

The essential raw materials of a ceramic product are clay and water. Non-plastics (also known as 'tempers' or 'openers') can be added to the clay mix and slips, paints or glazes may be required to finish the pots. Fuel is needed to fire the vessel.

Clay

Clays are complex materials but the two principal features are the very small particle size (less than 0.002mm in diameter) and the high proportion of 'clay minerals' in the mixture. The clay mineral component is ultimately derived from the weathering of rocks, and in particular igneous rocks. The small particle size and the plate-like characteristics of these clay minerals give clays the physical and chemical properties which allow them to be worked into shape and fired, creating ceramic.

Naturally occurring clays may be divided into two broad groups: there are those clays that derive directly from an underlying bed-rock by *in situ* decomposition, and there are those that are carried to their resting place by rivers, glaciers, wind or the sea. These are usually referred to as primary and secondary (or sedimentary) respectively. Most clays used for potting fall into the latter category.

Non-plastic inclusions

The great majority of natural clays include materials in addition to the clay mineral component. These *non-plastic* inclusions may, in the case of primary clays, include unweathered or partially decomposed fragments of the underlying source bed-rock. In the case of sedimentary clays a wider range of materials may become incorporated into the clay during the process of transportation, each of which has been through a different erosion cycle. As one of the most durable of the commonly occurring minerals, rounded quartz grains (the 'sand' of common parlance) are particularly common. Fragments of shell are also widespread in estuarine or marine clays.

The second source of non-plastics in ceramics are those that are added by the potter, usually deliberately, but also incorporated with the water or picked up from tools or working surfaces. In some cases these added non-plastics are simply more of those which occur naturally in the clay – a primary clay with fragments of the source rock may be supplemented by more of the original crushed rock. More commonly, the added materials are different to the non-plastics in the raw clay, and, as such, it may be possible to distinguish between them. A crushed rock which has been added to a sedimentary clay containing rounded quartz should be distinguishable.

The effects of these fillers on the behaviour of the clay mix are complex and choosing or creating the right combination of clay and filler is a matter of getting the balance right for the task in hand. As, unlike the clay, fillers do not hold water they reduce the proportion of water that can be held in the clay mix and hence the shrinkage of the clay and the drying time. The more filler is added the more the shrinkage is reduced (Jacobs 1983). Clays with a higher proportion of filler tend to have a higher 'wet strength' – they can support themselves better during the drying process. However the more non-plastics there are in the clay the more the plasticity is reduced and the more difficult it is to work. Clays with a very high proportion of filler may not be suitable for the manufacture of very thin delicate vessels or the use of a fast wheel.

Tempers other than those of geological origin are well known in both the archaeological and ethnographical record: crushed and burnt bone and shell (Steponaitis 1983, 20–43), dung (London 1981) and agricultural by-products such as straw or rice-husks have been recorded. The effects of organic materials on the behaviour of clays during forming and firing have been investigated in some detail (Crusoe 1971; Schiffer and Skibo 1989, 603–8). In particular excessively wet or plastic clays may be turned into workable pastes by the addition of dry organic material.

Water

The mixture of clay and water results in a plastic workable medium suitable for forming and firing. Soluble salts dissolved in the water may become incorporated in the clay. Common salt (NaCl) may be added with sea-water, either mixed with the clay before forming or by dipping the completed vessels in sea-water before firing (Rye 1976, 121–2). The combination of sea-water and a lime-rich clay may result in a white surface layer on the vessel (Peacock 1984) which has sometimes been confused with a slip.

Fuel

Fuel is required for the firing process, and perhaps also to facilitate drying and 'water-smoking', which drives off the excess moisture in the fabric. Fuels vary in both the quantity and quality (for example evenness) of the heat they provide and the amount of smoke they produce: these factors affect the suitability or otherwise of the fuel for a particular function. Modern potters recognise that fuels produce heat of a different character and may be more suitable for some part of the firing procedure than another, or may affect the product in other ways (Rye 1981, 104). Brears (1989, 7) relates a description of the changes in glaze colour caused by seasonal variation in the fuel, given by a potter from Truro in Cornwall. In spring the damp fuels produced an olive-green glaze, which changed with the passing of summer and autumn through khaki and buff, resulting in a bright orange-red glaze at the end of the season. Variations such as this must be considered when developing classification systems for archaeological ceramics.

In the archaeological record very few analyses have been made of the ash deposits from pottery firings to identify the type of fuel employed although, in principle at least, plant ash should show a wide range of variation and should be identifiable using advanced analytical techniques (Middleton 1984–5).

In the ethnographic record, wood is in widespread use as a fuel in traditional potting, but is often not of the highest quality. Rather, by-products of agricultural procedures such as prunings from fruit or olive trees, coconut husks, waste fibres or trimmings from timber shaping are commonly employed. Animal dung, usually in the form of dried dung 'cakes', is another common fuel. Modern pottery kilns consume oil or gas. Whatever the precise source of fuel, the quantities consumed by some of the largest pottery industries of the classical or medieval world must have been prodigious, comparable, in volume at least, with the supply of clay or the distribution of the finished products.

Pressure on fuel resources for cooking and heating in many modern potting communities is intense. Faced with the depletion of their traditional sources some potters turn to the wastes of industrial society, such as car tyres, while others turn their hand to activities other than potting (Arnold 1985, 54). The continuing depletion of fuel resources can only hasten the demise of an already declining craft.

Clay preparation

Almost all clay requires some form of preparation before it can be used for forming pottery, even if it is only a little light kneading. Clay preparation falls into two broad categories. Firstly there is purifying – the removal of extraneous unwanted materials such as roots and other organic matter, or large pebbles. Secondly, it may be necessary to alter the properties of the material. The aim is to produce a regular, uniform product from variable raw materials – a material whose properties are predictable and controllable, and suitable for the forming and firing procedures employed. A prepared clay mix suitable for hand-forming may not be suitable for wheel-throwing or moulding. The properties desired for the final fired product, such as its thermal characteristics, mechanical strength or porosity may also necessitate a range of preparations, and different clay mixes may be used for the production of different vessels according to their function.

In addition to simple mechanical sorting, more sophisticated preparation procedures may be employed. The clay may be mixed with water in large settling tanks (Peacock 1982, 54). The process of levigation allows the coarser fraction to settle out. Two or more types of clay may be mixed, perhaps with the addition of non-plastic tempers.

Forming

A very wide range of techniques are available to potters to form their wares. Many vessels are formed in several stages by a combination of methods which may be visible on different parts of the vessel (or, in an archaeological context, different sherds). The complete story of the formation procedure employed for a particular vessel is usually only recoverable from the consideration of all its parts.

Descriptions of the principal forming techniques are to be found in a number of publications – those by Rye (1981) and Rice (1987, 124–44) are particularly valuable. A broad distinction may be made between primary forming methods, which produce the basic form of the vessel, and secondary methods, which further define the details of the shape, even though in many cases the complex actions of the potter will somewhat blur the boundaries between these. The primary forming methods employed may be considered in two groups (Edwards and Jacobs 1986):

> Hand-forming – the building or forming of a pot by any means without the use of centrifugal force.
>
> Throwing – forming a vessel on a wheel which is rotated at a speed sufficient to allow the potter to use centrifugal force as an active agent in the forming and shaping of the vessel.

The forming techniques employed can be identified by a variety of methods. The surface and core of the vessel wall often retain traces (Rye

1981, 67–95 and Balfet et al. 1989, 52–63 provide useful sets of photographs and keys to identification), but for cases where these are unclear, or perhaps where several techniques overlap, resort to more sophisticated procedures such as radiography (Rye 1977; Glanzman 1983; Carr 1990) or tangential thin-sections (Woods 1984–5) is possible.

Hand-forming and building techniques

The simplest pots are made by pinching a hollow in the centre of a lump of clay and forming the shape of the vessel between the thumb and fingers. This technique is generally used only for the production of the simplest of small round-bodied vessels, or as a secondary technique to form additional pieces to be added to a vessel formed using another primary technique.

In slab-building, flat sheets of clay are joined together by squeezing or pinching them together at the edges. Although particularly suited for the construction of rectangular vessels, circular pots can also be made using this technique. Pots can also be formed by joining together a series of coils, either as rings or as a continuous spiral. Adjacent rings are invariably smoothed together but may show themselves as a series of corrugations, or even as weak lines where the vessel breaks or cracks.

Once a vessel being formed exceeds a certain size, it is invariably necessary to move the vessel around so that the face being worked on is nearest the potter. The pot may be placed on a simple mobile support such as a mat, a specially made pot support known as a batt (or bat) or even a large sherd from a broken pot. Bats are usually circular and made from wood or stone, or may themselves be made of a coarse ceramic (fig. 10.1).

One step up from such pot supports is the use of a simple turntable – a platform supported on a central spindle and capable of rotary motion. Such devices have been widely used in traditional potting and although they may be rotated, even continuously with the help of an assistant, they are not suitable for 'throwing' a vessel, as a true wheel would be (Edwards and Jacobs 1986, 50–3).

The use of moulds (or molds) to form pottery is widespread at many periods, but within this broad category a variety of techniques are available. In the simplest case a hollow object, such as a basket, the base of another pot or even a simple leather mould (Franken and Kalsbeek 1984) may be used to hold and shape the clay during hand-forming: this is closely related to the use of a flat pot support.

More sophisticated moulds are also used to form either entire vessels or particular parts of vessels. Of particular value are those with incised or impressed decoration on their inner face. Any vessels made in them will then have relief decoration on the surface. Simple basket moulds may leave traces on the vessel surface, but the classic example of the use of moulds is the early Roman arretine and samian industry. The study of samian moulded wares,

Fig. 10.1. A Berber potter from the Grande-Kabylie (Algeria) making large plates (used for cooking bread) by hand. The plate is formed on a large ceramic support, which is itself made from an old plate filled with clay. The outer wall is formed between the potter's hand and a shaped block of wood. (Photo: Paul Tyers)

and thus indirectly the moulds, has engendered a vast and apparently endless literature aimed at identifying the web of relationships between potters, mould-makers, styles and workshops, their chronology and organisation.

Wheel throwing

The process of throwing pots on a wheel is perhaps that most commonly associated in popular culture with the pottery production process. There are allusions in classical and later literature to the process of wheel-throwing, particularly the rise and fall of the pot on the wheel, the fluid changes of shape under the hands of the potter (e.g. Horace, *Ars poetica*, 21–2). This aspect of potting is well described by Rye and Evans, in a passage from their study of traditional pottery manufacturing in Pakistan:

> To any observer who has not attempted to make pottery, forming operations often appear to happen so effortlessly that it can mistakenly be assumed that 'anyone can do it'. This illusion is created partly by the plastic nature of the clay, which when soft deforms at the slightest touch, and partly by the skill and experience of the potter in controlling such a sensitive material.
>
> (Rye and Evans, 1976, 131)

Despite the clear evidence of their widespread use in the products, the archaeological remains of potter's wheels are slight and fragmentary at all periods. Various flywheels, spindles and sockets recovered from excavations on kiln sites have been identified as parts of potter's wheels but these are often difficult to interpret, and there is some risk of confusion with, for instance, mills and other rotary devices (Peacock 1982, 55–8).

Much of our detailed information on their structure and operation comes from contemporary illustrations or ethnographic sources. The history, construction and use of the potter's wheel has been discussed by several authors (Foster 1959; Rieth 1960; Scheufler 1968; Lobert 1984) who draw on illustrations of these devices in use, culled from a range of ethnographic and historical sources. Two broad classes of wheel are distinguished by most writers.

The simple wheel, also referred to as the stick wheel or single wheel – a single flywheel rotating on a central pivot (fig. 10.2(a)). Depending on the method of attachment between the wheel and the pivot, the flywheel may either come to rest at the horizontal or at an angle. The balance of the flywheel maintains an even, level rotation. The top surface usually has a small depression near the perimeter at one point and a short stick inserted in this socket rotates the wheel to start it up, or to speed it up when it is slowing down. The potter (or the assistant) is usually sitting or squatting beside the wheel while doing this, but may, more rarely, use a longer stick from the standing position.

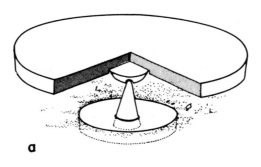

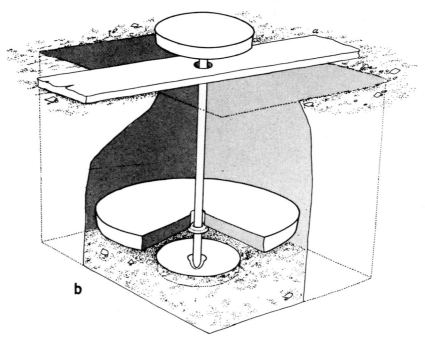

Fig. 10.2. The two basic types of potter's wheel. (a) the single wheel, and (b) the double wheel. (Rye 1981, fig. 58)

The pit wheel (or kick wheel or double wheel) is composed of two flywheels attached to a long central spindle and supported by a lower socket and an upper bearing (fig. 10.2(b)). The upper wheel is the throwing surface and is usually light and of relatively small diameter. The lower wheel is larger and heavier, and stores the

Fig. 10.3. A potter in Srinagar (Kashmir) (a) using a single wheel, and (b) the underside of the wheel, showing the pivot set in the ground. (Photos: Paul Tyers)

momentum which is applied by the potter who kicks the wheel, or, in modern wheels, by a motor.

Amongst modern traditional potters the single wheel is particularly characteristic of the Indian subcontinent, but the kick wheel is widespread throughout both Europe and Asia. The discussion of pottery wheels in Pakistan by Rye and Evans (where both types are found) is particularly valuable (Rye and Evans 1976, 116–18). In the Greek and Roman world it is probable that both single and double wheels were employed (Peacock 1982, 55–8). In medieval and later Europe the simple wheel was often in the form of a cartwheel mounted horizontally with the head attached to the centre, and a form of kick-wheel where the upper and lower flywheels were connected by a series of vertical struts was employed (McCarthy and Brooks 1988, figs. 8–10).

The different forms of wheel are not all completely interchangeable, each equally suitable for the manufacture of all types of vessel. The mechanics of the pottery wheel dictate, to a certain extent, the forms of vessel that can be produced, or rather the character of the wheel will reflect the requirements of different vessel types. Two important features are discussed by van der Leeuw in a consideration of the type of potter's wheels employed in the manufacture of sixteenth-century pottery at Haarlem in the Netherlands (van der Leeuw 1976, 124–5 and appendix D):

> The relationship between the weight of the wheel, its momentum and its optimum speed – a large heavy wheel will maintain its momentum for a longer period and revolve at a slower speed and resist friction from the potter's hands (and other sources) better than a small light wheel.
>
> The 'linear' speed, the speed at which the clay passes between the fingers of the potter, increases with distance from the centre of the wheel.

According to Hulthén (1974, 69) the minimum linear speed required to produce wheel-thrown pottery is 0.7m per second. A large heavy wheel, such as the single cartwheel type, will revolve at a slow speed, but for relatively long duration. The slow speed makes it suited to the manufacture of large-diameter vessels, for the linear speed will increase with the diameter of the vessel. A faster lighter wheel would not be suitable for large diameter vessels as the linear speed would be too high. Conversely, a faster wheel would be preferable for the forming of smaller diameter vessels, where the linear velocity would be adequate a short distance from the centre of the wheel. In Pakistan the simple stick wheels are often used for throwing small vessels 'off the lump' (Rye and Evans 1976, 116–18) and are unsuitable for the manufacture of larger diameter vessels (fig. 10.3). Thus, it may on occasion be possible to predict the character of the wheel employed for the manufacture of a particular group of pottery, even in the absence of direct archaeological evidence such as fragments of the wheel structures themselves (van der Leeuw 1976, 126).

Composite techniques

The broad distinctions made between hand-made and wheel-thrown pottery should not distract us from the recognition that many vessels are formed by a combination of techniques. In the simplest cases some alterations or additions may be made to the basic form created by the primary technique. A spout may be created by deforming the circular mouth to produce a 'pinched' effect, the body shape may be altered by 'folding' or parts of the vessel may be cut away. Pots may have handles, spouts, footrings or other features attached by hand after the primary forming stage. These subsidiary features may themselves be hand-made or wheel-thrown and in some cases the method of attachment varies significantly between potters and may be a valuable indicator of evolving manufacturing traditions (Pearce 1984). Whatever the precise alteration, these actions may mask or erase, at least over a small part of the final vessel, the traces of the underlying technique.

More complex combinations are also possible. Beating the wall of a vessel between a 'paddle' and 'anvil' (usually a rounded stone) to make it thinner is a common technique in modern India for the manufacture of large water jars and items of similar dimensions. The starting point may be a vessel that is either hand-formed or wheel-thrown and the effect of the beating is to produce a vessel of larger capacity, usually more globular in shape and with a higher volume-to-weight ratio. Several descriptions of the details of the technique are available (Miller 1985, 222–6; Saraswati and Behura 1966, 55–8). The finished vessel will exhibit traces of both the primary forming process, such as wheel marks, on the rim and upper shoulder, and the beating action, usually on the body. The latter leaves characteristic surface markings and finish (Rye 1981, 84–5). In fragmentary material it would be important to recognise the connection between the sherds from the two parts of the vessel.

Moulds are often employed in combination with other techniques. Vessels with a mould-formed lower part and a hand-formed or wheel-thrown upper part are known. Early Roman samian ware bowls are formed primarily in moulds but have rims and footrings added later. Samian production was a large-scale enterprise involving many potters and workmen each responsible for a particular stage of the procedure. Some workshops maintained quality and quantity control by the use of small stamps impressed on the surface of the pots by those carrying out the different operations (summaries of samian ware production and the use of stamps are given by Johns 1971 and Bulmer

1979). An understanding of the different stages of manufacture of such vessels is particularly important as the stamps often refer to only one stage of a complex procedure.

Surface treatments

There is no precise dividing line between some secondary forming procedures and surface treatments. Trimming or scraping serve as much to smooth the irregularities left by coil or slab construction and join the different parts together as to alter the appearance of the vessel. Some surface treatments can only be applied when the vessel has dried to the 'leather-hard' stage while others may be used while the vessel is still plastic.

One of the most common surface treatments is burnishing, where the leather-hard pot is rubbed with a smooth pebble or other tool. This compacts the surface and leaves a series of facets and a slight lustre on the surface. The burnishing may also have some effect on the heating effectiveness of ceramic vessels (Schiffer 1990) by reducing the passage of liquids through the vessel while it is being heated over a fire. There are many other possible types of surface decoration. Many involve penetrating, compressing or cutting the vessel surface with a tool. This may be a simple narrow-ended implement (a point) or something more complex such as a comb or a stamp (see p. 85).

Drying

Prior to firing, the finished vessel must be dried. This eliminates the water mechanically combined to the clay particles. Drying may take place in free air or in specially heated drying sheds. The vessel will shrink during drying which may set up stresses in the pot, resulting in drying cracks. The shape and position of these cracks reflects to some extent the procedures employed in the manufacture of the pot (Rye 1981, 66, fig. 46) – the S-shaped crack on the base of wheel-thrown vessels is one of the clearest examples.

Drying also has the effect of concentrating dissolved salts and fine clay particles towards the surface of the pot, drawn there by the movement of water through the wall. On enclosed vessels this effect is particularly marked on the outer surface. This in turn may affect the colour of the vessel during firing. It is important to distinguish these effects from slips, paints and other surface treatments.

Firing

The purpose of firing is to transform the clay minerals into a new material, ceramic. The necessary chemical and physical changes start to take place in some clays at about 550–600°C (Rice 1987, 90–3) and pottery which does not reach this temperature during firing will eventually disintegrate when immersed in water, even if it takes up to a year to do so (Skibo and Schiffer 1987, 85).

Two categories of pottery firing procedure are recognised:

> Open firings, also referred to as clamp firings or bonfire firings, where the pots and the fuel are in immediate contact and are arranged in a stack on the ground or in a shallow depression.
>
> Kiln firings, where the pottery and fuel are separate – the pot usually in a chamber which is heated by the hot gases and flames from the fuel.

Open firing

Open firings are common amongst traditional potters and would undoubtedly have been responsible for a substantial proportion of the material recovered from archaeological contexts. Many excellent ethnographic descriptions of the procedures are available (e.g. Gruner 1973; Rye and Evans 1976, 165–7; Arnold 1978, 351–7; Miller 1985, 228–32; see also Kramer 1985, 81). The usual method is to stack the pots over a layer of fuel and mix more fuel in and around the vessels, perhaps covering the entire stack with more fuel and/or a layer of waste sherds from earlier firings (fig. 10.4). The fuel is usually lit from below or at one end of the stack and burns through. Perhaps the most notable characteristics of an open firing are the fast rise in temperature during the initial stages and its short duration. It may only take a few minutes for the temperature to reach its maximum and fired pots can be removed from the fire shortly thereafter (Rye 1981, 102, table 3 records details of eleven such firings), although some other open firings take almost two hours to reach their maximum and the stack may not be opened until eight to ten hours later (Miller 1985, 230, fig. 71).

In the simplest open firings a very small number of vessels, perhaps only one or two, are fired in a small shallow depression in the ground. The ash remaining in the firing pit after the pots are removed may be collected for use as fertiliser (Rye and Evans 1976, 165) and the identification of such features in the archaeological record as evidence of pottery manufacturing would be rather problematic (Sullivan 1988, 33). Larger firing areas which are repeatedly reused are often thickly covered in broken and burnt pottery, although very little of this is distorted or fused. Again their identification might not be entirely clear, particularly if the area is later reused as a rubbish dump or midden. In fact, open-firing areas are only very occasionally identified in the archaeological record (Peacock 1982, 67, with references) although the assertion that a particular pottery type cannot have been produced in an area 'because no *kilns* have been found' is heard with surprising frequency.

Although undoubtedly a simpler technique than the use of kilns, open firings are perfectly adequate for the firing of many coarse wares and have the advantage of flexibility. Greater or lesser quantities of pots may be fired at a single session simply by making the stack larger or smaller. The potter is not confined to the cycle of producing and firing a complete kiln load. Although often associated with hand-formed coarsely tempered wares, open firings are

Fig. 10.4. An open firing in progress in the Grande-Kabylie (Algeria). The pottery is stacked over layers of firewood on the ground. (Photo: Paul Tyers)

Fig. 10.5. An early second-century Roman kiln from Highgate Wood in north London. (Photo: Bernard Brandham)

also employed by potters who use the wheel (e.g. Miller 1985) – we need not always seek kilns when faced with wheel-thrown pottery.

Somewhat intermediate between open and kiln firings are structures such as that described by Rye and Evans from Musazi in Pakistan (Rye and Evans 1976, 34–5). Here the firing area (3m × 10m) is enclosed by a wall two metres high on three sides. The pots (large jars) are surrounded by donkey dung for firing. The photographs of this structure being unloaded (Rye and Evans 1976, plate 26c) show remarkably little sooting or burning of the walls, or ash or wasters in the firing pit. Once more the identification of such a structure as part of a pottery manufacturing workshop might be difficult.

Kiln firing

Domestic ovens, such as bread ovens, may be pressed into service to fire pottery (Desbat 1989, 147) but it is more usual to build a specialised kiln structure (fig. 10.5).

The study of pottery kilns has generated a considerable body of litera-ture, both ethnographic and archaeological, and it is only possible here to point to the more significant elements. The classic studies by Hampe and Winter of modern pottery and tile kilns in Crete and Cyprus (Hampe and Winter 1962) and southern Italy, Sicily and Greece (Hampe and Winter 1965), with their excellent photographs, provide a wealth of valuable infor-mation on kiln and workshop structure and many other aspects of pottery manufacturing. They have proved to be the starting point for many others considering kiln morphology (for example kiln sections republished by Peacock 1982, fig. 12, 3–8 and McCarthy and Brooks 1988, fig. 21). Gazet-teers by Vossen and others of modern potteries in Spain (Vossen 1972; Vossen et al. 1980) and Morocco (Vossen and Ebert 1976) maintain this tradition. Kiln structure and operation is also considered in the surveys of pottery production in Pakistan (Rye and Evans 1972) and India (Saraswati and Behura 1966).

Turning to the archaeological record, classifications have been compiled for Roman kilns in Britain (Swan 1984), Gaul (Duhamel 1973) and Italy (Cuomo di Caprio 1971–2) and Peacock (1982, 67–70) has discussed the possible relationships between them. For medieval kilns in Britain we have the studies of Musty (1974; see also McCarthy and Brooks 1988, 40–54).

Thus anyone facing the prospect of excavating a pottery kiln has a bewil-dering quantity of comparative material to consider, but will hopefully avoid the pitfalls of the rather eccentric kiln reconstructions that have occasionally appeared in print. Swan (1984, 128) emphasises the importance of sufficient and detailed recording of the kiln structure itself and recommends in par-ticular a continuous section drawn across the structure and its infill from front to back, a section through the kiln structure at right angles to the flue axis and careful consideration of the stratigraphy in the flue. All fragments of kiln furniture and baked clay from the vicinity of the kiln should also be examined and recorded. Far too little is known about the superstructure of most excavated kilns to allow any potential information to slip by unrecognised.

11

POTTERY FABRICS

We here consider the role of the examination of fabric in pottery studies. Historically, form and decoration have received more attention from archaeologists than the details of the fired clay itself. Since the 1960s a more systematic approach to fabric analysis has come to take one of the central positions in pottery studies. It was seen as one of the means of breaking out of the strait-jacket of primarily chronological concerns and expanding the scope of the study into the areas of technology, trade and exchange. These developments cannot be divorced from other shifts in archaeological thinking and practice over the same period.

The methods of fabric analysis have been largely drawn from the geological sciences, for the reasons succinctly given by Peacock: 'Pottery can be regarded as a metamorphosed sedimentary rock and thus it can be argued that ceramics are best approached in a manner similar to that used in the geological study of the parent raw materials' (Peacock 1977, 26). The techniques have had their impact not only in the university research laboratory, but all the way down to the pot-sorter grouping and describing sherds in the finds hut.

Why look at fabrics?

The physical characteristics of the fired clay, its appearance and composition, are determined by:

    (i)   the natural composition of the raw material(s);

    (ii) the actions taken by the potter in creating the clay mix, such as settling out the coarser component, adding non-plastics, or combining two or more clays;

    (iii) the firing atmosphere and temperature;

    (iv) the use and post-depositional environment of the vessels.

Most of the stages of the manufacturing process (the workability of the clay, the size, shape, wall thickness and decoration of the formed vessel, the shrinkage rate during drying and possible firing techniques) and the technological properties of the finished product (its porosity, physical and thermal strength) are all to a great extent dependent on the character of the original clay mix, notably the frequency, size, shape and identity of the non-plastic inclusions.

The examination of pottery fabrics – the composition and structure of the fired clay body – gives valuable information on three broad themes: (1) the technology of the manufacturing process; (2) the physical characteristics of the fired product; and (3) its provenance.

Manufacturing technology

There are a variety of techniques that can be used to determine the maximum temperature reached during the firing cycle (Rice 1987, 426–7, table 14.3). Some require relatively simple equipment such as an electric kiln or a petrological microscope, whereas other techniques are confined to those with access to more complex facilities. Many of the techniques rely on the identification of changes in the clay body which take place at high temperatures, such as the changes in the porosity or level of vitrification of a fabric. Some of these changes rely not only on the maximum temperature achieved during the firing cycle, but also the time that the temperature is held and other variables such as the firing atmosphere. Thus maximum firing temperature is only being measured indirectly. The determination of firing temperature is important for two aspects of the pottery. Firstly there is the relationship between firing temperature and firing technology. A series of pots which are fired to a narrow range of temperatures may suggest a reasonably sophisticated level of control over the firing process. Secondly, a series of vessels consistently fired to a temperature exceeding the point of vitrification may be intended to be non-porous, and this may be an important indication of their original function.

The firing atmosphere has a significant effect on the fabric of a fired vessel, most notably on its colour. The fired colour of a fabric depends principally on the iron compounds and carbon that the clay contains and the duration, temperature and atmosphere during firing. Most clays, but in particular sedimentary clays, contain a proportion of organic matter. When heated in an oxidising environment (where there is an excess of free oxygen) the carbon will burn and form carbon dioxide, which will attempt to escape from the fabric. In some cases the escaping gas causes bloating or bubbling. Where there is no excess of oxygen (a reducing environment), or the duration of the firing is insufficient, the carbon will not all burn out, but will be visible in the final fired fabric as a dark grey or black core. This core may be particularly marked where the vessel is thick, such as at the rim or base, or in the section of the handle. However, carbon can also be deposited on the surface of the pot during firing in a process known as 'smudging'. This results in a very black surface and margins.

Iron compounds in the clay also react to the firing atmosphere. In oxidising conditions the iron compounds in the clay will usually be converted to ferric oxide (Fe_2O_3), which is red in colour, but this change will not usually take place until after the carbon has been burnt off. Even if the surplus of oxygen

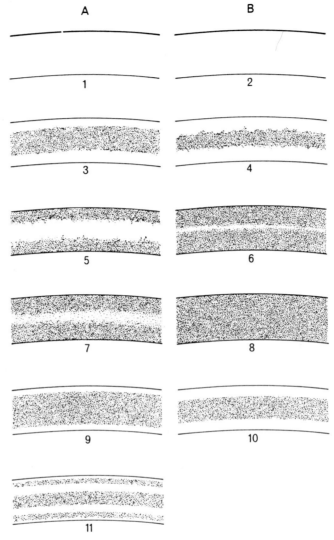

Fig. 11.1. Stylised cross-sections comparing variations in the appearance of firing cores in fine textured clays (Column A) and coarse-textured clays (Column B).

1: Oxidised, organics not originally present; no core

2: Oxidised, organics may or may not have been originally present; no core

3–4; Oxidised, organics originally present; diffuse core margins

5: Reduced, organics not originally present: diffuse core margins

6: Reduced, organics not originally present; black or grey may extend completely through the wall leaving no 'core'

7: Reduced, organics originally present; diffuse core margins

8: Reduced, organics may or may not have been originally present; no core

9–10: Reduced, cooled rapidly in air; sharp core margin

11: Reduced, cooled rapidly in air, reduced and cooled rapidly in air again; sharp core margins, 'double core' (Rye 1981, fig. 104)

is very marginal or prolonged firing will result in a red colour, but where there is a shortage an iron-rich clay will usually be grey (see p. 69).

The character of the atmosphere may alter several times during the firing cycle, and as the reactions described above are reversible the final colour of fabric may be quite complex. It is not unusual to see sherds with layers of colours from the surface to the core, each corresponding to a different stage of the firing and the extent to which its effect has 'penetrated' the wall of the vessel. The appearance of the section under different firing conditions (fig. 11.1) has been illustrated by Hodges (1962, 61, fig. 1) and Rye (1981, 116, fig. 104).

Provenance studies

Provenance studies are concerned with identifying groupings, usually known as fabrics or wares, which reflect their origin, and where possible determining their source. The 'ideal' arrangement may be where a single ware represents the output of a single workshop but this may not always be realised. Rather, a single fabric may represent the output of a group of workshops sharing the same raw materials and processing them in a similar manner, and conversely, a single workshop (or related group of workshops) may be responsible for more than one fabric (because of the use of different sources of clay processing systems). Recognising that this may be the case does not negate the procedure of fabric characterisation (as occasionally seems to be suggested), but merely adds another range of possibilities to the *interpretation* of the groupings.

We recognise three stages of examination: visual, petrological and compositional, reflecting a rising level of complexity (and cost), but decreasing accessibility and a consequent narrowing of the quantity of material that may be processed. The bed-rock of pottery processing procedures can only be accurate and informed visual examination, and where possible there must be feed-back from any results obtained from more sophisticated analyses.

Visual examination

With the realisation of the importance of consistent recording systems, capable of reuse and cross-referencing, it is now usual for pottery fabrics to be described using standardised categories and keywords on pro-forma sheets or cards (see p. 233). A number of such recording schemes have been described (Peacock 1977, 26–32; Orton 1979; Steinstra 1986; Bauer et al. 1986. Kunow et al. 1986; Schneider 1989) which follow broadly similar lines.

An initial aim of most studies is to sort the sherds in the collection into wares, giving a single description which covers the variation within the group rather than describing every catalogued item in detail. The visual examination should take place on a clean section through the sherd which exposes the core. The existing breaks may not be suitable because of minerals deposited on their surface during burial and it is usual to make a new clean break. Some workers have suggested that a flat section is preferred for this examination (Smith 1972; Glock 1975) which might necessitate the sawing of many thousands of sherds. Sections perpendicular to the rim might, it is suggested, also be an aid to drawing (Holladay 1976). Such a system is not widely employed and it is more usual to make a fresh break by snipping off a corner of the sherd with a large pair of pliers or pincers. Grains protruding from the surface of the break appear in three dimensions, making them easier to identify than they would be in a section and a break gives a better view 'under the surface' of the sherd. The quality of the fracture itself may be a valuable diagnostic feature. When making the break it is important to take account of the uneven distribution of inclusions in the fabric which might cause the break to occur along a weaker, but perhaps unrepresentative, zone. In wheel-thrown ware many inclusions will become aligned to the direction of throwing, so breaks at different angles through the sherd may give rather different views of the fabric of the pot. In the case of any doubt more than one break should be made. A small hand-lens ($\times 8$) or a higher power binocular microscope (up to $\times 30$) is invaluable as an aid to examination of the fabric and identification of inclusions. It is important to confirm the scale of any graticule in the eyepiece of a binocular microscope before using it for any measurements.

Colour

Since Shepard extolled the virtues of the Munsell colour system for the recording of pottery colour ('The advantages . . . are so great that it is hardly necessary to argue its superiority': Shepard 1956, 107) it has been widely employed in the Americas, and since the late 1960s (e.g. Franken and Kalsbeek 1969) in Europe.

Munsell colours are referred to by three variables, known as the hue, value and chroma. *Hue* refers to the position of the colour in the spectrum. In the Munsell system they are referred to by letters or pairs of letters:

R	Red	YR	Yellow-Red
Y	Yellow	GY	Green-Yellow
G	Green	BG	Blue-Green
B	Blue	PB	Purple-Blue
P	Purple	RP	Red-Purple

Working around the spectrum the hues are further subdivided by a numerical prefix from 0 to 10, with 0 towards the red end of the spectrum and 10 towards the purple. In the standard charts the prefixes are 2.5, 5, 7.5 and 10. *Value* refers to how light or dark the colour is, with 0 representing black and 10 representing white. The *chroma* is the saturation or purity of the colour, with 0 representing neutral greys and higher numbers indicating purer colours. A Munsell colour is expressed in the order *hue value chroma*, with a space between hue and value and an oblique stroke between value and chroma; thus 2.5YR 6/8. As a special case, pure white, grey and blacks (that is with chroma of 0) are prefixed N (neutral).

Although the Munsell notation provides a complete description of a particular colour it should always be accompanied by a brief verbal description. This indicates to the reader the general range of colours represented in the material and provides a means of deciding whether resort to the colour charts for a more precise representation of the colour is necessary. However, neither the colour names suggested by Munsell, nor Shepard's suggested system of modifiers (Shepard 1956, 110), have found wider favour.

The complete *Munsell book of color* is a large and unwieldy volume (not to mention expensive) and for most practical purposes the smaller *Munsell soil color charts* is preferred (Munsell Color Company 1975). The range of reds, browns and yellows in the latter covers most of the colours encountered in ceramic work, and the charts are contained in a durable, pocket-sized (13cm × 19cm) volume. The standard collection of soil colour charts contains seven hues: 10R, 2.5YR, 5YR, 7.5YR, 10YR, 2.5Y and 5Y. The sheets are perforated with holes through which both sherd and colour chip can be viewed at the same time, and masks are supplied which should be used to reduce interference from other colours on the chart when attempting comparisons. Two supplementary charts are available in the same format (7.5R and 5R) which are more red than 10R and may be useful for some material. Advice on recording Munsell colours will be found in the documentation distributed with the chart. Particular attention should be given to the recommendations on the lighting conditions and background when the chart is used.

An alternative to the *Munsell soil color chart* is the *Rock-color chart* produced by the Geological Society of America (1948), which employs the Munsell notation. The chart includes selections from hues 5R, 10R, 5YR, 10YR and 5Y which partially duplicate those of the *Munsell soil color chart*. In addition there are a small number of chips in yellow, green, blue and purple hues (5GY, 10GY, 5G, 10G, 5BG, 5B, 5PB, 5P and 5RP) which would be useful for glazes, slips and paints. The *Rock-color chart* is not perforated to allow the sample and colour chip and sherd to be examined at the same time, but it would be relatively easy to make it so.

Alternative colour systems have been used in the description of archaeological ceramics, particularly in continental Europe. Kunow and others recommend the use of Munsell for most fabric colours but supplement this with the Schwaneberger colour chart (designed for stamp collectors) for coloured glazes, largely on the grounds of cost and availability of the full Munsell system (Kunow et al. 1986, 33). In France, Germany and Switzerland the colour charts produced by the CEC (Fédération Européenne des Fabricants de Carreaux Céramiques), the DIN (Deutsche Industrie Normen) standard colours (DIN 6164) or the *code Cailleux* (Cailleux and Taylor 1963) are widely used (Schneider 1989, 39), although the Munsell system is gaining popularity. It would clearly be preferable if usage standardised around a single system, and Munsell offers the clearest advantage.

The use of the Munsell system is sometimes criticised for providing a 'falsely accurate' picture of the sherd or the colour divisions are considered 'too fine'. Such remarks suggest some misunderstanding about how and when colour charts should be used. When describing wares rather than individual sherds it is necessary to cover the range of colours represented, but also make it clear which are the most common variants. More seriously, the value of colour as a means of characterising fabrics at all has been questioned (for example Picon's dismissal of the value of 'codes de couleur compliqués': Picon 1984). It is undoubtedly true that variations in colour, and other factors such as porosity and hardness, may be due to firing or post-depositional conditions rather than differences in the original materials. But it is equally true that the slip or fabric colour produced by particular workshops are often quite precise and regular and provide a valuable means of distinguishing one producer from another.

If the colour is to be recorded it is better that it is with reference to some accepted and commonly available standard rather than in vague terms or colloquialisms in a foreign language. The reproduction of a list of oxide percentages from compositional analysis is not an adequate substitute, is of no value to anyone faced with the task of sorting material in the field, and in any case ignores the effects of firing. With experience it can be recognised when a colour is likely to be a significant element in the characterisation of a ware and when it is not.

Hardness
Hardness is usually expressed in terms of resistance to scratching. Mohs' 10-point scale of hardness is often used but an alternative test using a fingernail (Mohs 2 or 2.5) and a steel blade (6) has found wide favour (Peacock 1977, 30). Rice suggests that copper wire (Mohs 3) and window glass (4.5) can be used to mark other points in the scale (Rice 1987, 357; see p. 235).

Whatever the precise items in the scale, it is rather more difficult to determine exactly what is being measured in a composite material such as pottery. The length and duration of firing, porosity, grain-size distribution, post-depositional environment and mineral composition all contribute to the 'hardness' and although it should continue to be measured and recorded it should not be used as a precise indicator.

Inclusions
Special attention should be given to the inclusions in a fabric, for in many cases these provide the most reliable method of distinguishing between fabrics.

Identity

The type of inclusions should be determined using a simple key such as that published by Peacock (1977, 30–2; see p. 238). Where there is some doubt or difficulty it is better not to make a possibly erroneous and misleading identification – a simple description of colour and appearance will suffice.

By far the best way to approach the identification of inclusions in a pot sherd is to have access to a thin-section of the sherd (see below, p. 140). By moving from the section to the sherd and back again one can learn what inclusions that can be seen by eye look like in thin-section, enhancing the value of both methods of analysis. This is in fact the basic principle which geologists use – look at the hand specimen first and only then examine the thin-section. Working without access to thin-sections in a region with unfamiliar geology may well involve much extra work if the initial classification turns out to be based on false premises.

Frequency

The frequency of the inclusions should be estimated. The preferred system would be by reference to visual percentage estimation charts, although this is quite rarely undertaken. A recently prepared set of computer-generated charts covers a wide range of inclusion size-ranges and percentage values, and is available in both white-on-black and black-on-white (Mathew et al. 1991). A specimen chart is included here in the appendix (p. 238).

Size and sorting

The average, or more accurately the modal (that is most common) size of inclusions can be determined relatively easily, either by eye or by use of a graticule in the eye-piece of a binocular microscope, especially if you determine a range (for example 0.25–0.5mm) rather than an exact size. But this is only part of the story; not all inclusions will be the same size, and much useful information may be contained in the way in which the size of inclusions vary about their average: this is known as the 'grain-size distribution' (see below, p. 141).

Roundness

The shape of inclusions reflects their erosional history. In general, the longer this history the more rounded the grains will become until they ultimately ought to form tiny spheres, if they were free of blemishes or irregularities. Roundness can be estimated by comparing the shape in thin-section with a chart or it can be measured in a variety of ways using image analysis techniques. Most pottery researchers would use a simple classification such as 'angular', 'sub-angular', 'sub-rounded', and 'rounded'.

For inclusions such as mudstones and slates the sphericity may be useful in description. This is defined as the closeness of the grain's outline to a circle (or in three-dimensions the closeness of the grain's shape to a sphere). Note that an inclusion might be rounded but not spherical. Inclusions which cleave more in one plane than another will be less spherical while micas (which have only one plane of cleavage) will be completely flat. Sphericity can be measured by comparison with a chart or by measuring the longest and shortest dimensions of a sample of inclusions.

Petrological analysis

The techniques that have had perhaps the most impact on pottery studies since the 1950s are petrological techniques taken directly from the earth sciences. Ceramics share features with both rocks and sediments and many of the same tools and procedures can be employed.

Thin-sectioning

Prime amongst these is examination of thin-sections through a petrographic microscope. A thin-section is a thin slice of ceramic material mounted with a special adhesive or resin on a glass microscope slide. The ceramic slice is then ground down to a thickness of *c.* 0.03mm and a thin glass slip is glued over it. The grinding can either be done by hand, using glass plates and successively finer powders, or there are some semi-automated systems available. A particular problem with many ceramic thin-sections is the rather friable nature of the material. To counter this it may be necessary to impregnate the sherds with a resin prior to sectioning – this and other techniques are described by Nicholson (1989, 89–92).

When the slide is mounted in a microscope with a polarised light source (light which is vibrating in one plane only) and a rotating stage, the various minerals in the ceramic affect the light in different ways. Some display characteristic colours, others particular patterns, and these differences allow them to be identified (for details of optical mineralogy consult a standard textbook such as Kerr 1977).

An advantage that examining the minerals in a ceramic body in this way has over, for instance, an analysis of the composition of the clay (p. 144), is the large body of comparative data that is available in the form of geological maps and texts or rock samples and thin-sections held by museums and other research bodies. The minerals in a thin-section will often give valuable clues about the origin of the clay or filler. Some combinations can indicate that the clay derives from a very specific type of geology, for which there may be only one or two candidates in the region. In other circumstances it may be sufficient to identify a sherd as coming from outside a region – as in the case of a fabric tempered with granite fragments in a limestone area. Otherwise sherds may be grouped together on the basis of shared characteristics, even if a specific source cannot be suggested.

The most common inclusion type, at least in Europe and the Mediterranean world, is quartz. There are ways in which quartz can be studied petrologically with profit. For example, one can distinguish quartz crystallised as part of a granite from that formed by the induration of sedimentary rocks or that subjected to low-grade or high-grade metamorphism. It is rare, however, to find a sand deposit which can be characterised by classifying the quartz grains in this way and it is normal for those faced with classifying pottery containing quartz-sand inclusions to use some sort of descriptive statistics based on the size range of the inclusions.

Textural analysis
Textural analysis is not concerned with the identity of the minerals in a ceramic body but rather with the distribution of their sizes, and to a lesser extent, their shapes. The potential of the technique has been reviewed by Darvill and Timby (1982) and Streeten (1982) and details of the procedures are described by Middleton and others (1985).

There are two ways of approaching grain-size analysis. One is to describe the grain-size distribution for all the inclusions together and the other is to treat each identified inclusion type separately. If the inclusion types are of potentially differing hardness then the latter approach is essential. In the case of most fabrics with quartz sand inclusions the non-quartzose inclusions are rare enough to be ignored at this stage. Several methods of analysis have been used, each with its own advantages and disadvantages.

Some work from thin-sections and others from the sherd itself. The former is potentially more objective as it can eliminate much observer bias, but suffers from the problem that large grains may be reduced in diameter by the sectioning process itself, especially if they are larger than the thickness of the sections, while very small ones may 'disappear' altogether within the thickness of the section.

The simplest approach is to measure the smallest and largest inclusion in a thin-section and to use these data to compare sherds. At York, for example, this simple method was sufficient to show that a particular type of pottery was made using increasingly fine quartz sand during the tenth and eleventh centuries (Brooks and Mainman 1984, 69). Usually, however, the overall size range may overlap, or be identical, but one can still see a difference between fabric groups.

At the other extreme, it is possible to count the numbers of grains falling into various size ranges, and plot a histogram or frequency polygon of the sizes. To do this, a sample of grains is needed (there are far too many to count all of them, nor is it necessary, in order to estimate the size distribution). Some workers (e.g. Hamilton 1977) have done this by crushing sherds and extracting the grains, others by sampling from a view of the sherd, either visually or in thin-section. Such methods have not found general favour because they can be extremely time-consuming, although there is the possi-

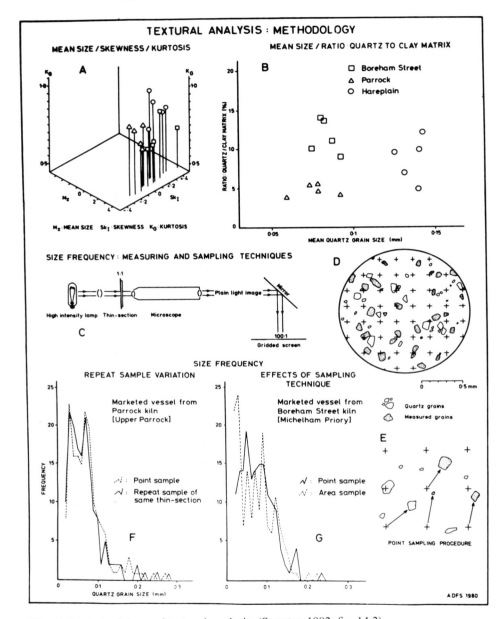

Fig. 11.2. Methodology of textural analysis. (Streeten 1982, fig. 14.2)

bility of semi-automatic analyses by coupling the microscope to an image analyser and micro-computer (Middleton et al. 1985, 64–6). A good way of characterising the size distribution visually and at the same time conveying a vivid impression of the texture of the fabric (which was our motivation for looking at size distribution) has been given by Streeten (1980; figs. 11.2 and

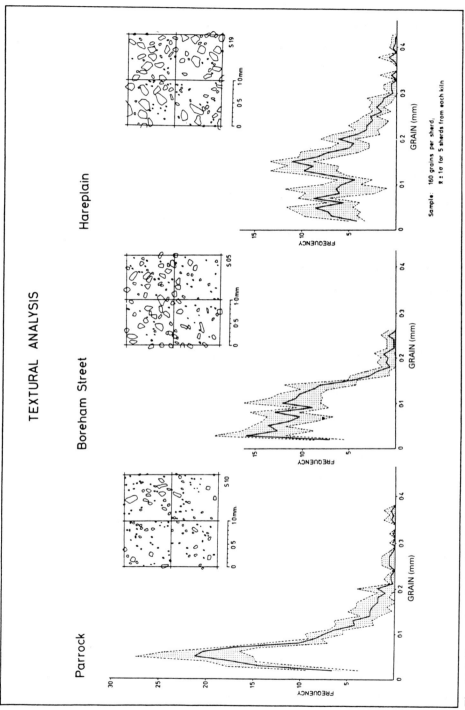

Fig. 11.3. Textural analysis of fabrics from three early sixteenth-century kilns in Sussex. (Streeten 1980, fig. 37)

11.3). This does not seem to have been followed up, perhaps because of the skill needed to produce such figures, but it seems to have great potential.

Heavy mineral analysis

Another technique that can be applied to ceramics with largely quartz inclusions is heavy mineral analysis. The principals and procedures have been reviewed and described by several writers (Peacock 1967; Williams 1979; van der Plas and van Doesburg 1987). Instead of concentrating on the characteristics of the quartz sand, this is ignored, and the focus shifts to the very rare, small grains of accessory minerals which are present in most sands, and which are themselves rarely picked up in other petrological techniques such as thin-sectioning. These minerals are usually dark in colour and dense (with a specific gravity greater than 2.9), and are extracted by mixing the crushed sherd with a high specific-gravity liquid such as acetylene tetrabromide or bromoform. The lighter component – the quartz-sand – floats to the surface of the mixture and the heavy minerals sink; a centrifuge may be used to hasten this. The heavy mineral grains are filtered out and identified with standard petrological techniques. It is suggested that several hundred grains are required to form an adequate sample; this is inevitably time-consuming and there seem to be no shortcuts. The suite of minerals can then be compared with that from sands of known source, or sherds may be grouped together on the basis of shared characteristics.

Heavy mineral analysis is essentially subsidiary to the other petrological techniques described above, but it may well be the only way of distinguishing between some otherwise homogeneous sand-tempered wares.

Compositional analysis

Compositional analysis (also referred to as elemental analysis, or more simply, chemical analysis) seeks to provide an assessment of the elements present in a ceramic body. The results are usually quantitative and are expressed in terms of the percentages of different elements present or, with rarer components, in parts-per-million (ppm).

The role of compositional analysis in pottery analysis has been surveyed by several writers (Wilson 1978; Bishop et al. 1982; Bennet et al. 1989) and the substantial review of Greek and Cypriot pottery by Jones (1986) includes much valuable information on the techniques. Compositional analysis is typically not concerned with description of the elemental composition *per se* but with the investigation of provenance: the determination of the source(s) of the analysed material. The analysis seeks to identify those characteristics of the composition that can be used to distinguish between material from different sources. In one case it may be that a high percentage of a particular element distinguishes between two sources, in another it may be characteristic ratios between two or more elements. Such factors are sometimes referred to as *markers* or *fingerprints*. The techniques are not confined to the study of the clay body. Slips, paints and (particularly) glazes have also been examined.

Most practical applications of compositional analysis fall under one of three headings:

(i) There is firstly the attempt to pin down the clay sources responsible by comparing the composition of the raw clay with that of fired vessels. This has been referred to as clay sourcing.

(ii) A second approach (perhaps the most common), is to compare only the composition of fired vessels, the origin of some of which is known – a procedure usually known as workshop sourcing. The vessels of known origin may be the products of a known kiln site, or they may be related in some other way, such as bearing the stamps or marks of a single potter, always bearing in mind the possibility that such potters may move from one production site to another during their active lifetime. If a particularly large geographical scale is being considered, it may be sufficient to take sherds whose exact origin is not known (down to the level of a named kiln site) but which represent the clays employed in a particular area.

(iii) The third approach compares sherds whose origin is not known. The aim may be to define clusters or groups which *may* reflect source, or simply to determine whether a series of samples may or may not belong to the same group.

The principal techniques currently employed in the study of archaeological ceramics are Atomic absorption spectrophotometry (usually abbreviated to AAS), Neutron activation analysis (NAA), Optical emission spectroscopy (OES) and X-ray fluorescence (XRF). These four main techniques are not completely interchangeable. Some are more sensitive than others to very low concentrations, and the level of precision that can be attained and the number of elements that are capable of recognition also varies. Although up to eighty of the ninety-two naturally occurring elements may be detected by NAA and XRF, in all such studies only a far shorter list, often only twenty or so, is actually considered. The exact choice varies from one project to another and some research laboratories traditionally include some elements that others regularly exclude (Jones 1986, 18–20). In addition to these common techniques, other more exotic procedures have been occasionally employed for the compositional analysis of ceramics – some, however, appear but once in the pages of one of the archaeological science journals and then sink without trace.

However, it will be relatively rare that a pottery worker will be faced with the problem of choosing between competing techniques or designing a research program 'from scratch'. More often the choice of laboratories able to participate in a project will be strictly limited, the choice of techniques and procedures will already have been made, and it will be a question of integration with an existing research program.

It is not intended to describe the physical and chemical basis of these techniques here – there are excellent summaries by Jones (1986, 16–22), Rice (1987, 374–5, 393–400) and others. Rather we will concentrate on the value of such compositional studies and their incorporation into a wider research program on pottery.

We can view the progress from clay to ceramic to compositional analysis as a series of links in a chain, or transformations, each introducing additional factors that must be considered when interpreting the results. These transformations are best summarised in the following table:

Table 11.1. *Transformations from clay to compositional analysis*

Clay preparation
   levigation and washing
   mixing of clays
   addition of non-plastics
   addition of water
Post-depositional environment
   addition of elements
   removal of elements
Sampling
   sampling errors
   contamination
   measurement errors
Statistical analysis

Clay preparation

In their simplest form the techniques of compositional analysis assume that the material being analysed is homogeneous. While this may be almost true with very fine fabrics, it is certainly not so with most coarser fabrics, and it is these that form the majority of those with which the archaeologist is concerned.

No single component of the fabric will be responsible for all the compositional variability. The clay and non-plastics both contribute to the mixture, and the widespread practice of potters to prepare their raw clays (p. 115) *reduces* the possibility of matching pottery and clay based on compositional data alone. Washing and levigation may remove material from the original clay, mixing non-plastics or water (perhaps containing contaminants) will add them. In some simple cases, such as when a single type of clay is combined with differing proportions of a single type of non-plastic inclusion, it may be possible to distinguish clusters in the final data that reflect this (Neff et al. 1988, 343–5).

This potential lack of correspondence between raw clays and ceramics made from them may or may not be a hindrance, depending on what type of application of compositional analysis is being undertaken.

Post-depositional environment

Ceramics are not always inert in their post-depositional environment but may react with it. Elements may be both added to and removed from sherds, which may in turn show up in the compositional analysis. Two alterations are particularly well documented. Pottery which has spent a long time under the sea, such as material from ancient wrecks, absorbs magnesium (Picon 1976; Jones 1986, 36–7).

Phosphate has been shown to be absorbed after burial (Lemoine and Picon 1982; Freestone et al. 1985), in some cases raising the concentration from *c.* 0.1 per cent up to *c.* 10 per cent. Precipitation from ground water is probably responsible as the phosphate concentrates around cracks and pores in the ceramic – it has been suggested that fertilisers applied to the soil above may be in part responsible for this (Lasfargues and Picon 1982). It has also been noted that the deposited phosphate may in turn absorb trace elements such as scandium, chromium, barium and others (Freestone et al. 1985, 1974). The implications of this for some provenance studies may be quite far-reaching.

Sampling and measurement

Prior to measurement a sample must be taken from the sherd or vessel to be analysed and prepared for examination. A small sample is usually removed from the vessel or sherd and reduced to a fine powder. Steps must be taken to reduce contamination from the equipment used to perform these tasks, such as the drill-bits (Attas et al. 1984), pestles and mortars. In order to adequately sample a heterogeneous material such as a coarse ceramic containing discrete inclusions it will be necessary to crush a relatively large sample and then take smaller sub-samples from this.

Three factors must be taken into account when considering the results of compositional analysis: sensitivity, precision and accuracy (Bishop et al. 1990). Sensitivity is the ability to measure very small quantities of an element, broadly the minimum that can be detected. Precision is the repeatability of the measurements. It is a measure of how similar a series of analyses of the same material would be. Accuracy is the relationship between the measurements and the actual values. Standards of known composition are usually employed to determine accuracy. Advanced techniques of compositional analysis such as those employed in the examination of archaeological ceramics do not provide absolute values but rather a series of values with a standard deviation attached. These ranges reflect factors inherent in the procedures combined with instrumentation and counting errors.

Statistical analysis

Finally, the raw results of any technique of compositional analysis are not open in any sense to 'independent' interpretation. On their own they only describe the sample, but as this is usually not the aim of the procedure some form of comparison with other data is normal. This requires the intervention of data analysis procedures.

The other data may be from the same laboratory, employing the same equipment, standards and procedures, or they may be from other laboratories – perhaps even employing different techniques. Some inter-laboratory and inter-technique comparisons have been performed (Harbottle 1982; Jones 1986, 38–45) but these have not always proved particularly encouraging. Clearly, extreme care must be taken when attempting to compare between measurements taken in such different environments. It may generally not be advisable to pick a set of results 'off the shelf', however tempting it may be, without at least considering the above factors. As has been pointed out (Bishop et al. 1990, 544–5), the precision and accuracy of the data becomes particularly important when commercial contractors are being employed to carry out analyses, rather than specialist research laboratories, where we might at least expect more internal consistency. If the goal of archives of reusable results is to be realised then more attention will have to be given to these points.

Several techniques for the analysis and representation of data are available, of which Principal Components Analysis (PCA) (Shennan 1988, 245–62) is one of the most common. PCA envisages the individual samples ('observations') as points in a geometrical space whose axes are defined by the variables, and which therefore has as many dimensions as there are variables. The space is rotated to a new set of axes so that the observations are as spread out as possible in the directions of the first few axes. This enables them to be plotted in a low number of dimensions (usually two), while preserving as much as possible of the original structure of the data. The benefits are: (i) we can see a picture of as much of the relationships between the original observations as can easily be plotted in two dimensions; and (ii) since the new axes can be related mathematically to the old ones (the variables), we can see which variables contribute most to the differences between the observations. The main disadvantage is that PCA is intended for use with variables that are all measured on the same scale. If, for example, we measured some variables in millimetres and some in centimetres, we would probably find that those in millimetres appeared 'more important' than those in centimetres, because they were larger numbers and (most likely) had a wider spread. For the same reason, one cannot combine different sorts of variables, such as lengths and weights or lengths and counts. This problem can be overcome to some extent by 'standardising' the data, that is by treating each observation as so many standard deviations above or below the mean value of its variable, but with a risk of giving too much importance to relatively minor variables.

Statistical analysis of percentage data (also known as compositional data) was revolutionised by the publication of the CODA (= COmpositional DAta) technique (Aitchison 1986). Aitchison pointed out that all existing methods were unsound because they ignored the spurious negative correlations that are induced by the fact that a complete set of percentage data always adds up to 100. This flaw had been known for many years, but had been conveniently overlooked or ignored. His new technique, CODA, was theoretically sound and overcame all the objections to earlier techniques. Unfortunately it had problems of its own, mainly an inability to cope with zeros in the data, which were not shared by earlier techniques. Analysts found that theoretical soundness did not necessarily lead in practice to better or more useful results (see Baxter and Heyworth 1989). The debate continues.

Comparison between techniques

A continuing problem with much of the published work on compositional analyses is the failure to make any attempt to apply the results of these analyses in such a way that they are of assistance to those faced with the problems of dealing with large quantities of material from sites. The warnings of Peacock, issued in 1977, that 'it is only by searching for and recording visual criteria corresponding to the chemical groupings that it will be possible to extrapolate the findings on a larger scale' (Peacock 1977, 25) have all too rarely been heeded. Undoubtedly in many cases the appropriate visual clues will not be forthcoming, but it is all too apparent from much of the published work that no attempt has been made to look for them, and some clearly see no benefit in so doing.

When faced with a list of elements present in a fired body it will not be immediately apparent how they entered it. In particular there is no simple 'translation' from the elements to the compounds that contributed them, particularly in the terms that a geologist, or a trained pottery worker in the field, would recognise. Picon suggests that, broadly, the aluminium, potassium, magnesium and titanium derive from the clay minerals, while silica and calcium are from the non-plastics (Picon 1973, 18–19). Some more specialised forms of compositional analysis eliminate some of these difficulties. The electron micro-probe allows the analysis to be confined to a small point in the fabric (the width of a beam of electrons) rather than providing the 'bulk' analysis of most of the other common techniques (Freestone 1982). If the point analysed is within a non-plastic in the fabric, the study could then combine the petrological approach – perhaps the identification of the inclusion as a feldspar or quartz – with detailed data on its chemical composition. Unfortunately, this type of equipment is not yet commonly available.

However, there are a number of studies that apply more than one form of

Table 11.2. *Analysis of Punic amphoras from Corinth*

Sample	Chemical analysis	Mössbauer spectroscopy	X-ray radiography	Petrological analysis
6	I	I	I	I
9	I/II	I	I	—
10	I	I	I	I
4	I	I	I	I
15	I	I	I	I
30	I	I	I	—
11	I	I	I	IIe
8	I	I	I	IId
27	I	I	II	—
16	I	I/II	I	IIe
31	I	I/II	II	IId
14	II	I/II	II	IIc
19	II	I/II	II	IIb
2	I	II	II	IIc
22	II	II	I	IIe
12	II	II	II	—
13	II	II	—	IIc
26	II	II	II	IIc
24	II	II	II	—
18	II	II	II	IIb
20	II	II	II	IIb
28	II	II	II	—
25	II	II	II	—
23	II	II	II	—
21	II	II	II	IIa
29	II	II	II	—
17	II	II	II	IIb
7	II	II	II	IIa
1	II	II	II	IIc
3	II	II	II	IIc
5	II	II	II	IIc

elemental analysis and also incorporate petrological and visual examination. The study by Maniatis and others (1984) of Punic amphoras from Corinth employed optical emission spectroscopy (OES), Mössbauer spectroscopy (MS), X-ray radiography (XRAY) and petrological analysis (PA).

The results are summarised in a table (see table 11.2), from which the relationships between the compositional groupings and the petrological and visual characteristics can be seen. The outcome of different classifications, as shown here, can be compared by using a new family of techniques known as consensus analysis (McMorris 1990).

Another example of the successful integration of compositional and visual

Table 11.3. *Comparison of visual and compositional groupings in stamped sigillata from Haltern*

Qualität	Arezzo	Italy	Lyon	Pisa	Total
i	0	2	0	24	26
ii	4	15	0	44	63
ii?	1	2	1	4	8
i/ii	0	0	0	4	4
ii/iv	1	4	1	19	25
iii	0	0	4	0	4
iii?	0	1	0	2	3
iv	0	4	61	8	73
iv?	1	7	2	5	15
iv/v	2	1	0	1	4
v	3	3	0	0	6
v?	0	2	0	1	3
Total	12	41	69	112	234

Source: von Schnurbein 1982.

classifications is related by von Schnurbein (1982) in his study of the terra sigillata from Haltern. He first divides the material, under a binocular microscope, into five categories ('Qualität').

The stamped pieces are then subjected to chemical analysis and assigned to one of five sources: Pisa, Lyon, Arezzo, Campania and Italy. The results of the compositional analysis are then compared with the visual groupings (table 11.3).

There are some strong correlations between the visual and compositional groups: of the 69 Lyon stamps, 61 (88 per cent) are in Qualität iv (and two further stamps are classed as iv?).

Studies such as these point the way forward to a more fruitful collaboration between compositional analysis and visual and petrological studies. The former have undoubtedly a great contribution to make but their relationship to the majority of pottery analysis, which must always be based on informed visual examination, must be strengthened.

12

FORM

When dealing with a collection of vessels, or indeed any other class of object, it is natural to group similar items together, and separate them from the groups from which they differ. Pottery, the product of an almost uniquely plastic medium, has been made in a very wide range of forms or shapes. There may be several different ways of classifying a collection of complete vessels – perhaps on their overall shape, or the details of their rim forms, the presence of handles and spouts, their decorative motifs and so on – and in many traditional methods of classification all such factors may be taken into consideration. When the material in question is composed largely of sherds, a different set of problems may arise. Rim sherds may, in some cases, be unique to a particular vessel form – in others the same rim may be shared by a number of forms, but it may be that all the vessels sharing certain characteristics in the rim form are products of a single workshop.

The purposes of classification are perhaps threefold. Firstly there is the practical one that the alternative to classification is treating each and every item as unique, which would undoubtedly generate a vast amount of information but equally would inhibit any clear view of the material (the wood-for-the-trees syndrome). The second is that the recognition of types allows patterns in the data to be recognised. Thirdly we can use the type as a 'label' to attach to other information and in the case of ceramics the most important additional information is a measure of quantity (see p. 166).

The attributes of a successful classification have been summarised succinctly by Orton (1980, 33):

(i)   objects belonging to the same type should be similar;

(ii)   objects belonging to different types should be dissimilar;

(iii)   the types should be defined with sufficient precision to allow others to duplicate the classification;

(iv)   it should be possible to decide which type a new object belongs to.

Approaches to the classification of shape

Pottery shape is influenced by a large number of factors. The decisions made by the potter, the tools and materials available and his skill (or otherwise) in manipulating them all contribute to the finished product. Most practical approaches to the classification of pottery fall into one of three categories:

152

(i) the (traditional) type series;
(ii) formal classifications and measurement-based systems;
(iii) classifications based on manufacturing sequences.

The type-series approach

A number of approaches are employed in traditional pottery classification systems. One common system is the identification of 'type vessels'. Vessels are grouped together on the basis of similar features and a single example is illustrated which thereby represents all the others. The type vessel need not come from the same site as the others – it may be a complete vessel from a museum collection which represents sherds from an excavated collection. As a means of summarising the material from a site this system has much to recommend it, but the problems may start when a type vessel is promoted to wider usage, beyond the limited group of material it was initially intended to represent. It may be perceived to fill a gap in an existing typology, or it may be taken to be a representative of a type with a wide distribution.

One of the best known, and most successful, of the standard typologies is Dragendorff's classification of samian ware (Dragendorff 1895). This was initially intended as an aid to the study of the material on sites in Germany, but quickly became the standard reference in Britain, France, Switzerland, Italy and beyond. In this case such usage was quite valid, as the pottery in Britain and elsewhere was the same – the products of the same workshops and potters – as the German material which formed the basis of the type series. Dragendorff was classifying a production assemblage as well as a series of site finds. Additions to the samian ware series were filled by other scholars working on further site finds or the material from kiln sites.

Typologies are not always so successfully employed. Particular difficulties arise when a type series intended for one area is transferred to another and applied indiscriminately. It may not be possible to transfer the chronology or other attributes of a particular form from one region to another. The developments in one region may not be mirrored outside a limited area.

The most satisfactory type series are perhaps those that define the types *within* a fabric or ware. These can be applied to any material of the same fabric.

Formal classification systems

A more formal scheme of ceramic classification has been described by Gardin (1985). The individual features of the vessel, the body form, base, neck, rim, handle, spout and so on are compared with drawn examples and appropriately coded. For example, handles are coded for their type, number, location of attachment, position on the vessel, overall form and cross-section (Gardin 1985, 76–85) – the section would be coded for the shape of its upper and lower faces – thus 0. .0' would be a handle of cylindrical section, 6. .2'

III   ÉLÉMENTS   ADDITIONNELS : PRÉHENSION   (suite)   J

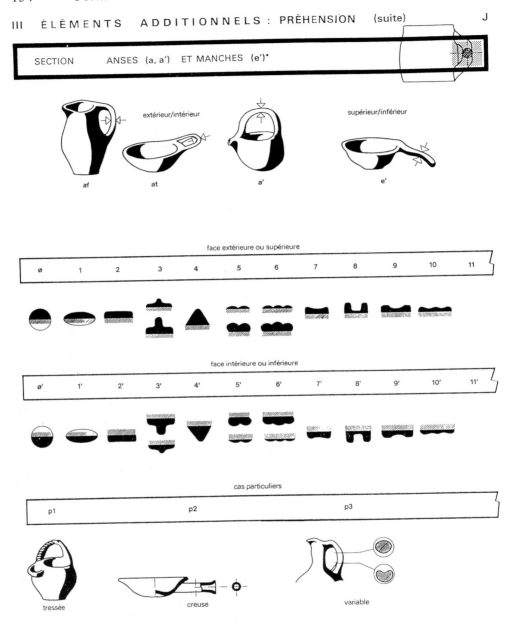

Fig. 12.1. An example of the formal description of ceramic shapes – handles. (Gardin 1985)

would have three ribs on the upper surface and a flat lower surface (Gardin 1985, 84). The details may be recorded on pre-printed forms (Gardin 1985, 102–7) and expressed as a sequence of letters and numbers (fig. 12.1). The original system is intended to be universal in the sense that it is equally

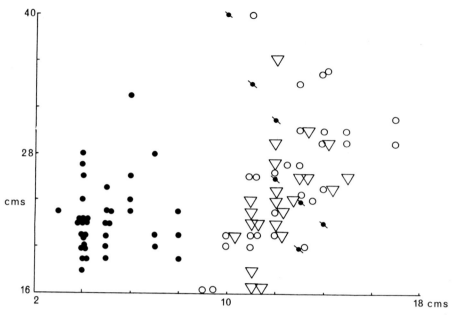

Fig. 12.2. The use of simple ratios and measurements to distinguish pottery of different tribal groups in Kenya. The maximum body width (vertical axis) and mouth width (horizontal axis) distinguish between Kokwa pots (filled circle) and those from the Chebloch and Tot (open circles and triangles) (after Hodder 1979, fig. 4)

applicable to all pottery types irrespective of date or origin. It clearly relies on finding appropriate matches amongst the illustrations for all the elements on the vessel to be classified, and new elements may be added when recognised. Such systems are not in widespread use but Hamon and Hesnard (1977) apply these principles to the problems of describing Roman amphoras. Such an approach may be of value in museum cataloguing or the design of computer databases to encode ceramic form.

Measurement-based classification

A simple, yet effective, method of classifying pottery is to define types in terms of the ratios of the principal dimensions. Such an approach is used by Webster (1964) in his description of the principal classes of Romano-British pottery types. Thus, a bowl has 'a height more than one third but not greater than its diameter', a dish 'a height less than a third of but greater than a seventh of its diameter' and a plate a height 'not greater than a seventh of its diameter' (Webster 1964, 5–16). Hardy-Smith (1974) describes a similar system for the classification of post-medieval ceramic forms employing the ratio between height and diameter to distinguish between plates, cups, bowls, jugs and so on. The value of such systems has been discussed by Millett (1979a, 36–7, fig. 12) and Orton (1980, 33–6). In many cases such simple ratios reflect traditional classifications reasonably faithfully, although there are marginal cases and some traditional divisions, such as that between Romano-British beakers and jars or plates and dishes, include criteria such as the quality of the fabric or decoration which are, or at least are intended to be, partly functional. However, even such simple measurements can, in some circumstances, be a powerful tool for dividing up groups of pottery. Hodder describes the pottery of several tribal groups in the Baringo district (western Kenya) and plots the maximum body width and mouth width of pots from the area (Hodder 1979, 15, fig. 4; fig. 12.2). There are clearly two groups – those with a mouth of less than about 10cm diameter and those with a larger mouth – and this difference in size reflects a difference in origin.

The next step after considering ratios is to take a more elaborate set of measurements as a basis for coding and/or classifying a pot. At least three sets have been proposed, known as the 'sliced' method (Wilcock and Shennan 1975a, 99), the 'mosaic' method (Wilcock and Shennan 1975a, 100) and the 'swept radius' method (Liming et al. 1989). The first idea is very simple: the profile of the pot is divided into a number of equally-spaced horizontal 'slices', and the radius at each is measured. They are usually expressed as percentages of the height of the pot to eliminate differences due only to size. The data can be used as input to a statistical technique such as cluster analysis, as was done by Wilcock and Shennan (1975b) on Central German Bell Beakers. The disadvantage is that many slices are needed to describe a shape accurately, but much of this information is redundant because the pot usually varies only slightly between one slice and the next. In the mosaic method, a grid of squares is overlaid on the profile, which can be seen to pass through some squares but not others. The squares through which it passes are coded in a hierarchical structure which describes the shape of the pot. As far as we know, this technique has not been used since it was first described.

By contrast, the swept radius method has been used successfully to provide data for a cluster analysis of forms. The first step is to choose a central point for the profile, conventionally halfway up the central axis. A radial arm is swept round from this centre (like a hand on a clock) and the radii are measured at equally spaced angles. They are usually expressed as percentages of the height. The advantage over the sliced method is that it can deal with asymmetric profiles and that it seems to require fewer data points, twenty-four being adequate for even quite complicated shapes (Liming et al. 1989, 370. It is also claimed to give better results than the tangent-profile method (see below p. 159).

A more sophisticated use of the sliced method is employed by Richards (1987) in his consideration of the shape of Anglo-Saxon burial urns. These hand-made vessels are of rather simple form with an apparently continuous gradation of size and shape rather than falling into discrete types. A simple rim diameter/height ratio would not be appropriate and a method is required

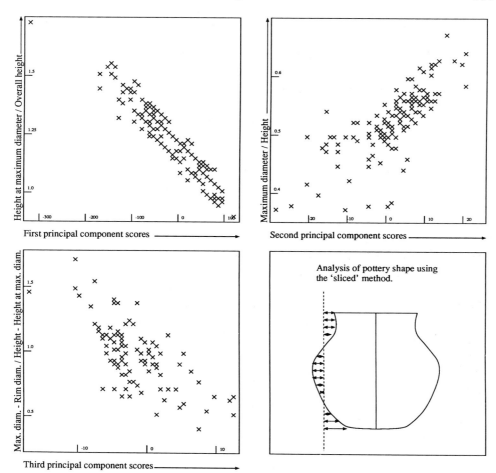

Fig. 12.3. An example of the use of principal components analysis to investigate the shape of pottery vessels. The first three components of the PCA represent ratios of maximum diameter/ height, height of maximum diameter/height and (maximum diameter − rim diameter)/ (height − height of maximum diameter). (Richards 1987, figs. 12–15)

which takes fuller account of the relationships between different parts of the vessel profile rather than simply the major dimensions.

The vessel profiles are first digitised using a digitising tablet and the data standardised to the same height, thus eliminating the overall size as a factor and concentrating purely on the shape element. The vessel is divided (conceptually) into 100 slices of equal height and their radii are calculated at each boundary. The resulting data are then subjected to the technique of principal components analysis (PCA; see p. 148). In the case of 100 burial urns from a cemetery at Spong Hill (Norfolk, Great Britain) 93 per cent of the variability is accounted for by the first three components. The first component (79 per cent) is broadly represented by the ratio *maximum diameter / height*, the second (9 per cent) by *height of maximum diameter / height* – a measure of how 'shouldered' the urn is – and the third (5 per cent) by (*maximum diameter − rim diameter*) / (*height − height of maximum diameter*) – a measure of how 'enclosed' the neck is (Richards 1987, 71–6; fig. 12.3). Experiments using the same analytical method with only 20 slices confirmed the results obtained with 100 measures. Most of the morphological variation in the vessels is thus encompassed by the four measures: rim diameter, maximum diameter, height and height of maximum diameter. These variables can then be used, as in the case described by Richards, in a broader analysis of the associations between form, decorative style and grave goods. However, the principal disadvantage of this and similar systems is that they cannot be applied to the sherd material which forms the majority of the pottery recovered from archaeological sites.

Geometric shapes

Many vessel forms can be classified by reference to geometric shapes, or *primitives* such as spheres, ellipsoids, ovaloids, cylinders, hyperboloids and cones (Shepard 1956, 233–5, figs. 23–4). The simple vessel shape may be represented by a solid with segments removed, or, more usually, a complex shape will be represented by many different segments. The vessel is divided into segments, each represented by a geometric shape or a part thereof. Thus a flagon may have a cylindrical neck, with a truncated oval as the body. By reference to such solids the overall volume of a vessel may be estimated. A number of coding schemes based on the division of forms into segments of geometrical shapes have been proposed (Castillo Tejero and Litvak 1968; Ericson and Stickel 1973; see also Traunecker 1984) although none has seen widespread use and as with measurement and ratio methods their application to sherd material is problematic.

The envelope system

An attempt to devise a system that could be used on sherds as well as whole pots was made by Orton (1987) while working on waste from a delftware kiln site. A basic typology had already been established (Bloice and Dawson 1971); the problem was to fit fragments to the defined shapes. If the profiles of several examples of the same broad form (for example bowl) are reduced to a common scale, and overlaid, a line can be drawn which encloses all the profiles (fig. 12.4). This is known as the envelope of the profiles of that form; clearly the more tightly defined the form, the thinner the envelope. It is useful for showing the range of variation possible within a type-definition, and can also expose inconsistencies in definitions, when one profile could belong to more than one type (Orton 1987, fig. 8). Potentially the most useful feature of the system is that drawings of sherds can be overlaid on the envelopes of different forms (provided that they can be correctly oriented to the horizontal,

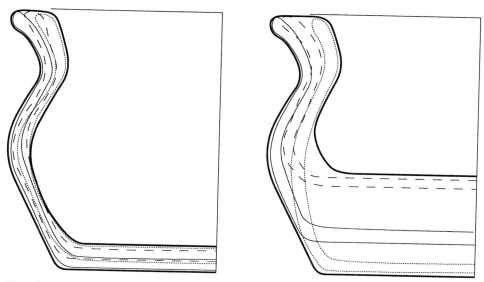

Fig. 12.4. Two examples of 'envelopes' of pottery forms. (Orton 1987, fig. 2)

which is usually possible for wheel-thrown pottery) to see to which types they could, or could not, belong. If the sherd crosses the envelope, it cannot belong to that type; if it does not, it may belong (fig. 12.5).

Mathematical curves as descriptions of shape

The thinking behind this family of techniques is that it may be easier and theoretically more valid to compare some mathematical representation of the shape of a pot (or other artefact) than the original shape. Four such representations have received recent attention: (i) the tangent-profile (TP) technique (Main 1981; Leese and Main 1983) and its derivative, the sampled tangent-profile (STP) technique (Main 1986); (ii) B-spline curves (Hall and Laflin 1984); (iii) the centroid and cyclical curve technique (Tyldesley et al. 1985); and (iv) the two-curve system (Hagstrum and Hildebrand 1990).

The TP technique starts by defining a reference point on the profile, which is digitised at selected points. For each of these points, its distance along the profile from the reference point (the 'arc-length') and the direction of the profile at that point (the 'tangent-angle') are measured (fig. 12.6). The graph of tangent-angle plotted against arc-length describes the shape of the profile. This representation allows a measure of the difference between two profiles to be made; this measure is said to match well with human perception (Leese and Main 1983, 173). The STP technique is very similar, but samples points at equal distances along the profile, thus making it easier to store the data and to compare profiles.

The B-spline is one of many curve-fitting techniques available on modern

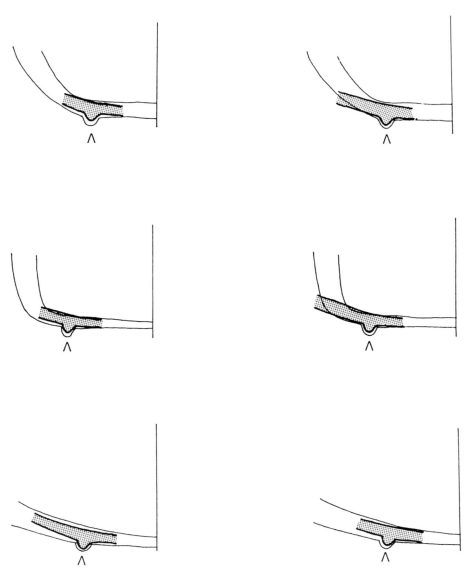

Fig. 12.5. Envelopes of bases of porringers of types A (upper), B (middle) and open (lower) from 'Mark Browns Wharf' (London). The smaller sherd (column 1) can be matched by two envelopes (upper and lower), and the larger sherd (column 2) only matches the lower envelope. (Orton 1987, fig. 6)

CAD (computer-aided design) packages, that can fit smooth mathematical curves through a selection of points. It is thought to be more suitable for describing pottery profiles than either cubic splines or Bezier curves (Hall and Laflin 1984, 180, 186). It has the advantage of being able to store a profile in a small amount of computer memory, but it is not obvious how it could readily be used to compare profiles or measure similarity.

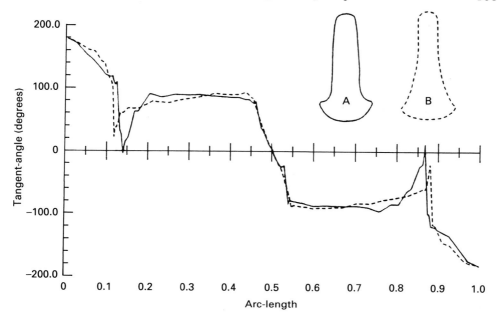

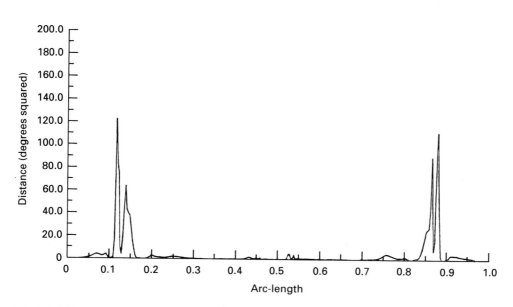

Fig. 12.6. Tangent and distance profiles for two contrasting axes. (Leese and Main 1983, fig. 3)

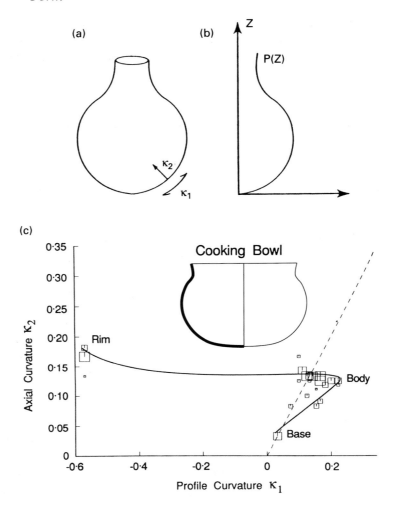

Fig. 12.7. The 'two-curve' method of analysing pottery shape. Two principal curvatures characterise the surface geometry of a ceramic vessel. (a) the profile curve (k1) gives the curvature along the vessel profile. The axial curvature (k2) gives the curvature perpendicular to the profile. (b) a surface of revolution results when a profile is rotated about its axis. (c) the plot shows the surface curvature (solid line) calculated from the profile and sherd curvature (boxes). (Hagstrum and Hildebrand 1990, figs. 1 and 3). Reproduced by permission of the Society for American Archaeology from *American Antiquity*, 55 (1990)

The centroid and cyclical curve method has been mainly used on skeletal data. It starts by drawing an arbitrary line through the centroid (centre of gravity) of a profile, dividing the profile in two. Each half has its own centroid; the line connecting them passes through the original centroid. It then records the angle between the arbitrary line and the new one that connects the centroids. The arbitrary line is then rotated through a set angle (for example 5°) and the process is repeated. When the arbitrary line has been rotated through a total of 180° we can plot a graph of the angles that have been measured between the pairs of lines for each position of the arbitrary line. This graph is called the 'cyclical curve' and it represents the shape of the profile. It can be used as input to statistical analyses.

The two-curve system is much more adapted to ceramic material, and, like the envelope system, is particularly suited for dealing with sherds. For complete pots, a series of points on the profile are chosen and at each the curvature of the pot is measured in two directions – along the profile (the 'profile curvature') and at right angles to it (the 'axial curvature'). The graph of axial curvature against profile curvature is plotted to give a curve whose shape is characteristic of the form of the pot (fig. 12.7). For sherds, we take the two measurements of curvature which we can plot as a single point on the graph. By comparing the scatter-plot of sherds in an assemblage with curves that are characteristic of known shapes of pots, we can estimate the proportions of pots of different shapes represented in the assemblage.

It must be said, however, that many such approaches seem to be more geared to the needs of efficient computer storage or the exploitation of software created for other purposes than to the characteristics of real pots. In some ways the target of a useful database of pottery shapes seems as far off as it did in the 1970s, with technological development appearing to hinder as much as help the relationship between the analyst and pot (see for example Lewis and Goodson 1991).

Classification of manufacturing stages
An alternative to the approaches outlined above is based on a classification of the methods of manufacture – describing the steps taken to produce a vessel rather than simply classifying the finished product. Instead of concentrating on the ratios, measurements or curves represented in the vessels the emphasis is instead on a careful examination of the traces left on the vessel which indicate the steps taken during the manufacturing process to create the shape. The steps will include not only the basic primary forming techniques (that is hand-formed or wheel-thrown) but also such details as the way the final shape is built up by luting separate pieces together, the sequence of smoothing and finishing techniques or the way that rims and bases are shaped. In the case of wheel-thrown wares it may be possible to deduce the actions of the potter by looking for tell-tale areas of stretching or compression on the finished vessel. Rye (1981, 75–8) gives clear descriptions of the principal steps in wheel-throwing and the traces they leave on the finished vessel.

Thus, in this approach it is the successive manipulations taken by the potter – the sequence of steps – which distinguish one 'type' from another. Evidently, the same (or very similar) morphological types (when viewed as a series of measurements, ratios, curves and so on) may result from different

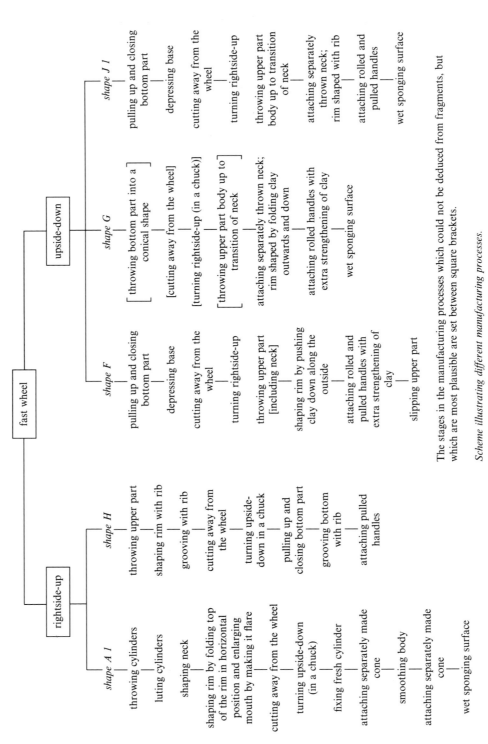

The stages in the manufacturing processes which could not be deduced from fragments, but which are most plausible are set between square brackets.

Scheme illustrating different manufacturing processes.

Fig. 12.8. An example of a decision tree describing a typology based on a study of the traces left during manufacturing. (Schuring 1984)

sequences of operation, and conversely one such sequence may result in a certain morphological range. Schuring (1984) gives an example of such an approach, applied to a group of later Roman amphoras. In this study it is proposed that 'everything produced in the same way, that falls within the variations in shape that the particular technique permits, can be classified as one type' (p. 148). The final classification is presented as a 'decision tree' showing the steps taken for the different vessels and indicating where the manufacture of one type diverges from another (fig. 12.8). The manufacturing traces observed on vessels should be recorded on the illustrations (see p. 89).

13

QUANTIFICATION

Introduction

This is a subject which has often generated more heat than light in recent years. Although it has been generally (but not universally) appreciated as a 'good thing', its aims and in particular its methods have been a source of controversy. To try to resolve this problem we must go back to basics. At its simplest, quantification is an attempt to answer the question 'How much pottery is there?' – whether in a context, feature, site or other grouping. An answer to this question as posed would be of little use, for two reasons. Firstly, we do not know how much of the archaeological record we possess: do we, for instance, have all a 'site' (and does the term 'site' really mean anything?), or was rubbish dumped beyond the confines of what we regard as the site? Or was it dumped on a midden and used to manure the fields? Secondly, even if we had a complete record (and could tell that we had) we would still not be able to relate our 'death' assemblage to a 'life' assemblage of pots actually in use, since the relative quantities depend on the average life-spans of the pots. An assemblage of ten pots, for example, might have been used simultaneously with a life of (say) five years each, or successively with a life of only six months each. Such differences are, at present, unresolvable.

The second step is to say that the main interest lies, not in the overall size of each assemblage (though that may be important when it comes to questions of reliability of evidence, p. 175), but in their compositions, that is the proportions of the various types that make them up. This overcomes most of the first problem (although we should note that large assemblages are statistically more likely to include examples of rare types than are small ones, simply by virtue of their size (Cowgill 1970)), but makes no impression on the second. For example, suppose our hypothetical assemblage of ten pots consists of nine drinking vessels and one storage jar. It may be that the average life of the former is, say, six months, while that of the latter is five years. If so, there would be roughly equal numbers of each in use in the life assemblage to which our death assemblage refers. But since we cannot obtain direct information on the relative life-spans, we cannot make such an inference. Ethnographic studies may suggest relativities (e.g. David 1972; DeBoer and Lathrap 1979), but unless they can be demonstrated to be more than a reflection of a particular society, we are still in the realms of educated guesswork when it comes to archaeological inference.

The third step is to give up this search, and to concentrate on comparing the compositions of different assemblages. The assumption needed for such comparisons to yield useful information about life assemblages is that the relativities between life-spans of different types remain constant between different but comparable assemblages. In concrete terms, if in one situation a storage jar lasts for ten times as long as a drinking vessel, then in another comparable situation this ratio should be preserved, although the life-spans may differ. It is not necessary to know, or even estimate, the actual life-spans. If even this minimal assumption cannot be made, then any difference between life assemblages will be confounded with changing relativities in life-spans, and while we would be able to observe differences, we would not know to which source to attribute them. In which case, there would be little point in studying pottery quantitatively at all, and much established methodology (for example seriation, spatial analysis) would be without foundation. To avoid despair, we accept this minimal assumption and proceed with courage, looking first at the theoretical ideal and then at what may be practical in particular circumstances.

The sampling basis

We are now in a position to treat our assemblages as samples from some parent populations, about which we wish to make inferences. The traditional statistical approach would be to talk about sampling fractions (the proportion of the population that is present in the sample) or, looked at another way, the probability that any particular member of a population is selected for a sample. This we cannot do, because we have no idea of the original size of the population. Further, it would not be an adequate description of the sampling process, because it does not take into account the fact that the pots are generally found broken and incomplete. To take account of this, we introduce the idea of the *completeness* of a pot in an assemblage (Orton 1985a; the term *completeness index* is also used, see Schiffer 1987, 282) – this is just the proportion of the original pot actually present in an assemblage (we shall look later at how we might measure it). For example, a particular pot might be 50 per cent complete in one assemblage and at the same time 10 per cent complete in another; if the assemblages are combined, the pot becomes 60 per cent complete in the new assemblage. We can now describe the sampling process in terms of the pattern of the distribution of the completeness; for example by saying that 10 per cent of the pots are between 10 per cent and 20 per cent complete, 5 per cent are between 20 per cent and 30 per cent complete, and so on. What we cannot do is to say how many are 0 per cent complete, that is do not appear in the assemblage at all. I spent some years trying to establish the shape of the pattern by computer simulation of the breakage, disposal and retrieval of pots (Orton 1982a), only to find much later that I did not need to know it. At about the same time, it was suggested that the pattern should follow what is known as a log-normal distribution (Fieller, *personal communication*) and recent measurements support this view.

The question then arises, do all types in an assemblage have the same distribution of completeness? The answer is, not necessarily. Completeness depends on the history of a pot from the time it is broken or discarded to the time its fragments are recovered. During this time, it undergoes a series of one or more 'events', at each of which it may become more broken and/or less complete. Such events might include sweeping-up off a floor, throwing into a rubbish pit, the digging of another pit through that one, and so on. We can expect types that have been through the same series of events to have the same pattern of completeness, but those that have been through more to have a different distribution, with a smaller average completeness. Such types are archaeologically called *residual*. We call an assemblage *archaeologically homogeneous* if all the types in it have the same post-depositional history. We shall meet *statistically homogeneous* assemblages later when we look at the problems of measuring completeness. Homogeneous assemblages are the most useful and the easiest to use statistically; inhomogeneous assemblages usually contain homogeneous fractions which can be examined separately.

Uses of comparisons of assemblages

Before we proceed to assess the various measure of the amount of pottery it is worth summarising the uses to which the compositions of two or more assemblages can be put, although these are dealt with separately in individual chapters. The first and most common is seriation (pp. 189–194): the attempt to order assemblages so that the proportion of each type follows a regular pattern of zero-increase-steady level-decrease-zero (or some part of this pattern, if for example a type is already in use by the date represented by the earliest assemblage). If this can be done, it is usually assumed that the order found is chronological, bearing in mind that there are other rarer possibilities. The second use is between-site spatial analysis (pp. 199–206) in which we examine the proportions of a chosen type at sites around its known or supposed centre of production in order to throw light on the possible means of trade or distribution. Finally, we have within-site analysis (pp. 207–216) (using 'site' in the broad sense to mean areas up to, say, the size of a town), where we look for variations in the proportions of different types which may indicate areas of different function or status. All these needs require us to be able to infer reliably from assemblages to populations.

Assessment of measures

We are at last ready to assess the value of the four measures commonly employed – sherd count, weight (or its close relatives, surface area and displacement volume), number of vessels represented and vessel-equivalents (p. 21). The argument that follows was originally presented in mathematical form (Orton 1975); here I shall try to make it seem plausible in natural language. We shall look at archaeologically homogeneous assemblages.

First, we consider the sherd count. In any one assemblage, the proportion by number of sherds of a type reflects two things: (i) the proportion of that type in the population; and (ii) the average number of sherds into which pots of that type have broken (known as their *brokenness*) in comparison with the brokenness of other types. In general, brokenness varies from one type to another, and also with size in the same type, so that those with a high brokenness will be over-represented in comparison to those with low brokenness. Statistically, we say that the sherd counts are *biased* as measures of the proportions of types. But worse is to come. If we take two assemblages with different overall levels of brokenness, the relative brokenness of two types is likely to vary from one to the other. For example, if one type breaks up much more easily than another, then the more that examples of the types are broken, the higher will be the ratio of sherds of the former type to sherds of the latter. This means that the bias in the sherd count varies from one assemblage to another (unless they happen to have the same overall level of brokenness). Thus if we compare two assemblages, and find a higher proportion of sherds of a certain type in the first assemblage, that does not mean that there were more pots of that type in the corresponding population: it may just reflect differences in the brokenness between that and other types. So sherd count cannot be reliably used for the purposes outlined above on p. 168.

Next, we consider weight. The proportion by weight of a type in an assemblage reflects: (i) the proportion of that type in the population; and (ii) the relative weight of whole pots of that type compared to other types. So heavy types will be over-represented in comparison with light ones: weight too is biased as a measure of the proportion of types. But, in contrast to sherd count, this bias does not vary from one context to another: the relative weights of different types stay the same. So weight could be used to compare proportions between assemblages, even though it cannot be used to measure proportions in any one assemblage.

The situation for the number of vessels represented is more complicated. Both completeness and brokenness can affect a pot's chance of being represented in a particular assemblage. When completeness is low, pots with a high level of brokenness stand a greater chance of being represented than those of types with a low level because there are more sherds from which to sample. For example, if from a population of ten pots of each of two types, one type breaks into ten fragments each, and the other does not break at all, then a (say) 10% sample may consist of sherds from up to ten pots of the first type, but only one of the latter. The proportion in the assemblage is therefore biased, this bias depending on the completeness of the assemblage and the brokenness of each type. The more complete an assemblage, the less the bias is likely to be (see fig. 13.1). We therefore cannot reliably compare the

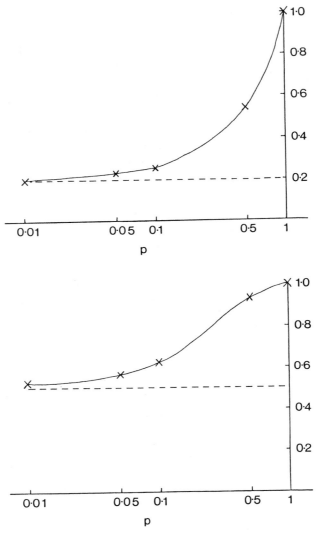

Fig. 13.1. Variation in bias for 'vessels represented' as the completeness varies, for two ratios of brokenness: (upper) 1:5 and (lower) 1:2. The horizontal axis measures completeness and the vertical axis measures bias; a value of 1 indicates freedom from bias

proportions in two assemblages unless they happen to have the same completeness and overall level of brokenness.

This shows, too, that the brokenness of types in an assemblage can affect the pattern of completeness, which only attains its theoretically ideal form when the pottery is very broken. When it is less broken, the distribution is more 'lumpy' (for example, if there are on average only two fragments per pot then completeness will be concentrated at or around 0%, 50% and 100%). In particular, the chance of zero completeness (that is that a pot is not represented) increases.

By contrast, the proportion measured by vessel-equivalent is not affected by either completeness or brokenness. Whatever the level of brokenness of a type, the amount present is governed only by the original amount and the completeness of an assemblage – whether it be 10% of ten whole pots making one whole pot, or 10% of ten pots, each of which had broken into ten equal sherds, making 10% of 100 = 10 sherds, or one vessel-equivalent (this is just for illustration, in practice there are better ways of doing this, see below). Differences in completeness between assemblages affect all types equally, so the proportions are not affected. Thus the vessel-equivalent is the only measure that is unbiased, both for measuring proportions within an assemblage and for comparing them between assemblages.

To sum up this long and complex argument, we have found that weight and vessel-equivalents can be used to reliably (that is without bias) compare proportions of types in different assemblages, while sherd count and numbers of vessels represented cannot. This is not quite the end of the story, because bias is a property of long-term averages, and we are concerned with individual values (that is the proportions of a particular type in two or more assemblages). As is well known, individual values are scattered about their average, their dispersal about it being measured by their standard deviation (sd). So two assemblages with proportions of (say) 40% and 50% of a certain type might, or might not, derive from two populations with the same proportion (for example 45%); the chance of this happening depends critically on the sds of the two proportions being compared. This makes it important to be able to measure sds as well as proportions, in order to be able to compare the proportions reliably. We note further that if two measures are both unbiased, the one that gives the smaller sds is to be preferred. We shall return to these points when we have considered some practical problems.

Practicalities

Theoretical considerations take us so far, but we must also look at practical issues. Chief among them is – how do we actually obtain the measure of a type in an assemblage? Sherd count and weight present no practical problem, provided that we have a typology that allows us to assign all sherds to a type. But if, for example, the definition of a type depends on a decoration that is present on only part of the pot, how could we tell whether we have part of an undecorated pot, or an undecorated part of a decorated pot? Such problems can introduce further, often highly variable, biases, and can affect all measures. The only sure answers are: (i) to base definitions of types entirely on fabric – this may be suitable for some questions but not for others; or (ii) to base the measure only on a part of the pot that can be confidently assigned to a type (very often the rim, see below).

The number of vessels represented can often be very difficult to count, as it requires sherds to be sorted into *sherd families* (all the sherds from the same pot, see p. 56: the term seems to be due to Smith 1983, 47). To avoid confusion we introduce here two further terms – the *nuclear sherd family* (all the sherds from the same pot in the same context) and the *extended sherd family* (all the sherds from the same pot in the same collection, for example, from a site). Depending on the type of pot and the skill of the worker, it can be very difficult to tell whether two sherds which do not join come from the same pot or not. Therefore in general (but not in all cases) it is not possible to simply count the number of vessels represented; it must be estimated. We have coined the term *evrep* (estimate of *v*essels *rep*resented) for this estimate. This problem has long been recognised and various estimates have been suggested – for example the 'minimum number of vessels' (that is when in doubt, assign unattached sherds to the same pot if at all feasible), the 'maximum number of vessels' (that is when in doubt, assign sherds to different pots), and the average of the two. These probably say more about the psychology of the worker ('lumpers', 'splitters' and 'fence-sitters', see p. 73) than about the pots. It has even been suggested that the vessel-equivalent could be used as an absolute minimum number of vessels represented. This has led to confusion, because while it undoubtedly is a lower limit to the evrep, it is often well below any reasonable minimum number, and makes the vessel-equivalent (one of the better measures) look like a poor attempt at one of the worst.

Finally, we come to the question of how to obtain vessel-equivalents. This can be done only if we have a way of saying how much of a pot each sherd (or nuclear sherd family, if they can be sorted correctly) actually is. Usually this cannot be done exactly, but there are exceptions, for example if the type is so standardised that we know within reasonable limits the weight of each type of pot represented. We can then simply divide the total weight of the sherds of the type by the known weight of a pot of that type to obtain the vessel-equivalent (the *standardised weight* approach). When feasible, which admittedly is not often, this should give very good results. But as a rule we can only estimate, and obtain an estimated vessel-equivalent (abbreviated to *eve*). To do this, we have to find a part of the pot that can be measured as a fraction of some whole. The most obvious is the rim; by using a rim chart (fig. 13.2) one can, unless a rim sherd is very small, abraded or not truly circular (as may happen with hand-made pottery) measure it as a percentage of a complete rim. One can then let the rim stand representative of the whole pot, and use this figure as the eve. Sometimes it is more appropriate to use another part of the pot – for example, if a type is defined as having one handle, one could count handles. Even this is not as easy as it sounds, since handles too can be broken, leading to handle-equivalents. As a rule of thumb, it's best to use a part of the pot whose proportion can be measured on as fine a scale as

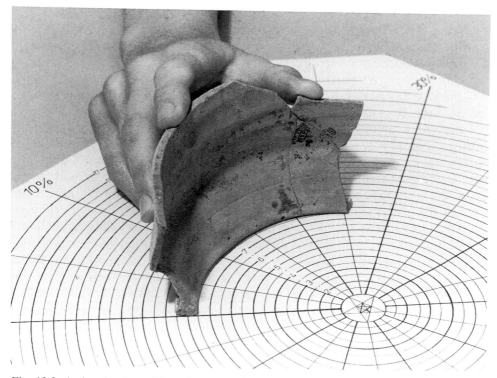

Fig. 13.2. A rim chart, used here for measuring a rim sherd as a percentage of a whole rim. (Photo: Trevor Hurst)

possible. Another important consideration is to match the part of the pot measured to the definition of the type. For example, if a type is defined in terms of its rim form, it would make sense to use the rim to obtain the eve (or *rim-eve*, as we could call it).

Other practical issues which must be taken into account are the speed and accuracy of using the measure, and the need to train workers. But this does not mean that inferior measures should be used simply because they are easier to carry out and require less training (for example the sherd count). The additional training needed, beyond the ability to recognise types, is relatively small.

Are the assemblages really different?

As we saw on p. 171, it would be extremely useful to be able to attach sds to our estimates of proportions, to help us assess the significance of differences observed between assemblages. Until recently, this was impossible. The project *Statistical Analysis of Ceramic Assemblages*, carried out in 1988–90 and 1991–92 by two of us and funded by the Science Based Archaeology

Committee of the Science and Engineering Research Council and the British Academy, solved this and other problems. We discovered that it was only possible to calculate sds if eves were used as the measure. We also discovered a piece of mathematics (christened the *pseudo-count transformation* or pct) that can be used to turn the eves of the types in an assemblage into numbers which have the same statistical properties as counts of objects, although they are not actually counts of anything and are not usually even whole numbers (Orton and Tyers 1990; 1991). We call the numbers that emerge from this transformation *pies* (pottery information equivalents) because one pie of pottery contains as much information (in the statistical sense) as one whole pot, and the technique *pie-slice*, because the total pie of an assemblage is being sliced up between the different types. This might seem to be a creature fit only for a mathematical zoo, except that it allows us to use all sorts of statistical techniques that were designed for use on counts, on compositions of assemblages. The main ones are log-linear-analysis and its cousin quasi-log-linear-analysis (Bishop et al. 1975, 177–228), which enable us to assess the differences between several assemblages in terms of two aspects of type, for example fabric and form, and correspondence analysis (Greenacre 1984) which enables us to display the data visually. Used together, they form a powerful tool, and have the added advantage that they enable pottery to be integrated into broader assemblages of classes of finds that can be counted.

It must not be thought that pie-slice solves all our problems, although it is a very useful piece of theory. Once one has performed the pct, practical problems crowd in. The most important is what we have called the problem of 'chunky types'. These are types for which the element selected for measuring eves (for example the rim) is less breakable than the same element of other types, for example flagons and amphoras. The effect is to distort the apparent pattern of the completeness of that type, since the pattern of (say) rims is in such cases much more 'lumpy' than that of the pot itself. In extreme cases the pattern polarises to one of 0% and 100%. This affects not only the type concerned but the whole assemblage, since it is necessary to pool the information from all types to obtain the best estimates of the statistics on which the pct is based. Fortunately, once the problem is recognised, the troublesome chunky types can be isolated and dealt with satisfactorily.

Another problem is that the pct frequently produces large tables of data, many of the entries of which are either zero or very small (near-zeros). Paradoxically, while the zeros can be accommodated by using *quasi*-log-linear-analysis in place of the more common log-linear-analysis, the near-zeros cause real trouble (in technical terms, the tables are *sparse*). The answer is to reduce the size of the tables by merging rows and columns (types and/or assemblages) until the entries are of a reasonable size. There is a side-effect here: merging two assemblages may bring together two nuclear sherd families from the same extended family (that is, the same pot). In strict theory, the two eve values should be combined (for example 50% + 10% = 60%, see p. 167). But we do not necessarily know that the 50% and the 10% are from the same pot, unless we re-examine the new joint assemblage (or look for sherd links between the two original assemblages, which amounts to the same thing). This is too much work simply to cope with a statistical nicety; fortunately unless the extent of sherd linking is severe (say more than 40% of the pots in the assemblages have sherd-links) we can safely overlook the problem. If sherd-links have been found for other reasons (see p. 209) that information can be used here.

How big should an assemblage be?
This is the question most commonly asked at conferences and seminars. Administrators would like to be told that there is a 'minimum viable sample size' below which it is not worth quantifying any assemblage, since they could then decline to fund work below this threshold. For the same reason, archaeologists approach this fearfully, although some have a nagging doubt about the equal value of all their quantification. No simple answer can be given, for two reasons:

(i) a lower limit would be in terms of pies, since we seek a lower limit on the information contained in an assemblage. But we cannot measure pies directly, only from eves through the pct. So to know whether we are below or above a threshold, we must quantify the pottery first, by which time it is too late to save time by not doing so;

(ii) we are working in a framework where we expect to merge assemblages into different groupings for different purposes, for example chronological groupings (phases) or functional groupings (possibly features). So even an assemblage that is 'too small' by itself may form a useful part of some larger grouping.

So, for the time being, we do not recommend that assemblages should be rejected for quantification solely on grounds of size. However, it sometimes happens that an assemblage is so very small that it cannot differ significantly from any other assemblage. Such assemblages confuse the program which merges assemblages, and are automatically omitted (or *pruned*, as we call it). But this can only be done on statistical criteria, not archaeological judgement.

Case studies
In this section we shall look at case studies undertaken as part of the Pie-slice project, concentrating on chronological and functional or social patterns. They have been reported in more detail elsewhere (Orton and Tyers 1991).

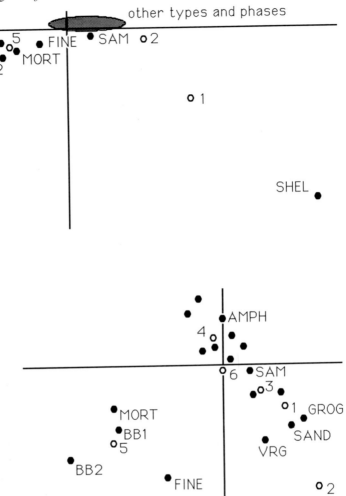

Fig. 13.3. Correspondence analysis plot of first- to second-century AD pottery assemblages from Lime Street, City of London (upper) as originally plotted, (lower) with the early fabric SHEL omitted. Key: open circles = contexts or phases; solid circles = fabrics

Chronological patterns
A chronological sequence should be represented by a 'horse-shoe' shaped curve (approximately a parabola) on a correspondence analysis (ca) plot (p. 192). Two such patterns are shown below, from Lime Street, London (AD70–160), and Silchester basilica (*c.* 15BC–AD60).

Lime Street
Comparison of fabrics with phases gave an apparently horse-shoe-shaped curve (fig. 13.3 (upper)), with fabric SHEL (shell-tempered ware) early in the sequence and BB1, BB2 (black-burnished wares) and MORT (mortaria) late

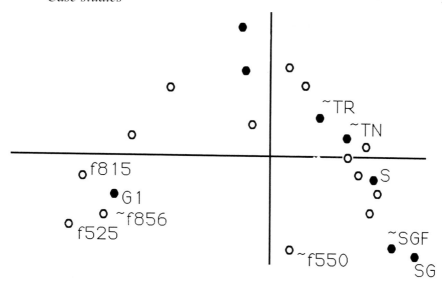

Fig. 13.4. Correspondence analysis plot of first-century BC to first-century AD pottery assemblages from the Silchester basilica. For key see fig. 13.3, p. 176

in the sequence indicated by the ordering of the phases, but with most of the points bunched in the apex of the curve. The removal of SHEL opens up the curve (fig. 13.3 (lower)). Phase 1 (which has become very small by the removal of SHEL) and phase 6 (always very small and possibly residual) are out of sequence, but the major phases (2, 3, 4 and 5) are in the 'right' order.

Silchester basilica

In the period to which the data relate, both forms and fabrics changed rapidly, with many introductions of new types. In the ca plot (fig. 13.4) the features and fabrics are arranged in the expected horse-shoe-shaped pattern. The 'early' end of the curve is the fabric G1 ('Belgic' grog-tempered wares) and feature groups ~f856, f525 and f815. The 'later' part of the curve includes the sequence ~TR, ~TN, and SG which is the expected order of introduction of the fine ware fabrics *terra rubra, terra nigra* and South Gaulish samian.

Perhaps more interesting than the expected horse-shoe are the deviations from it:

(i) at Lime Street, 'rag-bag' categories (for example FINE = fine imported wares) occupy locations well off the curve, towards the centre, because they are an amalgam of types of different dates, and therefore cannot be located in a strict chronological sequence;

(ii) at Silchester, the context-group ~f550, with both late material and a slightly above-average amount of the early fabric G1, lies off the inside of the curve. This location seems to be characteristic of contexts with a high proportion of residual material.

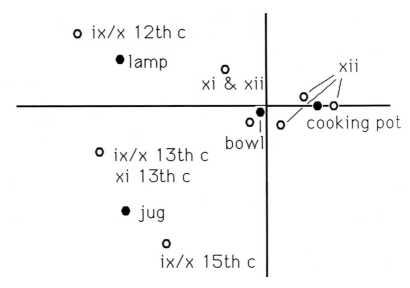

Fig. 13.5. Correspondence analysis plot of twelfth- to fifteenth-century AD pottery assemblages from medieval houses ix to xii at Brook Street, Winchester. Key: open circles = final phases; solid circles = forms

Functional/social patterns

So far the medieval tenements at Brook Street, Winchester (Biddle 1972; see Orton and Tyers 1991 for a more detailed account of the following analysis), have given the clearest indications of this sort of patterning. A preliminary analysis of forms by 'final phases' (phases within buildings) showed a three-way opposition between cooking-pots, jugs and lamps, with bowls (including bowl/ dish and bowl/jar) occupying a central, roughly neutral, position (fig. 13.5). The final phases that can be linked with these forms through the ca show an association of lamps with industrial activity (dyeing, metal-working), jugs with a stone-built house and cooking-pots with less substantial houses. The interpretation of these results is at an early stage and must be seen as provisional.

Spin-offs

As we noted briefly in the historical survey (p. 22), two measures together can give us information that neither could separately. We have already met the two most useful combinations – brokenness and completeness – in our theoretical discussion, when we were anxious to eliminate the effect of site formation processes. We can now define them formally at the level of an assemblage as:

brokenness = sherd count/vessel-equivalent,

completeness = vessel-equivalent/number of vessels represented,

noting that, for reasons discussed above, they will usually have to be estimated rather than measured. At the level of an individual pot, brokenness is an estimate of the total number of sherds into which it has broken, and completeness is the proportion of it present. They supplement the well-known average sherd size, that is weight/sherd count.

These statistics can all be used in the study of site formation processes. Brokenness and completeness both start from a value of one (the complete pot), but the former increases as a pot is subject to successive processes, while the latter decreases (if the context to which the assemblage belongs is properly defined). An important difference between them is that brokenness depends on both the type and the context, since some types are inherently more breakable than others, while completeness depends only on the context (in theory; problems of 'chunkiness' – see above – may affect this). This makes completeness potentially more useful as a pure indicator of site formation processes, but the snag is that it is more difficult to estimate as it includes in its formula the problematic number of vessels represented.

Comparing the statistics on different parts of a form can give us information on recovery bias. It is possible to show whether particular parts of a form are over- or under-represented if one knows the quantity to be found in a single vessel. All vessels have 360° of rim and 360° of base, but they may have one, two or more handles and three or more feet. If we know the number of handles or feet of a particular form, we can calculate different eve values based on different parts of the vessels, for example rim-eves, base-eves, handle-eves, and so on. If they do not agree, to within limits expected from sampling theory, this is evidence for differential retrieval of different parts of the vessels, that is recovery bias. As examples, Roman colour-coated beakers often have much higher values of base-eves than rim-eves, while for some medieval jugs handle-eves are greater than base-eves or rim-eves. Such evidence may be important if, for example, we are trying to estimate proportions of vessels with and without handles. It also has implications for the choice of the part(s) of a vessel used to measure eves.

A case study

We look at some pottery from the eastern terminal of the Devil's Ditch, a large linear earthwork in the Chichester area of Sussex, excavated by the Sussex Archaeological Field Unit in 1982 (Bedwin and Orton 1984). The fill of the terminal yielded about 1000 sherds (10 eves) of early Roman pottery from ten distinct contexts, some of which were separated by layers of sterile fill. Three hypotheses on the nature of the fill were considered:

  (i)   successive phases of silting and/or deliberate filling;
  (ii) phases of silting and/or deliberate filling, separated by phases of recutting or cleaning;
  (iii) simultaneous filling, presumed deliberate.

Table 13.1. *Values of brokenness for pottery assemblages from the Devil's Ditch*

Context	Brokenness = sherds/eves	
	All pottery	Roman coarse wares
155	67	170
152	101[a]	94[a]
129	59[a]	78[a]
191	92[a]	74
140	224	260
132	164	141
192	167	167
131	131[a]	149[a]
130	283	620
All	97	111
Fabrics		
A		103[a]
B		210
C		98[a]
D		41
E		168[a]
M		318
All		111[a]
Samian	32	
Other	113[a]	

Note: [a] More reliable figures

Conventional pottery analysis showed that most of the pottery could be sorted reliably into sherd families across the whole fill, and that there were many sherd-links between the different contexts, apparently ruling out hypothesis (i). It also showed that the final context, context $30 + 7$, was later than the rest. A full statistical analysis has been published (Orton 1985a); here we shall just look at the brokenness and completeness of the pottery from the nine other contexts (tables 13.1, 13.2). The former shows that the brokenness of the four lower contexts (contexts 155 to 191) is less than that of the five upper ones (contexts 140 to 130). Unfortunately these differences are confounded with differences between the fabrics; some fabrics are more broken than others (mainly because they are present as larger pots) and are also more common in some contexts than others. The table of completeness gives a more reliable impression, since variations in completeness between fabrics are smaller than variations in brokenness. In theory, there should be no variation in completeness, but in practice the more visible fabrics (for example samian, which is bright red) tended to be slightly more complete than others. Even

Table 13.2. *Values of completeness for pottery assemblages from the Devil's Ditch. (See table 13.1 for indication of the more reliable figures.)*

	Completeness = eves/vessel	
Context	All pottery	Roman coarse wares
155	0.10	0.03
152	0.09	0.09
129	0.12	0.11
191	0.12	0.13
140	0.05	0.05
132	0.04	0.04
192	0.06	0.06
131	0.05	0.05
130	0.04	0.02
All	0.10	0.09

allowing for this, we can see a distinct break in the sequence between contexts 191 and 140; the lower contexts lie in the range 9–12% and average about 11%, while the upper contexts lie in the range 4–6% and average about 5%, that is about half that of the lower group. The two groups were interpreted as a primary and a secondary fill, separated by a phase of recutting, in which material from the upper part of the primary fill was removed to form part of a bank, and subsequently returned as part of a secondary fill. Thus these statistics, especially completeness, added significantly to the interpretation of this feature. It must be noted, however, that this would not have been possible if the material had not been suitable for sorting into sherd families.

Discussion

It is clear that the statistical analyses are not a panacea, and make careful archaeological preparation and interpretation more, rather than less, necessary. The definitions of fabrics, forms and assemblages, and their grouping into larger units for specific purposes have to be carefully thought out. But provided this is done, there does seem to be scope for the detection of patterns which might otherwise have gone unnoticed.

14

CHRONOLOGY

Introduction

Pottery and dating are inextricably linked in archaeology, or at least in the minds of those involved in it. This link grew up in the typological phase, when sherds were treated as type-fossils of particular periods or phases (p. 9). It has sometimes appeared to have been submerged in the flood of interests that marked the contextual phase (p. 13), but has remained at or just below the surface of archaeological thought. The advent and/or wider application of techniques such as ^{14}C dating and dendrochronology has not significantly reduced the need for ceramic-based chronologies. A majority of excavation reports (83% in a recent survey of Romano-British site reports, see Fulford and Huddleston 1991, 5) continue to employ, to some extent at least, dates derived from the study of ceramics.

The abundance of pottery and its multiplicity of form, fabric and decoration, as much as the vast literature on the material, conspire to make pottery, in many ways, the ideal medium for carrying chronological information. Dating evidence acquired at one site or context, perhaps an association between a pottery type and a historically-dated event such as a destruction horizon (for example the Boudiccan destruction level of AD 61, see Millett 1987), may be attached to the pot, or an element such as its form, decoration or fabric. Its appearance may subsequently be employed to date other contexts, where other pottery types may be dated by secondary association.

It may further be recognised that particular forms vary in a consistent and predictable fashion, perhaps allowing a particular vessel to be placed at a point in a developmental (and hence potentially chronological) sequence. Many examples of such typological sequences have been described. The variation in rim and body shape of Romano-British black-burnished jars provides a good indicator of date, and the dimensions of the latticed zone on the body and the angle of the burnished lattice itself also vary through time. An examination of these variations as illustrated by Gillam (1957, nos. 115–48) shows that 'acute' lattice dominates in the second century AD, 'square' lattice in the third and 'obtuse' lattice in the fourth (fig. 14.1). Over the same period the proportion of the height of such jars taken up by lattice decoration falls from about 50% to about 25%. The development of several forms (globular pots, pitchers, jugs and so on) has been traced through four

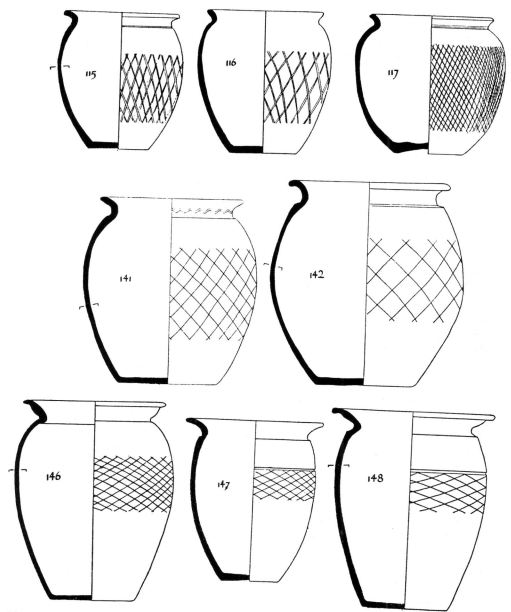

Fig. 14.1. Selected black-burnished ware jars showing the relationship between date and angle of lattice burnishing. Nos. 115–17 (acute lattice) are dated to within AD 120–160, nos. 141–2 (square lattice) to within AD 160–280 and nos. 146–8 (obtuse lattice) to within AD 280–370. (Gillam 1957, nos. 115–17, 141–2, 146–8)

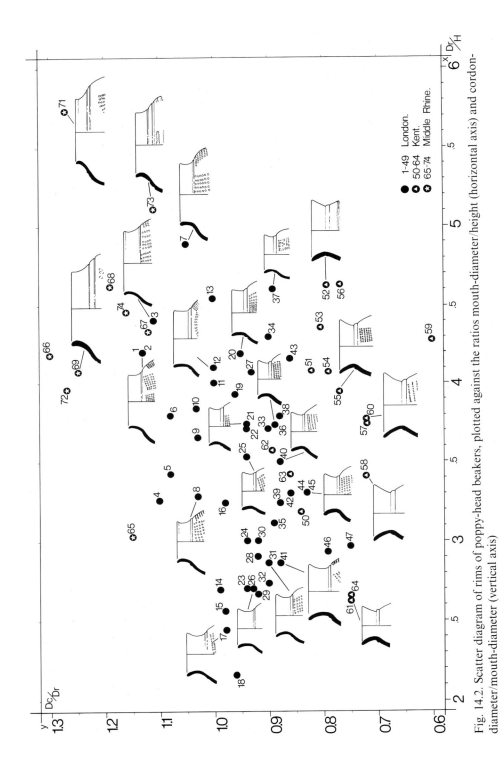

Fig. 14.2. Scatter diagram of rims of poppy-head beakers, plotted against the ratios mouth-diameter/height (horizontal axis) and cordon-diameter/mouth-diameter (vertical axis)

periods, from *c*. 1150 to *c*. 1300 AD, at the production site of Siegburg (Beckmann 1974). The variation in the details of the shape of some forms, expressed as ratios of measurements, may also contain a chronological element. As an example we can look at the class of Romano-British beakers known as poppy-head beakers (Tyers 1978). The shape of the rim can be described by three measurements – the diameter of the mouth, the diameter at the cordon (the bottom edge of the rim) and the height from mouth to cordon. Plotting the ratios between these measures (fig. 14.2) illustrates a trend from those where the diameter at the cordon is greater than the diameter at the mouth (thus the rim slopes in towards the mouth), to examples with a mouth-diameter greater than the cordon diameter (the rim flares out towards the mouth). The earlier group, from the middle Rhine, date to *c*. 70 AD, and the latest, from Kent, date to *c*. 200–250 AD. Thus a complex web may be built up describing the development of pottery types or styles in an area.

The process of matching features of a pot, often in an attempt to date it but more often in an attempt to understand its place in an assemblage, is usually referred to as 'searching for parallels'. The parallel may be for the form, fabric or decoration, or some combination of them. Searching for parallels, particularly with the purpose of accumulating dating information, has attracted widespread criticism. Certainly at some periods the indiscriminate citing of parallels, devoid of any understanding of the local context of the cited pot, can be seen to have been erroneous. More satisfactory results are obtained when the parallel refers not to some minor feature of the decoration or form, but refers to a pot in the same fabric – we are then dealing, at least potentially, with the products of the same workshop.

Pinning down dates

Before we look at how pots can actually be dated, we need to clarify a point of definition. At least two definitions of the date of an artefact are in use:

(i) the date at which it was made;
(ii) the range of dates within which artefacts of its type were commonly in use.

Despite the radical difference between these definitions, the outcomes may look very similar, especially as the former is usually quoted as a range to allow for the inevitable uncertainty about such a date. Confusion can and has arisen because it is often not clear which definition is in use in a particular report; the protagonists may not even realise that there is an alternative to their 'obvious' definition. Although we prefer the former, we accept both as valid definitions. The important thing is to make it clear which one is being used.

A point which is so obvious that it may seem not worth making is that the

Fig. 14.3. Example of a vessel inscribed with its date of manufacture: a cup from Colonial Williamsburg dated 1660, commemorating the restoration of Charles II. (Photo: Colonial Williamsburg Foundation)

date of a pot or a sherd is not necessarily the date of the archaeological context in which it was found. Apart from the problem of the life-expectancy of different vessels types (p. 207), whose effect will depend on the definition of date (see above), there is the question of the post-depositional history of the pottery. Between its original breakage and/or discard and its final resting place, it may have undergone several events (such as sweeping-up, removal to a rubbish pit, disturbance of that pit, and so on) spread over several years or even centuries. Recognition of this problem has led some archaeologists to the assumption that every assemblage has somewhere in it the *key* (or *latest*) *sherd*, which will date it. They then see the job of the pottery specialist as smelling out this sherd, like a pig hunting truffles, and dating it. Apart from the flattering but erroneous belief that any sherd could, if needed, be dated to a useful level of accuracy, and the fact that intrusive sherds (ones that are later than the context in which they are found) are not unknown, this approach ignores the information in the assemblage as a whole and should be resisted.

Having cleared the air, we can now look at the sorts of evidence that can actually date pots. In the historical period, a small number of pots can be considered as dated documents. Pots produced to commemorate particular events, such as coronations or weddings, often bear dates (Draper 1975; Hume 1977, 29–32; see fig. 14.3). Individual ceramic objects such as test-pieces may bear dates indicating their date of manufacture, perhaps with the name of potter and factory. A few pots bear such 'historical' dates almost by accident. There is an example of a flask in African Slip Ware (a fine ware made in Tunisia throughout the Roman period) which incorporates the impression of a coin amongst its decoration (Hayes 1972, 195, form 171.48, 199). The coin, which was issued between AD 238 and 244, thus provides a *terminus post quem* for the vessel and the decorative style (see also Hayes 1972, 313 for the impression of a coin on a lamp).

Vessels produced for, and perhaps by, governmental or other administrative institutions often bear dates. Painted inscriptions or stamps referring to the reigning monarch are known at some periods, perhaps combined with the year of reign. Sometimes a portrait can be related to a monarch on art-historical grounds, for example the supposed head of Edward II (1307–27) on a Kingston ware jug in the Museum of London (London Museum 1965, 223–4), but this sort of attribution is less secure. Such pots may then be placed at the appropriate place in a chronology built up from the study of king-lists, inscriptions and other documentary sources. Such evidence may not always be taken at face value. For example, in 1700 a law was passed in England that mugs used in the retailing of ale and beer had to bear a stamp containing the initials of the then ruling monarch, William III (WR). When he died in 1702 and was succeeded by Queen Anne, her initials (AR) were used by some potters for a short while until it was realised that the law specified, not the initials of the ruling monarch, but those of the monarch at the time the law was passed. The WR mark continued in use until 1876 when the law was repealed, by which time William III had been dead for 174 years (Bimson 1970). The WR mark is therefore of very limited use for dating, but the much rarer AR mark can be pinned down to a few years.

Some Roman amphoras bear painted inscriptions recording the contents, the name of estates and shippers and the date of bottling – usually in the form of a consular date. Although it is the contents that are being dated here rather than the container, in practice the date can usually be applied to the latter. From such sources it is not only possible to date the individual vessels but the overall date of production of a type or class can be ascertained (Sealey 1985).

At periods rich in documentary sources it may be possible to ascertain the dates of production of particular potters or workshops, using a combination of rent-books, receipts, wills and other legal documents (Le Patourel 1968). Pots which can be assigned to this source, whether to a particular potter or factory through a maker's mark or through features of form, style or fabric, may then be assigned to the known period of production. Linking kiln products with documentary evidence can have its dangers. For example, there is documentary evidence for the production of pottery in the medieval town of Kingston, Surrey [England] in the years 1264–6, in the form of royal orders or payments to the bailiffs of Kingston for batches of up to 1000 pitchers (Guiseppi 1937). The products of medieval pottery kilns have also been excavated in Kingston, notably at the Eden Walk (Hinton 1980) and Knapp Drewett (Richardson 1983, 289) sites. The temptation is to link the two pieces of evidence and date the excavated pottery to, say, the thirteenth century, or even to the middle or late thirteenth century. But the most detailed dating of Kingston wares comes not from Kingston itself, but from London, its main market. Here a series of deposits dumped behind waterfronts dated by dendrochronology show that Kingston wares were in use in London between *c*. 1250 and *c*. 1400 (Pearce and Vince 1988, 15–17), and that the known kiln products are typologically late in the sequence, say *c*. 1350–1400, about 100 years later than the documentary references.

Scientific dating techniques have been briefly discussed in our historical survey (p. 19); the one most likely to be of use is luminescence (either TL or OSL). However, it should be remembered that such techniques are expensive, require preliminary measurements on site and have error limits of between ±5% and ±10% of the age (Aitken 1990, 153). Careful formulation of questions and selection of samples are needed if such expensive resources are to be used wisely. Routine use cannot be envisaged.

It may be possible to divide the production period into a series of phases (a three-way division into early, middle and late is particularly popular). Similarly, documentary sources may be employed to date activity in particular structures, regions and towns, and by implication the period of use of any pottery recovered from them. Short-lived military sites may be especially useful in this respect (Fulford and Huddleston 1991, 43). Provided that reasonable caution is used with the interpretation and application of the documentary sources, a reliable framework for a ceramic chronology may be drawn up.

Bringing the evidence together

Associations between pottery and other datable artefacts provide another potential source of evidence. Coins are probably the most common class of such objects and (when they can be dated reliably) certainly provide a *terminus post quem* for the deposition of an assemblage and hence the final deposition of any pottery it contains. However, the dating of archaeological levels from coins is not without difficulty and such data must be used with great caution.

The key point is the degree of association between a pot and its external dating evidence. An example of tight association is that of a coin hoard buried in a pot. Unless an heirloom has been used, or the hoard represents savings accumulated over a long period in the same pot, there is likely to be a very close agreement between the date of the pot and that of the hoard, and such evidence can be very valuable (Bird and Turner 1974). On the other hand, the casual association of a pot, or perhaps just a sherd, with a coin in a soil horizon is not likely to give useful information. Either or both may be residual (p. 168), perhaps by hundreds of years.

Between these two extremes comes the association of pottery with dated structures. Sometimes a close association can be argued. For example, in the case of the London waterfronts (p. 168), the stability of the dated timber structures relied on the infilling dumps behind them, which must therefore be contemporary. The question that remains is – how long was the pottery deposited as rubbish (for example in a midden) before that dump was used to infill the waterfront? Here comparison of the wares present, together with the degree of breakage (p. 178) and of abrasion (p. 214) can help us. We can contrast this situation with one in which the filling may have occurred slowly over a long period. For example, a documented date for the digging of a castle moat may tell us little (except a *terminus post quem*) of the date of the pottery found in that moat.

Problems with ceramic dates certainly arise when the independently-dated elements are sparse and greater reliance is placed on chains of associations where little or no dating evidence is available. The danger of circular argument becomes acute, perhaps particularly when fine chronological divisions are being attempted. In addition, assumptions (often unstated) are usually made about factors such as the residuality of the material, which should more properly appear on a list of questions to be answered.

Seriation

A more formal approach is to try to order assemblages of types of pottery on the basis of the co-occurrences either of types in assemblages or of characteristics on types, the former being the more common. Assemblages which are similar to each other, in terms of the types present in them, may be close chronologically; conversely, types which commonly co-occur should have broadly similar date-ranges. The occurrence of types in assemblages can be described either in terms of their presence/absence, as used originally by Petrie (p. 11), or in terms of proportions using an appropriate measure (p. 168).

The principal technique for simultaneously ordering assemblages and pottery types is *seriation*. We have already seen how such techniques developed out of Petrie's work at the end of the nineteenth century. Whether performed manually or by a computer program, the aim is to recreate as far as possible for each type the ideal pattern described above, while using as much or as little additional information (for example stratigraphy) as may be available. The basic idea is contained in Petrie's Concentration Principle: '*if* the typology is 'chronologically significant', and when the graves have been correctly ordered, then the 'sequence-date'-*ranges* for the individual types will be found to have been individually *or in some communal way* minimised.' (Kendall 1971, 217), although it should be remembered that Petrie's work was on presence/absence, not quantified, data.

The underlying assumption is that the use of any type of pottery follows a regular pattern of not in use→increasing use→steady use→decreasing use→no longer in use. The exact shape of this pattern is not critical, provided there are no catastrophic collapses in usage. It does not matter if a type is already in use at the beginning of a period to be studied, or is still in use at the end, although a type which meets both of these conditions will be of little use in establishing a chronology and is probably best omitted from such an analysis (fig. 14.4). It is not necessary to assume that the chronological distribution of a type follows a normal distribution, although there may be superficial similarities.

All techniques rely, explicitly or implicitly, on the setting up of a *data matrix* in which (usually) the columns represent types and the rows represent assemblages. This arrangement is purely conventional, and may reflect the need for some computer programs to work with more rows than columns (there are usually more assemblages than types). The rows and columns are then re-ordered (or *sorted*) until the required pattern emerges (if indeed it was inherent in the data in the first place, which it may not have been). This is a trial-and-error approach, and there is no reason why it should have a single 'best' order, or if there is, that we should necessarily find it. The option of trying every permutation of rows and columns to see if it is the 'best' is not open to us – the number of possible permutations is so vast that we do not have 'world enough and time' (Marvell, *To his coy mistress*).

Manual techniques, such as the 'battleship curve' method (Ford 1962) and the close-proximity method (Renfrew and Sterud 1969) are best used when either the amount of data is small or when there are many external constraints (such as stratigraphy). The term 'battleship curve' has caused some puzzlement as to its origins. We have been told it is due to: (i) the similarity of the

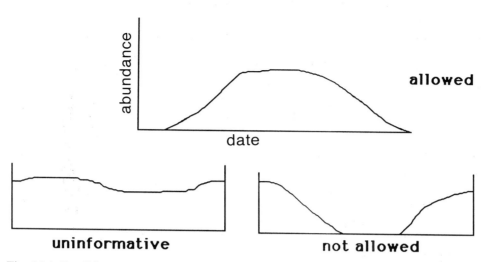

Fig. 14.4. Possible patterns for the production of pottery types: (upper) suitable for use in seriation; (lower left) usable but uninformative; (lower right) not suitable for use in seriation

ideal pattern of the occurrences of a single type to the view of a battleship seen in plan; and (ii) to a supposed parallel between the drawing of the percentage charts by blacking-in squares on graph paper to the children's game of battleships, in which the warring fleets are represented in a similar way.

Computer techniques, several of which are now available (Fletcher and Lock 1991, 145–76) are essential when there are many data, but have difficulties in coping with external constraints. There is a need for a technique which can deal with large amounts of data and serious but not overwhelming constraints; Bayesian statistics may be the best way forward (Buck and Litton 1991, 96). Mainstream techniques rely on explicit manipulation of the data matrix (either an incidence matrix for presence/absence data or an abundance matrix for quantified data), either in its own right or in the form of a similarity matrix derived from it (fig. 14.5). These approaches are superficially very different but have been shown to be mathematically identical (Kendall 1971, 220).

The benefits of correspondence analysis as a technique for exploring and displaying data were promoted from the 1960s onwards (Benzécri 1973), but did not make much impact on the Anglo-Saxon world until the 1980s (Greenacre 1984), and are still relatively little-known in British/American archaeology as a whole. The chief benefit is that rows and columns can be displayed on the same plot, so that each can be interpreted in terms of the other. Versions that use presence/absence data (for example 'model C' in Ihm, 1981) have formed the basis for seriation programs for some time. The

		types							
		A	B	C	D	E	F	G	H
contexts	1	1	3	0	0	0	0	0	0
	2	0	2	1	1	0	0	0	0
	3	0	1	2	2	0	0	0	0
	4	0	0	3	1	1	0	0	0
	5	0	0	2	0	2	1	0	0
	6	0	0	1	0	3	2	0	0
	7	0	0	0	0	1	3	1	0
	8	0	0	0	0	0	3	2	1
	9	0	0	0	0	0	1	3	2

	1	2	3	4	5	6	7	8	9
1	100	50	0	0	0	0	0	0	0
2		100	67	45	22	20	0	0	0
3			100	60	40	26	0	0	0
4				100	40	36	20	0	0
5					100	73	40	18	18
6						100	55	33	17
7							100	73	36
8								100	67
9									100

Fig. 14.5. Abundance matrix (left), showing numbers of pots of various types (columns) present in various contexts, for example graves. The corresponding similarity matrix (right). The abundance matrix is manipulated to show the similarities between the contexts in terms of numbers of pots of different types present (100 = complete similarity, 0 = complete dissimilarity). Since the matrix is symmetric we show only the upper part

use of correspondence analysis for abundance data has been delayed by its need for data in the form of counts, although when pottery has been found complete, as in cemeteries, analysis has been possible (Bech 1988).

Sherd count and vessels represented cannot be used, because although they are apparently counts they do not meet requirements of independence and/or lack of bias (p. 171). This impasse has been overcome by our discovery of the 'Pie-slice' technique and its use of pseudo-counts (p. 174), which enable us to use ca on suitably-quantified data. Some experimental analyses have been carried out (see p. 176), and we already know that in ideal conditions a chronological order will appear as a parabolic curve (Hill 1974, 348; Madsen 1988, 24). We are beginning to learn about the likely behaviour of types and assemblages that do not fit such a pattern, for example 'rag-bag' types and assemblages with high levels of residual pottery (see below), but more work is needed to enable us to fully interpret deviations from the theoretical ideal.

The application of seriation techniques to pottery assemblages whose ordering is constrained, but not determined, by stratigraphy, is a major problem in urban archaeology, and has been much discussed, notably by Crummy and Terry (1979) and Carver (1985). All agree that the main problem is that of residual material (material that has become incorporated into contexts that are later than its original date of deposition, for example by digging through rubbish pits). Carver suggests that this can be overcome by: (i) classifying contexts as 'secondary' or 'primary', according to whether or not they include material which is not related to the formation or use of the context; and (ii) relying heavily on the primary contexts. He defines the 'fade point' of a type as the context in a primary sequence in which it first fails to appear, and all occurrences later than that are residual. This approach seems to

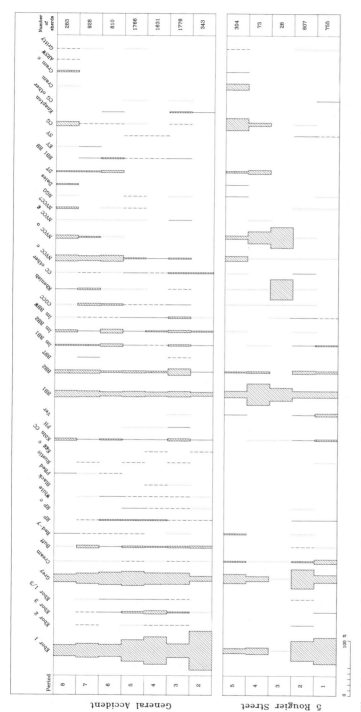

Fig. 14.6. Examples of seriation diagrams or seriographs. Values of 1% are represented by a solid line and of < 1% by a broken line. Presence (that is sherds of zero measure) is shown by a dotted line (from Perrin 1990)

be at risk of circular argument, unless one can be sure which contexts are primary, and it fails to tackle the problem of sample size and the functional variation between assemblages from primary contexts. Crummy and Terry (1979, 54–5) make some suggestions for what they call 'class 1' contexts, but say that they will be few on an urban site, while Millett and Graham (1986, 9) admit that they could not distinguish such contexts. We prefer an approach based on comparison of the parameters of different types in an assemblage, for example their brokenness and state of abrasion (p. 214).

Carver (1985, 360) goes on to discuss how the shape of the seriation diagram (or *seriograph*, fig. 14.6; see Perrin 1990) can be interpreted in terms of the site's development, with characteristics corresponding to steady and intense occupation, levelling (removal of deposits) and dumping (addition of deposits). While valuable, this seems to contain implicit assumptions about the regularity of the introduction of new types, and should be used with caution.

The ordering generated by automatic seriation need not necessarily be chronological; other factors such as geographical proximity, function or status may generate a similar pattern in the data. As always, an archaeological interpretation of the analysis must be made. Even if a chronological pattern is suspected, neither the direction nor the rate of passing of time can be deduced from the table alone. Chronological markets (such as the introduction of new types) cannot be assumed to occur at regular intervals. In either case, the formal study needs to be combined with understanding of the structure of pottery supply, which in turn relies on the combination of provenance studies and quantified data.

Meanwhile, research continues on more analytical approaches to seriation (Laxton 1976; 1987; Laxton and Restorick 1989). It seems likely that a combination of the two approaches, the exploratory and the more analytical, will be used in future.

A case study

We use Millett's (1979c) study of twenty-two stratified pottery assemblages dating from *c*. AD 75 to the fifth century, from the Romano-British small town of Neatham, Hampshire (Millett and Graham 1986). Using counts of rim sherds, he defined similarity coefficients between pairs of assemblages and used multidimensional scaling (mdscal; see Doran and Hodson 1975, 213–16) to produce a one-dimensional ordering (fig. 14.7). The problem of residual pottery was noted, with the comment that it may have made some early types appear to have continued later than they really did. In our view, the converse is also possible: the presence of a late type in an assemblage of mainly residual material could make it appear to start earlier than it really did. This might account for the apparent paucity of new types after *c*. 200 AD

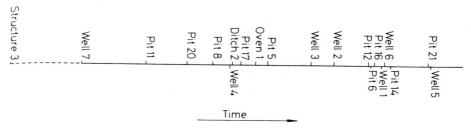

Fig. 14.7. One-dimensional ordering of assemblages from Neatham, using multidimensional scaling (from Millett and Graham 1986)

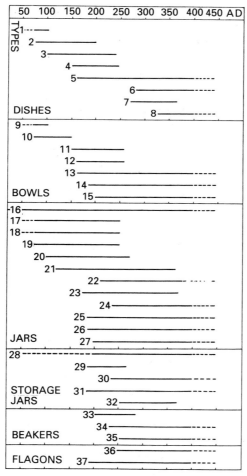

Fig. 14.8. The dating of the main forms of Alice Holt ware at Neatham, based on seriation (from Millett 1979c)

(fig. 14.8) and the dating to 180 AD of the start of types traditionally thought to start a century later (for example flanged bowls and hook-rimmed jars).

Summary

Chronology is clearly important to most (if not all) archaeological thought and it is not part of our purpose to say otherwise. As part of the attempt to understand factors such as trade, economics, function and so on it is important to be clear whether we are discussing contemporary systems, or a sequence of systems, or some more complicated chronological pattern. However, the frequently-heard claim 'I only use the pot for dating', or, more usually, 'Just give me the dates', ignores vital information and should be considered a misuse of the material. Pottery dates should be based on an appreciation and understanding of variations between assemblages, rather than the eccentricities of individual vessels, and any factor which is likely to cause such variation must be considered and if necessary eliminated before a date can be formulated. There should be continuous feedback between our understanding of trade-patterns, sources, site formation processes, function and chronology. The last cannot in any sense be placed in a separate box; it is only one of the factors controlling the variation within and between sites and cannot be considered without the others.

15

PRODUCTION AND DISTRIBUTION

When we consider the significance of an assemblage from a particular site we are then faced with the problem of placing the assemblage in its wider context. It is natural to try to compare the site's assemblage with that from contemporary sites in the immediate area, and perhaps also further afield, which brings us face-to-face with the problems of the interpretation of distributional evidence.

Information content of distribution

The recognition that the same pottery types are found on a number of sites is the first step in compiling distribution maps, but the significance that can be attached to the result is not always the same. When the types mapped are simply in the same general style, but not demonstrably in the same fabric, then the map represents an area where particular types are in use, but does not of itself give us much further information on the source(s) of the type, other than that it is likely to be within the known distribution rather than outside it.

However, when it can be demonstrated that the items mapped are in the same fabric and that this fabric is from a restricted source, (using the techniques of fabric analysis described on pp. 132–151) then the distribution map represents, in some way, the physical movement of pottery. The source may be represented by a kiln site and it is usual to plot this in addition to the find spot (a lozenge being the traditional symbol) or it may be the geological outcrop from which the temper or clay is derived. It may be helpful to plot the extent of the outcrop together with the find spots as an aid to the interpretation of the distribution (Peacock 1969, fig. 2; fig. 15.1). Distribution maps of objects of known source are far more valuable to the archaeologist concerned with the wider problems of economics and supply than distributions of types whose source is unknown. Many of the more powerful methods of distributional analysis are of little avail if the source of the item is not known.

When considering the particular problems of pottery trade and transport three factors deserve consideration. Despite the considerable evidence from the archaeological record for the transport of pottery, often over considerable distances and sometimes in large quantities, contemporary written sources (in literate societies) are often rather silent on the subject. For some areas and periods, such as the medieval period in England, it is possible to

197

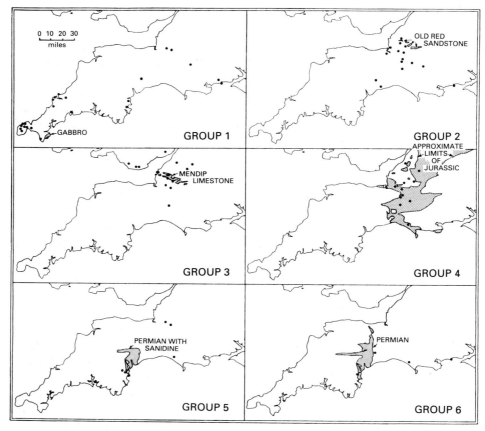

Fig. 15.1. Map showing the distribution of six groups of Glastonbury ware. The parent geological outcrops are shown stippled. (Peacock 1969, fig. 2)

build up a picture of the general character of pottery trade from port books and similar documents which may record the quantity, source and prices of materials entering (Le Patourel 1983), but on other occasions we have little if any contemporary documentation (see Cockle 1981 for a rare document from the Roman period). For instance, there are few if any references to the large-scale transportation of fine table wares during the Roman period. One explanation may be that the pottery trade is in some way 'parasitic' on large-scale movements in other goods. Thus the presence of a large quantity of pottery from an area may on occasion be an indicator of a trade in other materials, perhaps agricultural products or other items now perished. Pottery may thus be in some sense a marker for other movements of goods, or even people.

The second feature relevant to the interpretation of pottery distributions is its function as a container for other products, and in particular this is as a container for agricultural products. The amphora trade in the Graeco-Roman world is not an exercise in transporting amphoras *per se* but it is the items they contain that are important – wine, olive oil or fish sauces.

Such distributions reflect areas of production versus areas of consumption and in the latter the appearance of these new materials may have effects on other aspects of behaviour such as cooking or drinking habits. These may in turn generate a need for other items, such as specialised drinking or serving vessels, which may themselves be ceramic or made in other materials. Thus we may often be seeking a set of items, a service, as part of the underlying explanation for the appearance of the individual components.

Turning to the interpretation of distributional evidence we can examine the data from two viewpoints. The traditional approach is to plot the find spots of types and proceed from there. As evidence accumulates about the history and source of pottery types we can start to build up a picture of the sources of pottery recovered on a site and construct maps of pottery supply. The use of both types of map (discussed below) allows a full understanding of the pottery supply and distribution systems in a region to be investigated.

Distribution of artefact types

Distribution maps hold an important place in archaeology and the practice of compiling distributions of pottery types and interpreting them has a long history (Abercromby 1904). We can distinguish three types of artefact mapping, which should be viewed as a hierarchy of increasing information content. The simplest forms of distribution maps are those confined to the plotting of individual find-spots, perhaps on a base map showing outline topography, road-systems, towns and so on. When their limitations are recognised such maps provide a valuable summary of the overall extent of the distribution of a type and often provide the first stage in its study. Find-spot maps are particularly suitable for compilation from published sources. They record the presence of an item on a site and serve in part as an index or pointer to further information. However they provide no indication as to the relative abundance of a type and each point on the map carried equal weight. The density of points in a given area may however provide valuable information – if we were dealing with a map of a single fabric, for which we would expect a single source, we might expect a higher density of sites close to the source, and a lower density further away. A simple 'contour map' may be produced from site density data of this type using a technique such as grid generalisation (Orton 1980, 124–30; Hodder and Orton 1976), although the procedure must be applied with care.

The second form of distribution map is that where some quantitative element is attached to the points in the form of simple counts. The count may be printed on the map next to the point, or the counts are split into ranges (1–9, 10–19, 20–9 and so on), each with a different symbol, or the symbol may

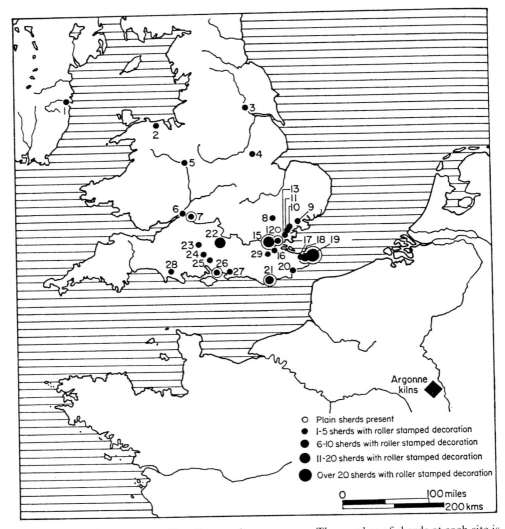

Fig. 15.2. The distribution of late Roman Argonne ware. The number of sherds at each site is shown by symbols of different sizes. (Fulford 1977, fig. 1)

change in size to indicate the number of items on a site (fig. 15.2). Although an advance over the simple point system, such maps should only be interpreted with the greatest care. The most serious difficulty is that the count of an item may be recorded, but there is no indication about the proportion of the assemblage that this represents – a count of five examples in an assemblage of twenty pots tells a rather different story to five examples in an assemblage of two thousand. Sites with a long history of excavation and publication are likely to be 'over-represented' on such a map – there may be a relatively large number of examples of a type, yet they form only a very small proportion of the assemblage. It is invariably necessary to interpret such maps in the light of archaeological knowledge. An additional advance over the find-spot map is to record appropriate sites where the type is absent, which is usually by using a symbol for the special count 'zero' – 'appropriate' in this context being sites considered to be contemporary with the type in question. Again the question of numbers is important – absence from a small assemblage being less significant than absence from a large assemblage. Such 'mapped counts' are often surprisingly difficult to compile from published sources – it is rare for complete catalogues to be available from all but a few sites and the introduction of counts into the picture opens up all sorts of complexities, which become even more acute in the case of the next type of map.

The most advanced of the three map types considered here is the quantitative distribution map, in which the 'symbol' represents the proportion of the assemblage formed by the type being mapped. Again symbols of different sizes may represent different ranges ($< 5\%$, $< 10\%$, $< 20\%$, $< 50\%$ and so on), or the symbol itself may be in the form of a pie-chart (fig. 2.1). A standard method of quantification is clearly essential (see above p. 168).

The quantitative distribution map may be adapted to answer a range of questions. If the pie-chart symbol is used it may be possible to plot more than one type on the same map using different shades or colours for the different groups. The values plotted on the map need not be expressed as proportions of the type in question in the whole assemblage. It may be appropriate to consider one table ware fabric as a proportion of all table wares, a cooking pot fabric as a proportion of all cooking wares or all amphoras as one group, or plot different varieties of one class of wares. It may even be suitable to confine the plot to the relative proportions of two types – perhaps the products of two different kilns – if one is only concerned with the relationship between them.

Fully quantitative distribution maps are more or less impossible to compile from published sources as the number of site reports including the appropriate data is very small. Even if a crude measure such as 'vessels represented' was felt to be sufficient, the number of reports where the values are recorded as a matter of routine is minimal – recourse may have to be made to making rough estimations by counting up the illustrations and deciphering comments in the text.

However, once available, a full measure is amenable to all manner of manipulation. Perhaps the most useful is the fall-off curve for which the type source must also be known. The classic application of regression analysis is to the distribution of Romano-British Oxfordshire ware (Fulford and Hodder 1974). The initial regression line calculated for the proportion of Oxfordshire products on thirty sites was not a good fit to the data – a better fit was obtained by separating the sites into two groups, those most easily reached by

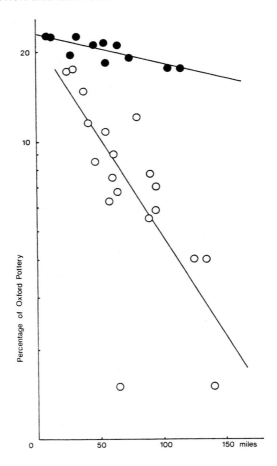

Fig. 15.3. Regression analysis of Oxfordshire pottery. A simple plot is not a good fit to the data, but this improves when those sites which can be reached by water (solid circles) are distinguished and analysed separately. (Fulford and Hodder 1974, fig. 3)

water and those reached overland. Two new separate regression curves were calculated which together were a better fit to the data (fig. 15.3). Thus in this case the quantified data help us to formulate an explanation for the mechanism behind the distribution process. It is interesting to note that their data were quantified by sherd count, which was the 'lowest common denominator' at all the sites included in the study. This means that although the broad trends are evident, one must be cautious about interpreting the data from any particular site (see p. 171).

Sources of supply to a site
Complementary to those distributions from the point of view of the producer are those compiled from the point of view of the consumer. In this case the assemblage of ceramics from a site is broken down into groups assignable to

different sources, which are plotted on a map. In the simplest form the source sites may be marked by a simple symbol, perhaps indicating the type of pottery produced. As a summary of the site supply such maps may be adequate for many purposes but the temptation to indicate the trade routes supplying pottery to the destination site with a 'join-the-dots' exercise should in most cases be resisted. The identification of the mechanisms responsible for the distribution process will only be possible by considering data on a larger scale than that presented by a single site.

A more sophisticated approach to site supply maps requires the use of quantitative data. One common approach is for the size of the source symbol to reflect the proportion of the assemblage supplied to a destination site. If appropriate it may be possible to split the destination assemblage into periods and illustrate the site supply at each period. A set of such maps have been compiled by Going, illustrating the supply of pottery to Chelmsford during the Roman period (Going 1987, figs. 52–9; fig. 15.4). The shifting patterns of supply are clearly demonstrated by examining a sequence of such maps. For this purpose, and many others, it is essential that the entire assemblage is quantified to give the complete picture of ceramic supply.

When enough analysis of this type has been carried out, it will be possible to start looking at the differences in supply pattern between contemporary sites in the same area. We might expect that different types of site may draw their ceramic supplies from different sources, depending on such factors as social status, occupation, wealth and so on of the inhabitants. Certain types of site may show preferential access to some products, but it is only against the background of a wider analysis that such patterns will emerge – it is not adequate to extrapolate from only one or two observations.

The identification of source from distribution

One particular aspect of the analysis of distribution evidence which deserves special consideration is the identification of likely source areas for pottery types based on the distribution evidence alone, and in the absence of production sites or other indications of the source.

In the basic model of distribution from a central point we may expect the highest concentrations nearest to the source and a simple fall-off curve in all directions. The 'concentrations' should be of three types:

(i)   an increased proportion of sites with the product;
(ii) an increased proportion of the product on those sites;
(iii) an increased range of types on those sites.

This ideal picture is rarely realised and many factors alter the final picture. As we have seen above, topography will intervene. Transport by river or sea rather than by land will distort the pattern, almost invariably to the advantage of the former over the latter.

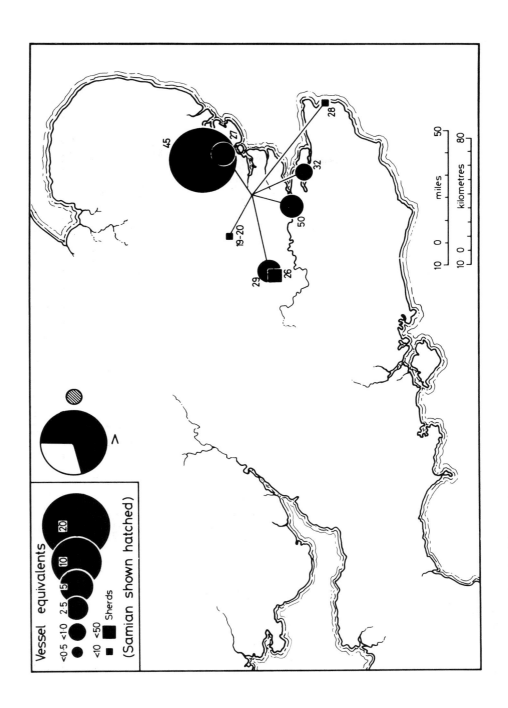

Vessel equivalents

<0.5 <10
<10 <50

Sherds

(Samian shown hatched)

miles

kilometres

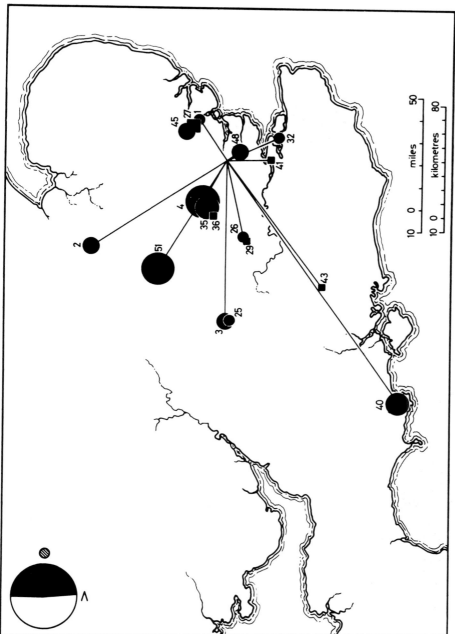

Fig. 15.4. Pottery supply to Chelmsford. (a) AD 60–80, (b) AD 360/370–400+. The size of the circles indicates the size of the assemblage from each source in estimated vessel equivalents. (Going 1987, figs. 52 and 59)

Much more complex patterns are also possible. Some distributions are directed towards particular groups of consumers, such as large stable military populations in frontier zones, or large cities or ports, and mostly bypass intermediate regions. There are many such examples from the study of Roman ceramics. The large globular olive oil amphora of the province of Baetica (southern Spain) has a distribution along the northern coast of the Mediterranean from Spain into France and Italy, up the Rhône valley and in particular along the Rhine, where large permanent garrisons were based at this period (Colls et al. 1977, 136, fig. 53). The type is largely absent from, for instance, northern Spain and western and northern France. We also have cases where different forms of vessel from a single centre are produced for different regional markets, and only distributed in those areas. A modern example will perhaps illustrate this most clearly. The potters at Agost, near Alicante in Spain, produced water jars (*botijo*) in a fine white local clay from the mid-nineteenth century onwards. By expanding production they eventually captured extensive markets in the other regions of Spain, but also in France and North Africa. For each region a slightly different form of jar was produced (Mossman and Selsor 1988, 219–20, fig. 4), which differed in the shape of the body, the form of the spouts or in other minor details. Such a pattern might appear in the archaeological record as a series of distinct distributions, but linked together by their common fabric. It is interesting to note that the *botijo* form is still in occasional use in North Africa today (although now made locally rather than imported from Agost), but it is still known as a 'Spanish bottle'.

16

ASSEMBLAGES AND SITES

Firstly we will examine some general theoretical considerations concerning the formation of archaeological deposits and the ceramic assemblages they contain. We will then consider one of the more important of the factors governing the relationship between the ceramics in use and that recovered from archaeological contexts – the use-life or life expectancy of the material. The value of sherd-link data is next discussed, followed by considerations of pottery collected from field walking and the role of quantification in the examination of site-formation problems.

Pottery life-expectancy

There is a small but valuable body of 'ceramic census data' collected by ethnographers and others detailing the types of pottery in use in individual households, which archaeologists have drawn upon in several ways as an aid in their interpretation of archaeological assemblages (Kramer 1985, 89–92).

The most useful of these studies provide lists or inventories detailing not only the types and numbers of vessels in use in particular villages, compounds or houses but also records of their age and from the latter may be derived estimates for the life expectancies of vessels of various forms or functions. An early study by Foster (1960) of life expectancy of pottery in Tzintzuntzan (Mexico) identifies five basic factors influencing breakage rates:

(i)   the basic strength of the vessel;
(ii)   the vessel function – its use as a cooking vessel, water jar, storage jar and so on;
(iii)   the method of use, such as the type of stove;
(iv)   the context of use – the care taken by the user, the activities of children, animals and so on;
(v)   the cost of the vessel.

At Tzintzuntzan cooking pots in daily use were estimated to have a life-span of about one year, but storage vessels lasted considerably longer. The study also includes the observation that 'a surprising amount of [the] breakage results from cats, chickens, dogs and pigs bumping pots or knocking them over' (Foster 1960, 608). Amongst the Kalinga in the Philippines dogs are apparently responsible for *c.* 10 per cent of all breakages (Longacre

Table 16.1. *Life-span of Fulani pottery (Cameroon)*

Type	Approx. capacity (litres)	Median age (years)
Bowls	1—2	2.7
Small cooking pots	3—5	2.7
Medium cooking pots	7—10	2.5
Large cooking pots	15—20	10.2
Storage	40—46	12.5
Other		4.2

Source: David 1972.

1985, 341, fig. 136) – useful reminders that the archaeological assemblage is not entirely composed of the results of human activities.

A similar picture is presented in the study by Bedaux and van der Waals (1987, 141–6) of pottery use amongst the Dogon of Mali. Here again pots in daily contact with fire, or pots regularly moved have the shortest life-span; those never heated and only occasionally moved have the longest. In this case, the age distribution of pottery varies between villages or compounds, and this seems to depend on whether or not pottery making is carried out there. Greater care in the handling of pottery in non-pottery making establishments is suggested, and there also seem to be differences in the age distribution of pots of the same type, but made by different potters.

David (1972) presents a set of figures for the life-span of Fulani (Cameroon) pottery. The ceramic assemblage is divided into six broad classes (bowls, cooking pots – small, medium and large – storage vessels and 'other') and the median age calculated for each group.

Taking as a starting point the number of vessels in use in an ethnographically recorded assemblage and using a simple formula it is possible to make projections for the number of vessels of each type we should expect to be broken (and thus potentially discarded) during periods of one year, five years, ten years and so on – assuming constant replenishment to maintain the same numbers in use at all times. DeBoer presents a table employing David's Fulani vessel life-expectancy data (DeBoer 1974, 338, table 1) which illustrated the proportions of types in these 'derived' assemblages (fig. 16.1). As we would expect the proportions in the 'derived' or accumulated assemblages will reflect not only the character of the original assemblage in use but also the breakage rates of the different types – those subject to most breakage being over-represented and those with the longest lives under-represented.

Combining this with our information on the types of vessels most likely to be broken suggests that cooking and serving vessels may be over-represented in the archaeological record, when compared with the 'life' assemblage, with

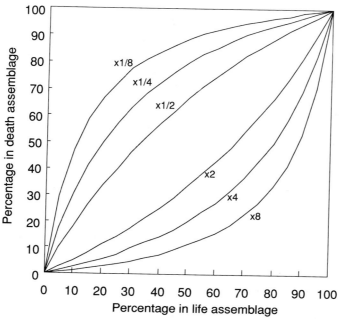

Fig. 16.1. The effect of different life-expectancies on the character of the archaeological assemblage. Each curve demonstrates the relationship between the proportions of a type in the 'life' and 'death' assemblages, where the life expectancy of the type is longer ($\times 2$, $\times 4$, $\times 8$) or shorter ($\times 1/2$, $\times 1/4$, $\times 1/8$) than that of the remainder of the assemblage

larger and more immobile storage jars and higher value items less represented. Vessels whose primary function is as a container for materials such as foodstuffs may have the shortest life of all and in some circumstances may come to dominate an assemblage – the number of wine bottles or jam jars passing through many households today greatly exceeds the number of new pots purchased. Non-replenishment or recycling of vessels will of course contribute considerably to the character of archaeological assemblages, further complicating their relationship with any activities that created them. The assumption that seems occasionally to be made, that differences between assemblages are in some way a *direct* reflection of differences in the assemblages in use on the site, is too simplistic. We should distinguish between two aspects of the ceramic assemblage – the character of an assemblage in use whose composition and size may reflect factors such as function and status, and the total assemblage of vessels discarded on a site which reflects both the range of types in use, and their discard and replacement rates.

Sherd-links

It is often recognised that parts of the same vessel are found in several contexts on a site – there are sherd-links or cross-joins between the contexts – and it is natural to want to try to do something with this information.

In our view, it is in most cases extremely difficult to make a quantitative study of sherd-links. Any such study would depend on being reasonably certain that one had found all (or almost all) the links on a site. The resources needed to do this for any but the smallest site would be enormous, in terms of both time and space, and even the most enthusiastic advocates admit that 'It will rarely be possible to assign every sherd in a group or deposit to a vessel, and in some groups there may be many sherds left over' (Moorhouse 1986, 88). This being so, it seems we are dealing with a qualitative and rather subjective form of evidence which is extremely difficult to interpret except either: (i) on atypical sites (for example Devils Ditch, p. 179); or (ii) in the most general terms (see below).

We can look at the problem in two parts. Firstly there is the question of what the sherd-links actually represent in different circumstances and secondly there are the practical questions of recognising the links and presenting the data in such a manner that they can be used by others.

What causes sherd-links?
In some cases sherd-links between contexts are simply the result of the context having been excavated and recorded in more than one section. It may be that the same context runs across more than one excavated area and has different numbers in each, or for some other reason it was excavated in blocks or areas. Links of this type should be expected and should be eliminated before proceeding with sherd-links between stratigraphic units.

Otherwise, sherd-links probably fall into three groups. The first is where a series of sherd-links between contexts indicate that they result from a sequence of closely spaced actions, the second is where material from existing levels is disturbed and re-deposited higher up in the stratigraphy, and the third is where parts of the same vessel have a genuinely different history, some parts surviving longer in use than others after breakage.

A series of tip lines in a pit may be excavated and recorded separately but may only represent a sequence of closely spaced actions, such as shovelling a rubbish accumulation into a pit. A series of sherd-links between such contexts would be expected and these too should be accounted for before proceeding with further work. The identification of sherd-links may be used as an aid in the interpretation of the sequence on a site. They may be used to demonstrate the possibility or otherwise that certain contexts are open at the same time, or may help to explain a sequence of dumping and levelling actions. An example of where this approach has been applied is Sandal Castle in West Yorkshire (Moorhouse 1983; fig. 16.2) although, as noted, this work 'depends on a method of quantifying pottery based on the individual vessel – where all sherds or pieces from the same unique vessel are brought together' (Moorhouse 1986, 85–6). The possibilities of meeting this requirement are discussed below.

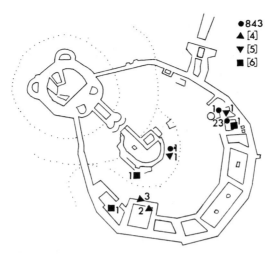

Fig. 16.2. The distribution of sherd-links at Sandal Castle (West Yorkshire). The numbers on the plan refer to numbers of sherds found at each location. (Moorhouse 1983, fig. 63 [C]: Vessels linking early occupation of stone castle buildings with Barbican ditch level 5)

Perhaps the most common type of sherd-link is that where parts of a vessel are disturbed and re-deposited in higher levels. Such sherds are 'residual' in their final resting place and relate to earlier phases of activity on the same site.

The final category of sherd-link is where parts of the same vessel are incorporated into archaeological deposits at different times, reflecting a genuine difference in usage. One possibility is that some parts of broken vessels remain in use while others are discarded. For instance the rim part may have little value once broken, but the base may be trimmed off and remain usable or broken handles may be discarded while the remainder of the vessel stays in use. There may be occasions where these processes are observable.

Recognising and presenting sherd-links

In many circumstances it will be possible to recognise all the individual vessels from a single context, provided that it is of relatively limited size, by grouping together all sherds that come from the same vessel. Destruction horizons and similar assemblages of complete or semi-complete vessels are particularly suitable for such treatment. We may be able to extend this to a larger number of contexts, or even the whole site in some circumstances. Given the combination of distinctive vessels and a skilled ceramics researcher, it may be possible to arrive at figures for the absolute numbers of vessels recovered, even when they are spread over several contexts or a large area. Brown (1985) describes a method of illustrating diagramatically the sherd-links between a series of contexts.

We must recognise, however, that such a procedure is by no means universally applicable. At some periods pottery forms and techniques are so standardised that it is not possible to separate the sherds from different vessels, even rims and bases. Body sherds are often impossible to match. Some types of site are also rather less amenable to this approach than others – deep complex stratification may be less suitable to the recognition of sherd-links than more simple single-period sites. On kiln waste heaps it would be impossible. The practical problems of both time and space must be considered – it is often not possible to acquire sufficient of either to ensure that all sherd-links have been recorded. In many cases the recognition of sherd-links will be confined to the more distinctive vessels in the group, and in practice this often means the finer decorated wares or other rarer vessels – often the 'imports' to the site. This part of the assemblage may behave rather differently to the remainder, the great mass of relatively undiagnostic coarse wares where the majority of the sherd-links would undoubtedly be found, if they could be recognised. An approach to pottery quantification requiring the identification of the same vessel across the site cannot be recommended in anything other than very special circumstances, and prime amongst these will be destruction horizons and similar primary deposits. This may seem to conflict with our earlier recommendation about sorting sherd families (p. 56). But there we only needed links within contexts while here we are talking about links between contexts, which requires far greater resources if they are to be found.

Field survey data

A specialised aspect of ceramics analysis is the investigation of field survey assemblages – also known as surface assemblages or surface artefact patterns. This material is usually recovered from the surface or amongst the plough soil during field walking. There is a growing literature on the theoretical aspects of the formation and interpretation of such scatters (e.g. Lewarch and O'Brien 1981; Haselgrove et al. 1985; Odell and Cowan 1987, with comments by Dunnell 1990 and Yorston 1990) and many useful case studies.

It is clear that many factors contribute both to the formation of surface scatters, and to the recovery of material from surfaces. When we turn to the variables affecting recovery, the character of the soil and the vegetation cover, which may be stubble from crops, are clearly important. Brighter or more distinctively coloured sherds are more likely to be recovered than sherds whose colour resembles that of the underlying soil, and different individuals may be better at data collection, resulting in an apparently greater density of sherds, or may preferentially collect sherds of different types (perhaps skewing the date distribution of the assemblage). These and other variations are discussed by Haselgrove (1985, 21).

Some workers have studied the concentration of sherds on the surface and

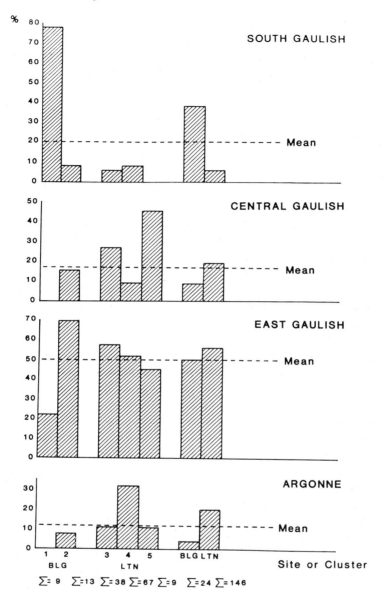

Fig. 16.3. Using the samian ware from surface collection to compare the dates of the underlying stratigraphy. BLG – Beaurieux, Les Grèves; LTN – Limé, Les Terres Noires.

sought to interpret variations in density, often in relation to some centrally located site. Wilkinson (1982) describes the results of an extensive field survey around Tell Sweyhat, a tell site in Syria dating to the third millennium BC. A total of fourteen transects were set up radiating from the tell, and the sherds seen on the surface were counted in a series of 10m × 10m squares at 100m or 500m intervals. The sherd densities observed allowed a contour map to be constructed which suggested a gradual fall-off from the tell, with the greatest densities within 3km of the centre. Wilkinson suggests that this equates with a manuring zone about 30–35 minutes walk from the centre. Extrapolating from the data obtained from the sample squares it is estimated that there are 8–10 million sherds on the surface within 3km – approximately 56 tons of pottery – and many times this quantity would be incorporated in the underlying soil.

The survey in the area of Maddle Farm on the Berkshire Downs yielded a more complex picture (Gaffney et al. 1985). Here pottery was collected from a series of 100m north–south transects at 25m intervals. The densities from these transects, subjected to a trend-surface analysis, suggested a number of high-density concentrations at some distance from the central settlement which seem unrelated to permanent occupation and are interpreted as points of seasonal activity such as dung-heaps or hay-ricks. Lower density concentrations nearer the central settlement are interpreted as areas where sheep were folded, which would not need manuring (Gaffney et al. 1985, 103, fig. 8.5).

Others have attempted to use the material from surface assemblages to illustrate the chronology of the underlying activity. Haselgrove (1985, 26–7) compares the dates of occupation of Roman sites in the Aisne Valley (France) using the overall balance of the samian assemblage as a guide (fig. 16.3).

Sherds after burial

The size and shape of sherds does not just depend upon the inherent characteristics of the original vessel, although these cannot be ignored. If sherds are left on a surface used by man or animals they will be further fragmented until perhaps an equilibrium has been reached. Sherd size may be a valuable indicator of the type of activity carried out in a particular area of the site, although one must bear in mind that few sherds actually get buried where the vessels broke and most go through several cycles of deposition and redeposition. Size and fragmentation are related so closely to fabric and form that it is not possible to make use of such data independent of fabric and form. To give one example, sherds of Roman amphora may be individually as large and as heavy as complete colour-coated beakers. In these circumstances variations in average sherd size or weight between contexts will be affected unduly by the presence or absence of particular vessel types.

In sedimentology it is possible to classify detrital fragments by the degree of roundness of their edges. The edges of sherds too will reflect the degree of weathering they have undergone and it can be important to note whether the edges and surfaces of a sherd are fresh and even perhaps to try to assess the degree of roundness. Allen (1989) describes such a system, employing techniques derived from sedimentology. This type of data might help to identify buried soil profiles and distinguish them from dumped deposits which were buried before weathering processes could affect the sherds within them. The study of the effects of abrasion on sherds has only recently started (Skibo and Schiffer 1987; Needham and Sørensen 1989). Sherds that have been in contact with plant root systems may become covered in a network of fine dark lines (Rye 1981, 121, fig. 108).

Sherds which have been subjected to the action of water are immediately recognisable and may even be colonised by bryozoan or other organisms. Such sherds can be found in the fills of drains and distinguish deposits contemporary with the use of the drain from those thrown into the drain after its abandonment.

After burial, changes continue to affect sherds. In particular certain chemicals may be removed from the sherds by leaching whilst others may be deposited on or in the sherd. Leaching of shell or limestone inclusions after burial must be distinguished from leaching due to use. If the vessels have been buried in an acidic matrix then the leaching will be even all over the sherd. If, however, the acid is derived from rainwater or urine acting on sherds lying on a surface then the effect may be limited to one side only. The presence of leached and unleached sherds of identical fabric in the same deposit may be evidence that not all the sherds in the deposit had the same depositional history. Deposits on sherds may consist of: vivianite, a blue iron compound deposited in anaerobic conditions; iron pyrites, which has the same depositional requirements as vivianite and is often mistaken for a deliberate slip or even traces of gold; iron panning, which occurs in the lower parts of soil profiles affected by heavy leaching; calcium phosphate, derived from bone and cess and particularly common on sherds deposited in cess pits; salts, such as gypsum and rock salt, which are deposited at the surface in hot climates by efflorescence and 'furring' which is deposited by running water saturated with minerals. The latter was particularly common on the potsherds found within a medieval culvert at Bath, in south-west England. It was therefore possible to identify sherds which had originally been part of this deposit but which were residual in later contexts. Rigorous, routine recording of this type of evidence is time-consuming but there may well be occasions where it is worthwhile.

The role of quantification

We have already seen, both in theory (p. 168) and practice (p. 176) how quantified data can give us useful information about site formation processes. Contexts can be characterised by the brokenness and completeness (p. 178) of the pottery they contain, but it must be remembered that a 'primary' context may nonetheless have a very high level of brokenness (for example pottery trampled *in situ*). When comparing contexts, the different parameters of different types of pottery must be taken into account if there are different proportions of different types in the contexts. But provided such 'nuisance' parameters are allowed for, useful information can be obtained.

17

POTTERY AND FUNCTION

The problem of function is perhaps one of the more difficult faced by those studying archaeological ceramics. The topic can be approached from three points of view: firstly at the level of the function of the individual vessel; secondly the functional information that can be recovered from archaeological assemblages; and thirdly the overall orientation of a particular industry – the sector of ceramics usage at which the principal products are aimed. To tackle all these aspects adequately it is necessary to draw together information on form, nomenclature, fabric, technology, trade, distribution and site formation processes as well as historical, ethnographic and literary references. It is perhaps not surprising that so much remains to be done, for some of the necessary tools, such as the appropriate statistical techniques for comparison between assemblages or the analytical techniques for identifying organic residues, have only recently become widely available. It is also not entirely clear what results may be expected from studies of vessel or assemblage function or how such information is to be integrated into site reports or regional surveys.

Individual vessel function
Artefacts made of fired clay are ubiquitous and their functions are diverse. Ceramic bricks, tiles, pipes and other forms of building materials are very common, and tubes, funnels and fittings for other industrial processes take advantage of the refractory properties of fired clay. Moulded and fired clay figurines have a long history and the use of clay as a medium for figurative art continues to this day. Pottery baths, sarcophagi, portable ovens and similar exotica have been produced at some periods, but perhaps the most important function of ceramics, both now and in the past, has been its use as containers, particularly for the storage, preparation, movement and serving of food.

Functional categories
The functions of pottery containers can be divided into three broad categories: storage, processing (which includes various cooking methods) and transfer (including serving and eating) (Rice 1987, 208–9). Without too much difficulty we can imagine that a vessel employed as a long-distance transport container for a liquid will tend to have characteristics (durability, ease-of-handling and stacking, weight/volume ratio, low porosity, sealable top and so

on) that are rather different from those required by a vessel whose primary function is the frying of eggs (thermal shock resistance, accessibility, smooth or non-stick surface, perhaps even a nice flavour – Arnold 1985, 138–9). An extension of this approach is to survey ethnographic and historical records for correlations between aspects of form, technology or other characteristics and vessel function (Hendrickson and McDonald 1983; Smith 1985). Rice has summarised the 'predicted archaeological correlates' for five broad functional categories: storage, cooking (food preparation with heat), food preparation without heat, serving and transport (Rice 1987, table 7.2). Such summaries may be a useful means of organising the available information, but many of the decisions taken during the manufacturing process require compromises between competing requirements, so in a particular instance a predicted correlate may be masked by some other factor. There will also be vessels that have to fit into more than one category. Cooking vessels produced for an export trade may acquire some of the characteristics of transport containers, such as stackability and uniformity of size.

Written sources and pictorial representations

When we turn to the problems posed by particular vessel types there are a number of potential sources of information on function. At the head of the list may be placed those vessels which proclaim their function explicitly with inscriptions. Fine beakers and jugs produced in the Mosel valley (western Germany) during the second and third centuries AD occasionally included painted or barbotined inscriptions amongst their decoration. These texts are dominated by such phrases as NOLITE SITIRE ('Thirst not') and DA MIHI VINUM ('Give me wine') and the association between these vessels and the consumption of wine would seem to be reasonably clear (Bös 1958). By extension, vessels of the same form from these factories, but without the inscriptions, should also be drinking vessels (fig. 17.1).

In literate societies there may be references to various aspects of ceramics and particularly indications about the function of particular vessel types. The simplest references may be merely names of pottery types, perhaps culled from lists or inventories or scratched on the pots themselves, but with no other immediate indication as to function. At the other end of the spectrum there may be complete printed catalogues of the products of particular industries and descriptions of their use and manufacturing.

A further source of valuable information is the representation of pottery in figurative art (Jacobs and Peremans 1976), which has the dual advantage that the vessels are shown in use and can often be precisely dated (p. 16; fig. 1.4). By cross-referencing all these sources it is possible to build up a reasonable picture of the range of pottery types in circulation at some periods – broadly equivalent to the folk taxonomies compiled during ethnographic observations (such as for Roman vessel types, Hilgers 1969; White 1975). The

Fig. 17.1. A beaker made in the Mosel valley during the third century AD with a painted inscription suggesting that the vessel was intended for drinking wine. (Photo: David Allan)

information on pottery use that can be derived from the examination of such pictorial sources extends to such items as the wicker handles added to jars to turn them into water carrying vessels (e.g. Faure-Boucharlat 1990, 92), or the basketwork used to protect vessels during transport (Laubenheimer 1990, 82, 85, 101). These of course would rarely survive in archaeological contexts. In areas where traditional pottery is still in common usage it will often be the case that the best clues about the function of the pottery types recovered from archaeological levels, as well as other aspects of the vessels, are to be had by examining their modern counterparts.

Physical properties

Just as there is a relationship between shape and function, so the physical characteristics of the fired clay will be relevant to the use to which the finished product will be put. Investigations have concentrated on three principal areas of interest: the thermal properties, particularly thermal stress resistance and heating efficiency, the mechanical strength and the porosity. When ceramic materials are heated, either during firing or during use, the constituents of the fabric will expand at differing rates – they have different coefficients of thermal expansion. Combined with temperature gradients through the vessel, stresses are set up which may lead eventually to cracking or spalling. Although this much is certain there is rather more of a debate about the significance of thermal stress as a factor in the choice of tempering or the shaping of vessels intended for cooking. One view is that proposed by Rye (Rye 1976), who suggests that the problems of thermal stress can be reduced by manipulating three factors: the shape of the vessel, the porosity of the fabric and the mineral inclusions of the clay. Thermal stress should be minimised by the manufacture of round-based globular pots with an even but thin wall rather than flat-based or angular vessels, where stresses will tend to concentrate along the angles. Fabrics with large pores may inhibit the formation of large cracks as a developing small crack will be intercepted by the pore and arrested. Some minerals, quartz in particular, have a thermal expansion coefficient that is markedly higher than that of a typical clay, whereas others such as feldspar and calcite expand at roughly the same rate (Rye 1976, fig. 3). Those in the latter category should cause less stress to build up and thus might be preferred.

However, these factors are clearly not universally applied to the problem of reducing thermal stress. Plog's (1980) review of ethnographic data from the American southwest highlights a number of examples of apparently contrary behaviour and Woods (1986) points to the wide range of flat-based, quartz-tempered cooking pots in use in western Europe during the Roman and medieval periods. In the ethnographic literature it is often recorded that cooking pots have relatively thick walls (Hendrickson and McDonald 1983, 632–4). It is clear that whilst some potters may be aware of, and take account of, the thermal shock problem, what might be considered to be the 'appropriate' solutions are not universally applied.

Porosity, in addition to being a potential factor in the reduction of thermal stress, has a bearing on the problem of heating efficiency. A porous fabric may allow liquids to seep through from one surface to another. For some vessel types this is advantageous, indeed a basic requirement. In water jars employed in hot climates the permeability of the fabric allows water to evaporate and hence cool the contents, a process which is further encouraged by light coloured surfaces. What may be an advantage in these circumstances will be rather less beneficial in others – the long-term storage or transportation of liquids for example. In a vessel employed for cooking any seepage of liquid through the wall of the pot will reduce heating efficiency prolonging the heating process and wasting valuable fuel. Without reducing the porosity of the fabric it is possible to reduce permeability by treating one or both surfaces. Schiffer (1990) describes a series of experiments that demonstrate the relationships between heating efficiency and permeability, and the advantageous effects of different surface treatments. It is clear that the application of resins, slips and even burnishing the surface are sufficient to raise heating efficiency, while still retaining the potential benefits of a porous fabric. Even in areas and at periods where glazes are in common usage and capable of providing a perfectly impermeable surface, they are not often applied to cooking vessels. There are references in the ethnographic record to the application of clay slips or other sealants to the surfaces of pottery to reduce permeability, but these are not always to cooking vessels and include vessels for storage as well.

The mechanical strength of vessels can be considered under a number of headings: there is resistance to sudden impacts, dropping the vessel for example, and there is resistance to more gradual processes such as abrasion. If vessels are to be stored or used in exposed environments then resistance to frost shattering may be an important consideration. Strength is not only important in the finished product but also during manufacture. It may be advantageous to produce thin-walled vessels for a particular purpose, perhaps to improve the volume/weight ratio for transportation, but this may require special procedures. It may be necessary to make the vessel in stages, or in parts which are only assembled when they are partly dried, or the vessel may be trimmed or beaten to produce a thinner wall.

It is usual to record the 'hardness' of a fabric as one of the characteristics considered during the standard process of pottery description (see p. 138) and a simple scheme such as reference to Mohs' scale is generally employed. More sophisticated mechanical techniques for the assessment of impact strength have been devised (e.g. Marby et al. 1988) and there have been experiments with test briquettes to determine the relationship between the quantity and type of temper, firing temperature and impact resistance. Bronitsky and Hamer (1986) suggest that the incorporation of finely ground tempers made the finished product significantly more durable. Schiffer and Skibo (1986, 606) record that tempered briquettes were less resistant than those that were untempered and the difference in impact strength increased with firing temperature. Briquettes tempered with organic materials were less durable than those tempered with sand. Abrasion resistance has also been investigated experimentally (Skibo and Schiffer 1987) and in this case it seems that a high percentage of coarse temper offers the greatest resistance to abrasion, and particularly so when wet.

It is apparent that the various physical characteristics of fired clays outlined above are not only interrelated, but the steps which might result in the optimum conditions for one factor will in some cases have adverse effects on others. Investigations of the precise effect of, for instance, particular types of tempering or surface treatment increase our understanding of the behaviour of traditional ceramics, and as such are valuable. They may help to explain some of the characteristics of a vessel of known function – a cooking pot or water jug – but they do not by themselves provide immediate and direct indication of the function of a ware or vessel.

Traces of use and wear
Many of the operations performed on ceramics will leave physical traces which can give valuable clues about these activities. An individual observation may, by itself, be of limited interest, but regular associations with an identifiable activity will lead to functional interpretations which are of wider value.

It may be possible to identify the general function of particular forms, as cooking pots, storage vessels and so on. In other cases a more specific association between form, source and function may be uncovered, suggesting that a particular producer was specialising in the manufacture of vessels which themselves had a specific and specialised function.

Many pots retain traces of their role as cooking vessels. When a vessel is used over an open fire traces of soot will often be deposited on the external surface, or the colour of the surface will alter. In some cases fine cracks may develop. Hally (1983) describes the variations in sooting patterns which develop under differing conditions – in particular a vessel suspended or supported over a flame will tend to develop sooting over the entire lower surface, whereas vessels set in a fire or amongst hot ashes or embers will tend to develop sooting in a zone around the lower body of the pot, but not directly on the base. Unfortunately these distinctions are of less value than they should be because it is probable that most sooting is removed during washing and processing during post-excavation, leaving only the barest traces surviving. Medieval drip-pans and pipkins are often sooted and burnt on one side only, that opposite the handle, suggesting that they were placed on the side of the fire rather than within or above it and contemporary manuscript illustrations would seem to confirm this (Moorhouse 1978, 7).

There is a potential source of confusion when examining discolourations on the surface of vessels due to heating or burning between those caused by cooking fires and those resulting from the original firing procedure. Localised

Fig. 17.2. A third-century AD bowl in 'black-burnished ware' from Ewell, Surrey, showing wear on inside of base. (Photo: University College London, Institute of Archaeology)

colour variations known as 'fire-clouds' (Shepard 1956, 92) usually result from contact between the vessel and fuel or hot gases during the firing cycle. They may occur in any type of kiln, but are more common in open or pit firings where the fuel is arranged around the vessels.

In addition to cooking or heating, many other food preparation processes such as scraping, cutting or stirring will leave traces on sherds which may be identified (fig. 17.2). Some Roman mortaria, bowls which often had coarse grits embedded on the internal surface, were certainly used for grinding or pounding, and most probably for the preparation of wheat and other cereals. The grits and the part of the fabric of the pot are often worn away – in a few extreme cases this has resulted in a hole right through the vessel. The character of the product resulting from this mixture of cereal, grit and pottery can be imagined.

Repeated stress on a vessel in a particular area may eventually result in other types of breakage, but may also be compensated for by thickening or strengthening. Weak points may exist wherever separate elements were luted together, and in particular the attachment of handles to vessels. Extra strips of clay around part of a vessel may have been added in reaction to a perceived fault and it may be possible to observe changes in the construction of vessels through time to strengthen such weak points.

Some classes of pot were made to be used once and then broken, indeed the breakage was an important part of their function. The Roman writer Pliny describes a type of bread or cake known as 'Picenum bread' which was baked in pots in an oven. These were broken to get at the contents, which was then soaked in milk and eaten (Pliny, *Natural History*, 18, 106; André 1961, 72).

Organic contents, deposits and residues

Ceramics are used at most stages of food processing and in many cases these operations leave organic traces which may be identified. However the value of this information is very varied. The identification of the contents of, for instance, a transport container has a potential value that is quite different to the identification of the organic contents of an individual cooking pot. In the former case there will probably be implications far beyond the vessel in question; the immediate implications of the latter lie, at least initially, in the context and site.

Occasionally a vessel will be recovered with the remains of contents which seem to provide unequivocal evidence of its original function. Amphoras, the ubiquitous storage and transport containers of the Graeco-Roman world, are commonly found on wrecks or other underwater sites and a very small number of these vessels are recovered complete with their contents. There are amphoras containing olive stones from a number of wrecks in the Mediterranean and, more surprisingly, one from the Thames estuary (Sealey and Tyers 1989, 57). A number of amphoras containing fish bones (from fish-based sauces) have been recorded (Sealey 1985, 83) – there are even a few vessels which still contain wine (Formenti et al. 1978). In addition to their ceramic connections, such large hoards of Roman foodstuffs are important archaeological resources in their own right, with the potential to provide important insights into agricultural or food-processing practices.

On a rather smaller scale are occasional vessels which contain remains of their last contents recovered from destruction deposits and similar 'primary' contexts. Plates in Pompeian-red ware from the AD 79 Vesuvian destruction of Pompeii are recorded as containing the remains of flat loaves – 'somewhat overcooked' (Loeschcke *in* Albrecht 1942, 38; Greene 1979, 130).

It has long been noted that some pots recovered from archaeological contexts contain traces of deposits or encrustations on their surfaces. Some of these derive from the soils in which the vessels were discarded or buried but others relate directly to the function the vessel fulfilled during its life. The deposits may be burnt or charred, either on the interior or exterior of the pot and probably resulting from cooking, or they may be similar to the limescales created in modern vessels used for boiling water for prolonged periods, such as kettles.

However, in addition to these visible traces of use, it has more recently become clear that organic compounds can be absorbed and retained by porous ceramic materials but leave no visible trace on the vessel. Thus we cannot confine the analysis of organic residues in pottery to that (possibly) small proportion of the assemblage with visible deposits – rather we may have to consider the potential of a very large group of material. The necessary procedures for the analysis of such residues have only become widely available in recent years. The principal technique is gas chromatography. Progress with the analysis of organic residues in archaeological material has been reviewed by Evans (1983–4). Two main points are worth consideration when planning a program of such analyses, or interpreting their results:

> The results of the analysis in its 'raw' form are expressed in terms of various fatty acids and glycerides – the building blocks of the original compounds. To translate these into the original items of interest is not without difficulty as some compounds alter over time, while others disappear. To identify the 'original' material analysis of modern samples for comparison may be required where published descriptions do not exist (Hill 1983–4).

> A vessel used for cooking a range of substances, at the same time or separately, may absorb organic residues from all of them. In addition, absorption from the post-depositional environment is also possible. In a feature such as a rubbish pit or midden, contact with organic compounds would seem inevitable. Analysis of the surrounding soil may help to identify and eliminate sources of possible contamination, but this would seem to rule out the use of material from old collections, and even most material from recent excavations.

It is evident that the reconstruction of any 'original contents' from the extant or altered parts of a mixture of compounds, complicated by possible contamination and reuse of vessels, demands great care and any interpretation of these results requires a full appreciation of the potential difficulties. It is also apparent that many of the compounds retrieved from some classes of vessel (such as amphoras) relate more to the tars, resins and other substances applied to seal the inner surface of the pots than the commodities they carried (Heron and Pollard 1987). Similarly it is common practice to 'prove' earthenwares by rubbing the inner surface with oil and baking them in a hot oven.

An interesting example of the value of contents and residues is reported by Bonnamour and Marinval (1985). They identify a group of early Roman jars from a number of sites in the Saône valley (central France) with burnt deposits of millet. It is suggested that the deposits result from the preparation of a gruel or beer. Many of vessels are of a similar form (a jar with a rilled neck) and it may be that this was 'chosen' to match the function. It would be most interesting to know if the pots are not merely of the same form, but from the same source. It could be that this function required not only '. . . a pot of that form . . .' but one from a particular source.

This leads us on to the identification of a sub-set of cooking wares which are not 'general purpose' but related to specific functions, perhaps even to the extent that they are associated with the preparation of particular recipes. A modern example will illustrate the point. The famous bean dish of south-west France, the *cassoulet*, apparently takes its name from the original clay pot produced by the potters at Issel – hence Cassol d'Issel – which was considered necessary for the dish (David 1959, 93). We can imagine that with growing popularity other potters would attempt to make inroads into this market by producing their own versions of the *cassol*, imitating features of the form, finish or refractory qualities of the original. The later history of such a 'type' might be marked by the decline and loss of the link with the original recipe and its integration into the range of general purpose cooking vessels. In the archaeological record such a mechanism might appear as the initial wide distribution of vessels from a single source, followed by 'imitations' produced in secondary centres. This is only one instance of the general problem of attempting to label a vessel type in a single functional category – a glance at the contents of any kitchen, particularly during moments of stress, will see all manner of vessels and containers which are not being used for their 'proper' function.

The final point to make about the identification of organic residues is the importance of communication between the various specialists involved in writing up a site. Those responsible for reporting on, for example, the fish bones from a site will need to know that some of the amphoras from the same contexts originally carried fish-based sauces (Partridge 1981, 243).

Function, production and distribution

Clearly related to the preceding is the overall emphasis of a production assemblage. A producer of, for instance, transport containers for agricultural products will be subject to economic influences and constraints which will have little, if any, effect on a producer of lamps or pottery statuettes.

In addition to a consideration of the individual forms in the production assemblage the distribution of the products may be used to distinguish between different functional categories. In general the 'fall-off curve' for high- and low-value products will differ sharply – high-value products having a broader but more even and lower level distribution contrasting with the high concentrations but more restricted distribution of low-value items. Certainly during the Roman period the majority of the long-distance move-ment of pottery relates to either its use as bulk containers for agricultural products or as fine table wares but there is increasing evidence that long-distance movements in apparently utilitarian cooking wares was possible if they were deemed to have particularly desirable characteristics. The example of black-burnished ware category 1 (BB1) in Britain is instructive here (Peacock 1982, 85–7). These coarse hand-made cooking wares (jars and bowls) were produced in south-west England throughout the Roman period, and indeed the origin of the industry precedes the conquest. Before about AD 120 they were largely confined to their homeland, but after that date they were distributed widely, being particularly common on military sites in the north of the country. Within a short time many of the pre-existing industries in the south and east of the province begin producing their own versions of the characteristic black-burnished forms, but often in wheel-thrown wares, and these eventually become the typical cooking pot forms of the later Roman period. We have here an indication of the dramatic possibilities when local forms are plucked from their source, promoted on a wider market and then assimilated into the repertoire of competing industries. The question which arises is whether the similarity of form can also be taken to indicate a similarity in function. In the case of BB1 and the wheel-thrown versions the answer may be yes, but it will not always be the case.

Symbolic meaning

In addition to their functions as cooking pots, table-ware and so on, pots (indeed any artefacts) may serve as transmitters of information about their producer, owner or user. Thus some classes of vessel may suggest high status, while others indicate religious, social or tribal affiliations. There is a view that artefacts are part of a 'material culture language', a means of communicating information between individuals and groups, and more than this, a medium through which social conflicts can be expressed and even resolved (Hodder 1986, 122–4). Some of the flavour of this view of the symbolic functions of a pot have been summarised in these words: 'It [a pot] may mean that I, as the ancient owner of this vessel, belong to *this* group, and believe *these* things, that I have *this* level of wealth, and *this* much status. I am also of a specific sex, and perform *these* labors defined by my sex, and this vessel correlates with *this* sex and *these* labors' (Strange 1989, 26).

Food preparation and consumption, and the myths and rituals that surround it, are one of the central aspects of culture (Goody 1982). Eating and drinking behaviour are, on the one hand, subject to deeply held beliefs about what is 'clean' and 'unclean' (or good:bad, inside:outside and so forth), but on the other, an area of culture open to outside influence in the form of new materials and techniques and a means of expressing or promoting status and difference. Pottery, the principal accessory to food preparation, storage and serving, will be inevitably touched by many of the same taboos and become stepped in ritual and symbolic meaning. Pottery has a demonstrable role in many cultures as a means of distinguishing between groups, of dividing 'them' from 'us'. The signals may be particular design elements, typological features, colours or manufacturing techniques. In some instances, it is suggested, pottery becomes a medium for inter- and intra-group power relations, a way of communicating information covertly that cannot be expressed openly (Braithwaite 1982).

But how are we to apply these ideas to pottery in the archaeological record? It is difficult enough through ethnographic observation, when vessels can be observed in use and the individuals involved in the drama are at least on hand to be questioned about their actions – or at least what they understand by their actions.

The answer lies in the soil

The solution, if there is one, lies in the most powerful resource we have – the structure of the archaeological record itself. We are concerned with the 'multi-dimensional' location of pots in their complete context, their relations to other pots and other classes of artefacts, and with archaeological features and layers. The methodological tools needed if one is to pursue this approach are now available through the quantification of entire assemblages and the stratigraphic relationships between them.

CONCLUSION:
THE FUTURE OF POTTERY
STUDIES

So where lies the future of pottery studies?

We have, on the one hand, an ever increasing range of tools at our disposal with which to examine our material. These are applicable not only at the level of the individual sherd or fabric, but also to the relationship between assemblages. These patterns are not only 'internal' – between different types of ceramics – but also with other classes of artefact. On the other hand the multiplicity of techniques and approaches now available holds out the prospect of ceramics study taking an increasing proportion of what are often reducing archaeological budgets. More than ever before, pottery studies must argue actively for a place at the 'high table' of archaeology.

The combination of abundance, near indestructibility and the almost unique plasticity of the medium conspire to make the ceramic assemblage one of the most important resources from an archaeological site. Although the questions that we are posing in archaeology have altered as ideas in the subject shift and develop, it is often pottery to which we turn to test new hypotheses. Unlike some other classes of archaeological material – glass or metalwork for instance – pottery is not continuously recycled so large parts of the assemblage do not disappear from the archaeological record. We also have the possibility of studying the development of technological and stylistic traditions over long periods of time, and thus the effects of social, political and economic change on a small group of individuals, namely the potters themselves.

If there were areas of current practice that deserve further attention we would perhaps pick out three:

(i) an increased awareness and understanding of the raw materials and manufacturing technology and the interaction between them;
(ii) the increasing use of appropriate methods of quantification to attack the problems posed by the assemblage;
(iii) the construction of reusable resources for ceramics study such as databases of quantified data, standard fabric descriptions, the results of compositional analysis and distribution data.

But we should perhaps not ignore other factors in ceramics: the immediacy of pottery; the message from the past at an everyday and sometimes intensely personal level – who has not placed their fingers in the marks left by that long-dead potter as he formed the jar, stopped and thought for a moment . . .?

> Time's wheel runs back or stops
> potter and clay endure.

Robert Browning, *Rabbi ben Ezra*, xxvii

APPENDIX:
SUGGESTED RECORDING SYSTEMS
FOR POTTERY FROM
ARCHAEOLOGICAL SITES

Introduction

The following recording scheme for pottery is based to a great extent on the systems devised for the Department of Urban Archaeology of the Museum of London in the mid-1970s (Orton 1979). This in turn draws heavily on earlier work in Britain (at Winchester and Gloucester for instance) and abroad (for example Carthage: Peacock 1977, 26–33).

Recording forms and cards

Sample recording forms for the quantification of pottery (fig. A.1), and cards for the description of fabrics (fig. A.2) are reproduced here – the relationship between them, and a record card for holding reproductions of drawings, is shown in fig. A.3.

Descriptive keywords for fabric description

The pottery-fabric descriptions used in reports and on fabric record cards are based on visual and tactile examinations of the surfaces and fresh breaks, both in the hand and using binocular microscope at ×20 or ×30 magnification.

The following characteristics are recorded: colour, hardness, feel, visual texture, inclusions, surface treatment, slip and glaze (if any). The conventions used in each of these categories are described below:

Colour	Munsell colour names and numbers are used. The colour of the core is always given, followed by the colour of the margin(s) (if different from the core) and the surface(s) (if different from the margins). Mixed colours are indicated by a solidus (/) – for example 'red/brown' – while partial colours (for example a core that fades out in places) are enclosed in brackets: '(grey) core, red margins' means that the grey core fades out in places, leaving an entirely red section.

231

Ceramics Recording Form	Site:		Context / Fabric:

Period:	Phase:	Date:	Sheet:

Fabric / Context:	Part	Form	Radius (cm)	Eve (%)	Weight (g)	Corpus	Comment

Notes:

Compiled by: __/__/__

Fig. A.1. Sample quantified pottery recording sheet

Hardness   The terms used are:

soft:	can be scratched with a fingernail.
hard:	cannot be scratched with a fingernail.
very hard:	cannot be scratched with a knife.

Table A.1. *Mohs' hardness scale and substitutes*

Scale	Mohs mineral	Substitute
1	Talc	
2	Gypsum	
2.5	—	Fingernail
3	Calcite	Copper wire
4	Fluorite	
4.5	—	Window glass
5	Apatite	
6	Orthoclase	Steel blade
7	Quartz	
8	Topaz	
9	Sapphire	
10	Diamond	

Publication reference:	**Fabric code:**
Context ref. of type-sherd(s):	**Common name:**

Colour: core:	ext.margin:	ext.surface:
	int.margin:	int.surface:

Hardness:	Feel:	Fracture:

Inclusions:				
Frequency:				
Sorting:				
Size:				
Rounding:				

Forming: Primary:
Secondary:

Slip: extent:	colour(s):
Glaze: extent:	colour(s):

Fig. A.2. Sample fabric recording card

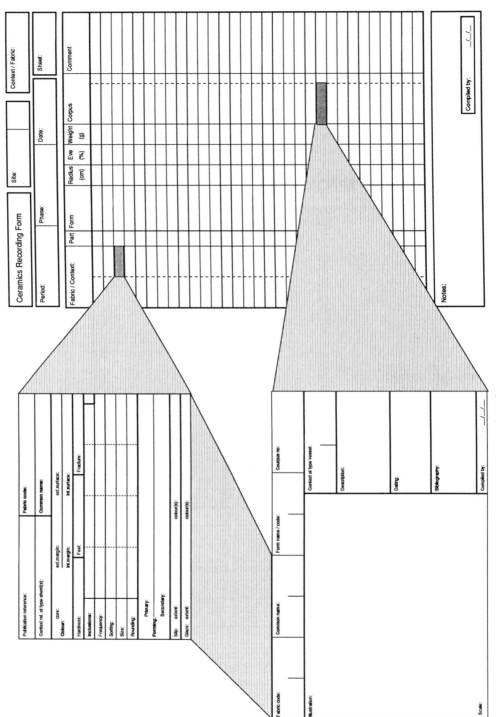

Fig. A.3. Relationship between data on recording sheets and cards

Feel   Basic terms employed are:

harsh: feels abrasive to the finger.
rough: irregularities can be felt.
smooth: no irregularities can be felt.

Two other terms which can be used are soapy and powdery. All refer to a surface in its basic state (for example without burnishing, which is described separately).

Texture   The terms at present used to describe a freshly broken section are:

subconchoidal: breaks somewhat like glass or flint.
smooth: flat or slightly curved, no visible irregularities.
fine: small, closely spaced irregularities.
irregular: larger, more widely spaced irregularities.
hackly: large and generally angular irregularities.
laminated: 'stepped' effect.

Descriptions refer to the section as seen by the unaided eye: for smooth fabrics, it is useful to add the texture as seen at ×20 magnification (for example 'smooth; irregular under lens').

Inclusions   Identification of inclusions is based on Peacock's algorithm (Peacock, 1977, 30–2; here table A.2.) A magnet is used to identify inclusions of iron ore and dilute hydrochloric acid to identify limestone, shell and so on. Colour is given when necessary – Munsell colour names are used, plus the terms clear (transparent, no intrinsic colour) and colourless (transparent or translucent, taking up colour of clay matrix to some extent).
Frequency. The frequency of inclusions is indicated on a three-point scale – abundant, moderate or sparse – or by reference to a percentage inclusion chart such as that on p. 238.

Table A.2. Key to identification of inclusions in pottery

A No inclusions visible – voids

1 Voids plate-like – sometimes curved and with striations — shell
2 Voids form perfect ovals or spheres c. 1mm across — oolite or limestone
3 Voids from rhombs — calcite
4 Voids irregular — limestone
5 Voids elongate with striations down length — grass or straw

B Inclusions react with dilute hydrochloric acid

1 Plate-like, curved, laminated or with structure at right angles to surface — shell
2 Inclusions form perfect ovals or spheres with concentric structure — oolite
3 Inclusions form perfect ovals or spheres without concentric structure — well rounded limestone
4 White or clear rhombs — calcite
5 Irregular lumps angular or rounded — limestone

C Inclusions homogeneous and do not react with acid

CC *Light coloured*

1 Glistening flakes — white mica
2 Clear glassy grains harder than metal — quartz
3 White glassy grains harder than metal — quartzite
4 Clusters of white glassy grains not well cemented together — quartz sandstone
5 Dull white or light grains
  a Easily scratched with metal
    1 Rhombs — dolomite
    2 With curved structure — calcined bone
  b Not easily scratched with metal
    1 Rectangular or subrectangular crystals – cleave well — felspar
    2 No visible crystals form, with conchoidal fracture — flint

Table A.2 (cont.)

CCC *Dark coloured*
1 Glistening flakes — *dark mica*
2 Red earthy grains
  a Well rounded
    1 Slightly magnetic – sometimes bright ochreous in colour — *red iron ore*
    2 Dull brown – clay-like — *clay pellets*
    3 Dull brown – clay-like but with laminations — *metasediment*
  b Angular
    1 Slightly magnetic, sometimes bright ochreous in colour — *red iron ore*
    2 Dull brown – clay-like — *grog*
3 Black grains
  a Shiny grains
    1 Metallic appearance. No crystal form, often well rounded — *black iron ore*
    2 Elongated rods often with striations down length, glassy appearance — *probably ferro-magnesian minerals*
  b Dull grains
    1 Soft, earthy, angular — *grog*
    2 Harder, flat grains, sometimes laminated — *metasediment (e.g. slate)*
    3 Not scratched with needle, no crystal structure, conchoidal fracture, angular — *flint*
    4 Scratched with needle, hackly fracture, formed of minute crystals — *basic igneous*
4 Hard red grains
  a Transparent or translucent — *quartz or quartzite*
  b Opaque rectangular or subrectangular crystals, cleave well — *felspar*
  c Opaque, conchoidal fracture — *flint*
  d Scratched with metal, hackley fracture, formed of minute crystals — *basic igneous*

D Inclusions heterogeneous and do not react with acid — *rock fragments*

Source: based on Peacock 1977, 30–2.

Size in mm

| Percentage | 0.5 to 1.0 | 0.5 to 2.0 | 0.5 to 3.0 |

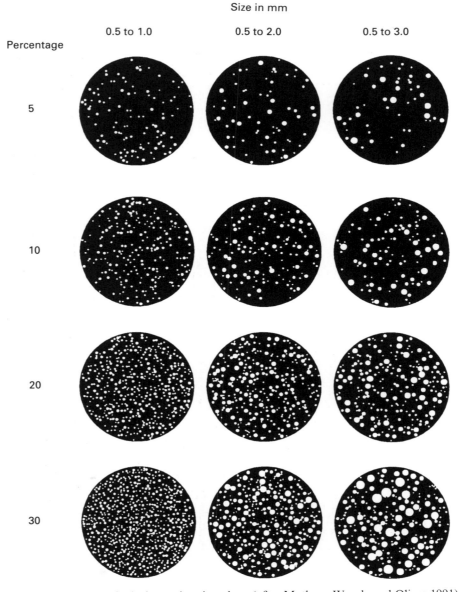

Fig. A.4. Percentage inclusion estimation chart (after Mathew, Woods and Oliver 1991)

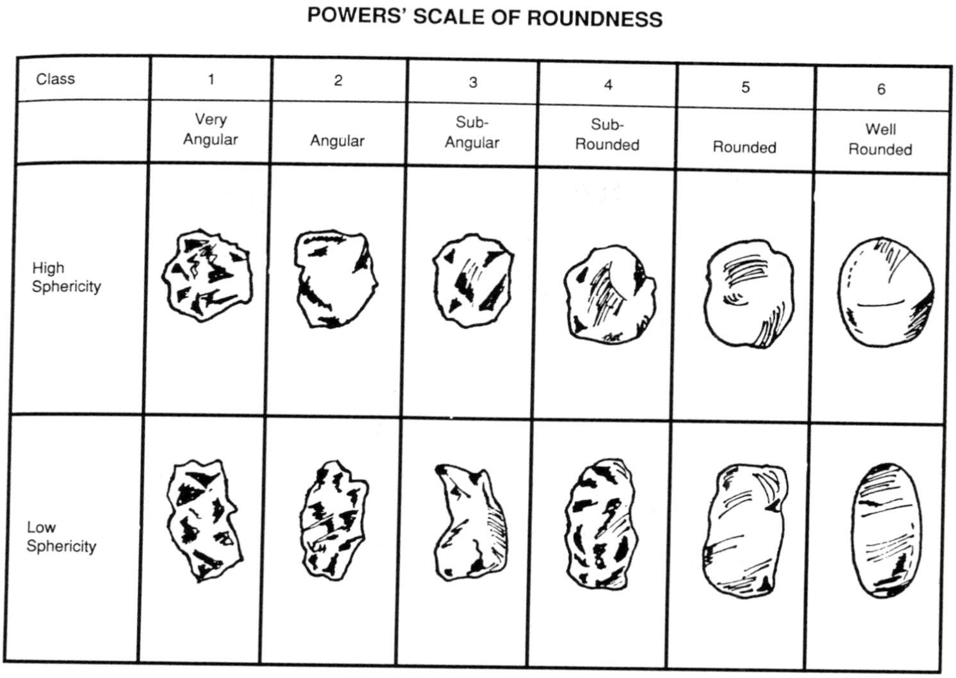

POWERS' SCALE OF ROUNDNESS

Class	1	2	3	4	5	6
	Very Angular	Angular	Sub-Angular	Sub-Rounded	Rounded	Well Rounded
High Sphericity						
Low Sphericity						

Fig. A.5. Sphericity/roundness estimation chart (from Barraclough 1992)

Scale for Pebble Sorting

Very Poor	Poor	Fair	Good	Very Good
1	2	3	4	5

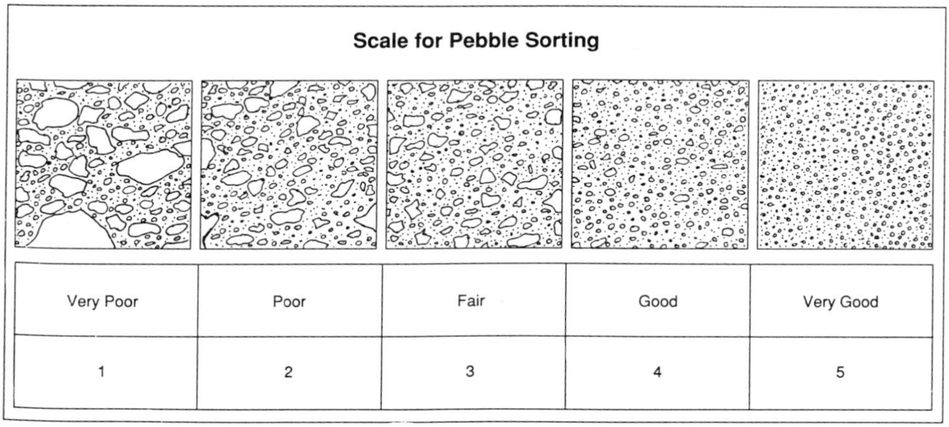

Fig. A.6. Inclusion sorting chart (from Barraclough 1992)

Size of inclusions. The terms used are based on the United States Department of Agriculture standard sizes for sand grains and are as follows:

very fine:	up to 0.1mm.
fine:	0.1 to 0.25mm.
medium:	0.25 to 0.5mm.
coarse:	0.5 to 1.00mm.
very coarse:	larger than 1.0mm.

Coarser inclusions are given to the nearest millimetre. The predominant size range is given – ranges in which lesser proportions are present are shown in brackets.

Sorting. Sorting indicates the homogeneity (in size) of the inclusions. Well-sorted grains are all about the same size, ill-assorted grains are not.

Rounding. The terms used are:

angular:	convex shape, sharp corners.
sub-angular:	convex shape, rounded-off corners.
rounded:	convex shape, no corners.
irregular:	convex/concave shape.
flat:	two-dimensional shape.

Reference may be made to a rounding/sphericity comparison chart such as that given in figure A.5.

Surface Treatment

The terms used are: wiped, smoothed, burnished, knife-trimmed, fingered and throwing marks.

Glaze

The extent, colour and finish are described. Terms used for extent are: all-over, areas, zones (that is areas with horizontal upper and lower edges), patches, streaks, runs, dribbles, spots.

Colour. The apparent colour (that is as actually seen) is given, except that obviously clear glazes are described as clear. Colourants in the glaze, and effects of inclusions in the clay, are described where possible.

Finish as seen at ×20 is preferred to an unaided description. Terms used are: lustrous, glossy, dull, sparse, pitted, crazed, smooth, thick, thin.

Slip   The convention is used that large zones of slip are a fabric characteristic but details are dealt with as decoration. Terms used are therefore:

(for extent):   all over, zone (plus location on vessel), see decoration.
(for finish):   continuous, sparse, smooth, lumpy, thin, micaceous, iron-rich.

Fabric coding scheme

The following simple coding scheme can be used to catalogue and organise a type-fabric collection. The coding describes the principal inclusion types and primary features of the construction and surface treatments.

Table A.3. *Moderate/abundant inclusions – upper case letters*

C	Organic
F	Flint
G	Grog
H	Shell
I	Ironstone
L	Limestone
M	Mica
N	Wares without obvious inclusions
S	Sand (quartz/quartzite)
V	Volcanic/igneous
X	Other/unknown

The code is given in dictionary order: thus GSby is a hand-formed, burnished fabric with abundant inclusions of grog and quartz sand. If sherds are stored so that fabrics with similar inclusions (that is similar codes) are kept together, then it is possible to match new sherds or fabrics by coding them and using this as a signpost to the most likely location of a match.

Table A.4. *Construction and surface treatments – lower case letters*

b	burnished
d	tin-glazed
f	salt-glazed
g	copper-stained glaze
k	other glaze
m	mica-slipped/dusted
n	slipped 'white' (high Munsell value)
o	other slipped
t	knife-trimmed
w	definitely wheel-made in whole or part
x	moulded
y	wheel not used/doubtful
z	other treatments

BIBLIOGRAPHY

Abercromby, J. 1904. 'A proposed chronological arrangement of the drinking cup or Beaker class of fictilia in Britain', *Proceedings of the Society of Antiquaries of Scotland*, 45: 323.

Adams, W. Y. 1979. 'On the argument from ceramics to history: a challenge based on evidence from medieval Nubia', *Current Anthropology*, 20: 727–44.

Aitchison, J. 1986. *The statistical analysis of compositional data* (London: Chapman and Hall).

Aitken, M. J. 1958. 'Magnetic dating – I', *Archaeometry*, 1: 16–20.

1990. *Scientific dating methods in archaeology* (London: Longmans).

Albinus, P. 1589. *Meissniche Chronica* (Dresden).

Albrecht, C. 1942. *Das Römerlager in Oberaden. Heft II: Die römische und belgische Keramik*, Veröffentlichungen aus dem Städt. Mus. für Vor- und Frühgeschichte Dortmund ii.2 (Dortmund).

Allen, J. R. L. 1989. 'A quantitative technique for assessing the roundness of pottery sherds in water contexts', *Geoarchaeology*, 4: 143–55.

Amé, E. 1859. *Les carrelages émaillés du Moyen-Age et de la Renaissance* (Paris).

André, J. 1961. *L'alimentation et la cuisine à Rome*, Etudes et Commentaires 38 (Paris: Klincksieck).

Arnold, D. E. 1978. 'Ethnography of pottery making in the Valley of Guatemala', in Wetherington, R. K. (ed.), *The ceramics from Kaminaljuyú, Guatemala*, Monograph series on Kaminaljuyú (University Park, Penn.: Pennsylvania State University Press), 327–400.

1985. *Ceramic theory and cultural process*, New studies in archaeology (Cambridge: Cambridge University Press).

Artis, E. T. 1823. *The Durobrivae* (London).

Attas, M., Fossey, J. M. and Yaffe, L. 1984. 'Corrections for drill-bit contamination in sampling ancient pottery for Neutron Activation analysis', *Archaeometry*, 26: 104–7.

Baif, L. 1536. *Lazari Bayfii annotationes* 2 De Vasculis (Paris).

Balfet, H. 1965. 'Ethnographical observations in North Africa and archeological interpretation', in Matson, F. R. (ed.), *Ceramics and man*, Wenner Gren Foundation for Anthropological Research, Viking Fund Publications in Anthropology 41 (Chicago: Aldine), 161–77.

Balfet, H., Fauvet Berthelot, M. F. and Mozon, S. 1989. *Lexique et typologie des poteries: pour la normalisation de la description des poteries* (Paris: Presses du CNRS).

Bamps, A. 1883. *La céramique americaine au point de vue des éléments constitutifs de la pâte et de sa fabrication*, Congrès des Americanistes Cinquième Session.

Barraclough, A. 1992. 'Quaternary sediment analysis: a deductive approach at A-level'. *Teaching Geography*, 17: 15–18.

van Bastelaar, D. A. 1877. *Les couverts, lustres, vernis, enduits, engobes, etc., de nature organique employés en céramique chez les Romains* (Anvers).

Bauer, I., Endres, W., Kerkhoff-Hader, B., Koch, R. and Stephan, H.-G. 1986. *Leitfaden zur Keramikbeschreibung (Mittelalter–Neuzeit). Terminologie – Typologie – Technologie*, Kataloge der Prähistorischen Staatssammlung Beiheft 2 (Munich).

Baumhoff, M. A. and Heizer, R. F. 1959. 'Some unexploited possibilities in ceramic analysis', *Southwestern Journal of Anthropology* 15: 308–16.

243

Baxter, M. J. and Heyworth, M. P. 1989. 'Principal components analysis of compositional data in archaeology', in Rahtz, S. P. Q. and Richards, J. D. (eds.), *Computer applications and quantitative methods in archaeology 1989*, British Archaeological Reports, International Series 548 (Oxford: BAR), 227–40.

Beals, R. L., Brainerd, G. W. and Smith, W. 1945. *Archaeological studies in northeast Arizona*, University of California Publications in American Archaeology and Anthropology 44 (Berkeley).

Bech, J.-M. 1988. 'Correspondence analysis and pottery chronology. A case study from the late Roman Iron Age cemetery Slusegard', in Madsen, T. (ed.), *Multivariate archaeology*, Jutland Archaeological Society 21, 29–35.

de la Beche, Sir H. and Reeks, T. 1855. *Catalogue of specimens illustrative of the composition and manufacture of British pottery and porcelain from the occupation of Britain by the Romans to the present time* (London: Museum of Practical Geology).

Beckmann, B. 1974. 'The main types of the first four production periods of Siegburg pottery', in Evison, V. I., Hodges, H. and Hurst, J. G. (eds.), *Medieval pottery from excavations* (London: John Baker), 183–220.

Bedaux, R. and van der Waals, D. 1987. 'Aspects of life-span of Dogon pottery', *Newsletter. Department of Pottery Technology* (*University of Leiden*), 5: 137–53.

Bedwin, O. and Orton, C. R. 1984. 'The excavation of the eastern terminal of the Devil's Ditch, West Sussex, 1982', *Sussex Archaeological Collections*, 122: 63–74 and fiche.

Bennett, W. J., Blakeley, J. A., Brinkmann, R. and Vitaliano, C. J. 1989. 'The provenience postulate: thoughts on the use of physical and chemical data in the study of ceramic materials', in Blakeley, J. A. and Bennett, W. J. (eds.), *Analysis and publication of ceramics*, British Archaeological Reports, International Series 551 (Oxford: BAR), 31–44.

Benzécri, J. P. 1973. *L'analyse des données: II. L'analyse des correspondances* (Paris: Dunod).

Biddle, M. 1972. 'Excavations at Winchester, 1970 ninth interim report', *Antiquaries Journal*, 52: 93–131.

Bimson, M. 1956. 'The techniques of Greek Black and Terra Sigillata Red', *Antiquaries Journal*, 36: 200–4.

  1969. 'The examination of ceramics by X-ray powder diffraction', *Studies in Conservation*, 14: 85–9.

  1970. 'The significance of 'ale-measure' marks', *Post-medieval archaeology*, 4: 165–6.

Binns, C. F. 1898. *The history of the potter* (London).

Binns, C. F. and Frazer, A. D. 1929. 'The Genesis of the Greek Black Glaze', *American Journal of Archaeology*, 33: 1–10.

Birch, S. 1858. *History of Ancient Pottery* (London).

Bird, D. G. and Turner, D. J. 1974. 'Reigate: fifteenth-century coin hoard', *Surrey Archaeological Collections*, 70: 166–7.

Birkhoff, G. D. 1933. *Aesthetic measure* (Cambridge: Cambridge University Press).

Bishop, R. L., Canouts, V., Crown, P. L. and De Atley, S. P. 1990. 'Sensitivity, precision and accuracy: their roles in ceramic compositional data bases', *American Antiquity*, 55(3): 537–46.

Bishop, R. L., Rands, R. L. and Holley, G. R. 1982. 'Ceramic compositional analysis in archaeological perspective', in Schiffer, M. B. (ed.), *Advances in archaeological method and theory* 5 (New York: Academic Press), 275–330.

Bishop, Y. M. M., Fienberg, S. E. and Holland, P. W. 1975. *Discrete multivariate analysis* (Cambridge, Mass.: MIT Press).

Blake, H. 1980. 'Technology, supply or demand?', *Medieval Ceramics*, 4: 3–12.

Blake, H. and Davey, P. 1983. *Guidelines for the processing and publication of medieval pottery from excavations*, Directorate of Ancient Monuments and Historic Buildings Occasional Paper 5 (London: HMSO).

Blanchet, A. 1899. *Les ateliers de céramique dans la Gaule-romaine* (Paris).

Bloice, B. J. 1971. 'Montague Close part 2', *London Archaeologist*, 1(11): 250–1.

Bloice, B. J. and Dawson, G. J. 1971. 'Norfolk House, Lambeth: excavations at a delftware kiln site', *Post-medieval Archaeology*, 5: 99–159 (119–29).

Boardman, J. 1976. *Athenian red-figure wares: the archaic period, a handbook* (London: Thames and Hudson).

Bonnamour, L. and Marinval, P. 1985. 'Céramiques gallo-romaines précoces avec dépôt du millet dans la moyenne vallée de la Saône', *Revue archéologique de l'Est et du Centre-Est*, 36: 321–5.

Bös, M. 1958. 'Aufschriften auf rheinischen Trinkgefässen der Römerzeit', *Kölner Jahrbuch für Vor- und Frühgeschichte*, 3: 20–5.

Bradley, R. and Fulford, M. G. 1980. 'Sherd size in the analysis of occupation debris', *Bulletin of the Institute of Archaeology*, 17: 85–94.

Brainerd, G. W. 1951. 'The place of ordering in archaeological analysis', *American Antiquity*, 16: 301–13.

Braithwaite, M. 1982. 'Decoration as ritual symbol: a theoretical proposal and an ethnographic study in southern Sudan', in Hodder, I. (ed.), *Symbolic and structural archaeology* (Cambridge: Cambridge University Press), 80–8.

Braudel, F. 1981. *The structures of everyday life* (London: Collins).

Brears, P. 1989. 'The continuing tradition', *Medieval Ceramics*, 13: 3–8.

Brongniart, M. A. 1844. *Traité des arts céramiques, ou des poteries, considérées dans leur histoire, leur pratique et leur théorie* (Paris).

Bronitsky, G. 1986. 'The use of materials science techniques in the study of pottery construction and use', in Schiffer, M. B. (ed.), *Advances in archaeological method and theory* 9 (New York: Academic Press) 209–76.

Bronitsky, G. and Hamer, R. 1986. 'Experiments in ceramic technology: the effects of various tempering materials on impact and thermal-shock resistance', *American Antiquity*, 51: 89–101.

Brooks, C. and Mainman, A. 1984. 'Torksey Ware viewed from the North', in Addyman, P. V. and Black, V. E. (eds.), *Archaeological papers from York presented to M. W. Barley* (York: York Archaeological Trust), 63–70.

Brown, D. 1985. 'Looking at cross-fits', *Medieval Ceramics*, 9: 35–42.

Browne, Sir T. 1658. *Hydriotaphia. Urne burial* (London).

Bryant, G. F. 1977. 'Experimental kiln firings at Barton-on-Humber, S. Humberside, 1971', *Medieval Archaeology*, 21: 106–23.

1978–9. 'Romano-British experimental kiln firings at Barton-on-Humber, England, 1968–1975', *Acta Prehistorica et Archaeologica*, 9/10: 13–22.

Buck, C. E. and Litton, C. D. 1991. 'A Bayes approach to some archaeological problems', in Lockyear, K. and Rahtz, S. P. Q. (eds.), *Computer applications and quantitative methods in archaeology 1990*, British Archaeological Reports, International Series 565 (Oxford: Tempus Reparatum), 93–9.

Buko, A. 1981. *Wczesno-średniowieczna ceramika Sandomierska* (Warsaw: Polish Academy).

Bulmer, M. 1979. 'An introduction to Roman samian ware', *Journal of the Chester Archaeological Society*, 62: 5–72.

Bunzel, R. L. 1929. *The Pueblo potter* (New York: Columbia University Press).

Burgh, R. F. 1959. 'Ceramic profiles in the Western Mound at Awotovi, Northeastern Arizona', *American Antiquity*, 25: 184–202.

Byers, D. S. 1937. 'On standards for texture in pottery', *American Antiquity*, 3: 76–7.

Cailleux, A. and Taylor, G. 1963. *Code expolaire* (Paris: Boubée).

Carr, C. 1990. 'Advances in ceramic radiography and analysis: applications and potential', *Journal of Archaeological Science*, 17(1): 13–34.

Carver, M. O. H. 1985. 'Theory and practice in urban pottery seriation', *Journal of Archaeological Science*, 12(5): 353–66.

Castillo Tejero, N. and Litvak, J. 1968. *Un sistema de estudio para formas de csaijas*, Technologia 2 (Mexico: Departmento de Prehistória, Instituto Nacional de Antropologío e Historia).

Catling, H. W., Blin-Stoyle, A. E. and Richards, E. E. 1961. 'Spectrographic analysis of Mycenean and Minoan pottery', *Archaeometry*, 4: 31–8.

 1963. 'Correlations between compositions and provenance of Mycenean and Minoan pottery', *Annual Report of the British School at Athens*, 58: 94–115.

de Caumont, A. 1850. *Quelques produits céramiques du moyen-age* (Caen).

Celoria, F. S. C. and Kelly, J. H. 1973. *A post-medieval pottery site with a kiln base found off Albion Square, Hanley, Stoke-on-Trent, Staffordshire, England SJ 885474*, Archaeological Society Report 4 (Stoke-on-Trent: City of Stoke-on-Trent Museum).

Chase, P. G. 1985. 'Whole vessels and sherds: an experimental investigation of their quantitative relationship', *Journal of Field Archaeology*, 12: 213–8.

Childe, V. G. 1929. *The Danube in prehistory* (Oxford: Clarendon Press).

Church, A. H. 1870. *Catalogue of the specimens of the Old English pottery in the collection of A. H. Church* (Cirencester).

Ciolek-Torillo, R. 1984. 'An alternative model of room function from Grasshopper Pueblo, Arizona', in Hietala, H. J. (ed.), *Intrasite spatial analysis in archaeology* (Cambridge: Cambridge University Press), 127–53.

Cochet, Abbé 1860. *Archéologie céramique et sépulchrale; ou l'art de classer les sépultures anciennes à l'aide de la céramique* (Paris).

Cockle, H. 1981. 'Roman manufacture in Roman Egypt. A new papyrus', *Journal of Roman Studies*, 71: 87–97.

Coleman-Smith, R. 1971. 'Experiments in ancient bonfire-fired pottery', *Ceramic Review*, 12: 6–7.

Colls, D., Etienne, R., Leuement, R., Liou, B. and Mayet, F. 1977. *L'Epave Port Vendres II et le commerce de la Bétique à l'époque de Claude*, Archaeonautica 1 (Paris: CNRS).

Colt Hoare, R. 1812. *The ancient history of south Wiltshire* (London: Miller).

Colton, H. S. 1939. 'Primitive pottery firing methods', *Museum notes, Museum of Northern Arizona*, 11(10): 63–6.

 1953. *Potsherds. An introduction to the study of prehistoric southwestern ceramics and their use in historic reconstruction*, Museum of Northern Arizona Bulletin 23 (Flagstaff, Arizona).

Colton, H. S. and Hargraves, L. L. 1937. *Handbook of north Arizona pottery wares*, Museum of Northern Arizona Bulletin 11 (Flagstaff, Arizona).

Combe, C. and Jackson, J. 1787. 'Account of the discoveries in digging a sewer in Lombard-street and Birchin-lane, 1786', *Archaeologia*, 8: 116–32.

Conyers, J. 1675. *Sloane MSS 958, f. 105, f. 108ff* (London: British Museum).

 1677. *Sloane MSS 958, f. 106–7* (London: British Museum).

Cornwall, I. W. and Hodges, H. W. M. 1964. 'Thin sections of British Neolithic pottery: Windmill Hill – a test site', *Bulletin of the Institute of Archaeology of London University*, 4: 29–33.

Cowgill, G. L. 1970. 'Some sampling and reliability problems in archaeology', in *Archéologie et calculateurs: problèmes sémiologiques et mathématiques* (Paris: CNRS), 161–75.

 1972. 'Models, methods and techniques for seriation', in Clarke, D. L. (ed.), *Models in archaeology* (London: Methuen), 381–424.

Crummy, P. and Terry, R. 1979. 'Seriation problems in urban archaeology', in Millett, M. (ed.), *Pottery and the archaeologist*, Institute of Archaeology Occasional Publications 4, 49–60.

Crusoe, D. L. 1971. 'The missing half: the analysis of ceramic fabric', *Southeastern Archaeological Conference Bulletin*, 13: 108–14.

Cuomo di Caprio, N. 1971–2. 'Proposta di classificazione della fornaci per cermica e laterizi nell'area italiana', *Sibrium*, 11: 373–464.

Cushing, F. H. 1886. *A study of Pueblo pottery as illustrative of Zuni culture growth*, Annual Report, Bureau of American Ethnology 4 (Washington, DC: Bureau of American Ethnology).

Darvill, T. and Timby, J. 1982. 'Textural analysis: a review of limitations and possibilities', in Freestone, I. C., Johns, C. and Potter, T. (eds.), *Current research in ceramics: thin-section studies*, British Museum Occasional Paper 32 (London: British Museum), 73–87.

Davey, P. and Hodges, R. 1983. 'Ceramics and trade: a critique of the archaeological evidence', in Davey, P. and Hodges, R. (eds.), *Ceramics and trade. The production and distribution of later medieval pottery in north-west Europe* (Sheffield: Department of Prehistory and Archaeology, University of Sheffield), 1–14.

David, E. 1959. *French country cooking* (Harmondsworth: Penguin).

David, N. 1972. 'On the lifespan of pottery, type frequencies and archaeological inference', *American Antiquity*, 37: 141–2.

David, N. and Hennig, H. 1972. *The ethnography of pottery: a Fulani study seen in archaeological perspective*, Addison-Wesley Modular Publications 21 (Reading, Mass.: Addison-Wesley).

Davis, N. 1971. *Paston letters and papers of the fifteenth century; part 1* (Oxford: Clarendon Press).

DeBoer, W. R. 1974. 'Ceramic longevity and archaeological interpretation: an example from the Upper Ucalayi, Peru', *American Antiquity*, 39: 335–43.

DeBoer, W. R. and Lathrap, D. W. 1979. 'The making and breaking of Shipibo-Conibo ceramics', in Kramer, C. (ed.), *Ethnoarchaeology: implications of ethnography for archaeology* (New York: Columbia University Press), 102–38.

Déchelette, J. 1904. *Les vases céramiques de la Gaule romaine* (Paris).

Dempsey, P. and Baumhoff, M. 1963. 'The statistical use of artefact distributions to establish chronological sequences', *American Antiquity*, 28: 496–509.

Desbat, A. 1989. 'Aperçu et réflexions sur les techniques traditionelles des céramiques à partir d'exemples marocains', in Rivet, L. (ed.), *Actes du Congrès de Lezoux 4–7 Mai 1989* (Marseille: Société Française d'Etude de la Céramique Antique en Gaule), 143–52.

DeVore, I. 1968. 'Comments', in Binford, L. R. and Binford, S. R. (eds.), *New perspectives in archaeology* (New York: Aldine), 346–9.

Doran, J. E. 1971. 'Computer analysis of data from the La Tène cemetery at Münsingen-Rain', in Hodson, F. R., Kendall, D. G. and Tautu, P. (eds.), *Mathematics in the archaeological and historical sciences* (Edinburgh: Edinburgh University Press), 422–31.

Doran, J. E. and Hodson, F. R. 1975. *Mathematics and computers in archaeology* (Edinburgh: Edinburgh University Press).

Dornbusch, J. B. 1873. *Die Kunstgilde der Töpfer in der abteilichen Stadt Siegburg* (Köln).

Douglas, F. H. and Raynolds, F. R. (eds.) 1941. 'Pottery design terminology – final report on questionnaires', *Clearing House for Southwestern Museums Newsletter*, 35.

Dragendorff, H. 1895. 'Terra sigillata', *Bonner Jahrbücher*, 96: 18–155.

Draper, J. 1975. *Dated post-medieval pottery in Northampton Museum* (Northampton: Northampton Museum and Art Gallery).

Drier, R. W. 1939. 'A new method of sherd classification', *American Antiquity*, 5: 31–5.

Drury, P. J. 1981. 'The production of brick and tile in medieval England', in Crossley, D. W. (ed.), *Medieval industry*, Council for British Archaeology Research Report (London: Council for British Archaeology), 126–42.

Duhamel, P. 1973. 'Les fours céramiques gallo-romains', in Duval, P.-M. (ed.), *Recherches d'archéologie celtique et gallo-romaine*, Hautes études du monde gréco-romaine 5 (Paris–Geneva: Centre de recherches de l'histoire et de philologie de la IVème section de l'Ecole Pratique des Hautes Etudes, III), 141–54.

Dunnell, R. C. 1970. 'Seriation method and its evaluation', *American Antiquity*, 35: 305–19.

1990. 'Artefact size and lateral displacement under tillage: comments on the Odell and Cowan experiment', *American Antiquity*, 55(3): 592–4.

Dyer, D. 1982. 'The social and economic changes of the later Middle Ages and the pottery of the period', *Medieval Ceramics*, 6: 33–42.

Edwards, B. J. N. 1974. 'A pottery drawing aid', *Antiquity*, 48: 230–2.

Edwards, I. and Jacobs, L. 1986. 'Experiments with stone pottery wheel bearings – notes on the use of rotation in the production of ancient pottery', *Newsletter. Department of Pottery Technology (University of Leiden)*, 4: 49–55.

Egloff, B. J. 1973. 'A method for counting ceramic rim sherds', *American Antiquity*, 38(3): 351–3.

Emeleus, V. M. 1960. 'Neutron activation analysis of samian ware sherds', *Archaeometry*, 3: 16–24.

Ericson, J. E. and Stickel, E. G. 1973. 'A proposed classification system for ceramics', *World Archaeology*, 4: 357–67.

Evans, C. and Meggars, B. J. 1962. 'Use of organic temper for Carbon 14 dating in lowland South America', *American Antiquity*, 28: 243–5.

Evans, J. 1983–4. 'Identification of organic residues in ceramics', *Bulletin of the Experimental Firing Group*, 2: 82–5.

Falbe, C. T. 1843. *Vases antiques de Pérou* (Copenhagen).

Farrar, R. A. H. 1973. 'The techniques and sources of Romano-British black-burnished ware', in Detsicas, A. P. (ed.), *Current research in Romano-British coarse pottery*, Council for British Archaeology Research Report 10, 67–103.

Faure-Boucharlat, E. (ed.) 1990. *A la fortune du pot; la cuisine et la table à Lyon et à Vienne Xe-XIXe siècles d'après les fouilles archéologiques* (Lyon: Musée de la Civilisation Gallo-Romaine).

Fleming, S. J. 1966. 'Study of thermoluminescence of crystalline extracts from pottery', *Archaeometry*, 9: 170–3.

1970. 'Thermoluminescence dating: refinement of the quartz inclusion method', *Archaeometry*, 12: 133–45.

1979. *Thermoluminescence techniques in archaeology* (Oxford: Clarendon Press).

Fletcher, M. and Lock, G. R. 1991. *Digging numbers: elementary statistics for archaeologists*, Oxford University Committee for Archaeology Monograph 31 (Oxford).

Ford, J. A. 1954. 'The type concept revisited', *American Anthropologist*, 56: 42–53.

1962. *A quantitative method for deriving cultural chronology*, Pan American Union Technical Manual 1 (Washington).

Ford, J. A. and Quimby, G. I. 1945. *The Tchefuncte culture, an early occupation of the lower Mississippi Valley*. Memoirs of the Society for American Archaeology 2 (Menasha, Wis.).

Formenti, F., Hesnard, A. and Tchernia, A. 1978. 'Une amphore Lamboglia 2 contenant du vin dans l'épave de la Madrague de Giens', *Archaeonautica*, 2: 95–100.

Foster, B. 1963. *The local port book of Southampton 1435–36* (Southampton: Southampton University Press).

Foster, G. M. 1959. 'The potter's wheel: an analysis of idea and artefact in invention', *Southwestern Journal of Anthropology*, 15: 99–118.

1960. 'Life-expectancy of utilitarian pottery in Tzintzuntzan, Michoacan, Mexico', *American Antiquity*, 25: 606–9.

Franchet, L. 1911. *Céramique primitive: introduction à l'étude de la technologie* (Paris: Geuthner).

Franken, H. J. and Kalsbeek, J. 1969. *Excavations at Tell Deir 'Alla*, Alla 1 (Leiden).
   1984. 'Iron Age pottery from Haren (Northern Brabant, The Netherlands)', *Newsletter. Department of Pottery Technology (University of Leiden)*, 2: 17–26.
Freestone, I. C. 1982. 'Applications and potential of electron probe micro analysis in technological and provenance investigations of ancient ceramics', *Archaeometry*, 24: 99–116.
Freestone, I. C., Meeks, N. D. and Middleton, A. P. 1985. 'Retention of phosphate in buried ceramics: an electron microprobe approach', *Archaeometry*, 27: 161–77.
Fulford, M. G. 1975. *New Forest Roman pottery*, British Archaeological Reports, British Series 17 (Oxford: BAR).
Fulford, M. G. and Hodder, I. 1974. 'A regression analysis of some later Romano-British pottery: a case study', *Oxoniensia*, 39: 26–33.
Fulford, M. G. and Huddleston, K. 1991. *The current state of Romano-British pottery studies*, English Heritage Occasional Papers 1 (London: English Heritage).
Fulford, M. G. and Peacock, D. P. S. (eds.) 1984. *The Avenue du President Habib Bourguiba, Salammbo: the pottery and other ceramic objects from the site*, Excavations at Carthage: The British Mission I, 2.
Gaffney, C., Gaffney, V. and Tingle, M. 1985. 'Settlement, economy and behaviour? Micro-regional land use models and the interpretation of surface artefact patterns', in Haselgrove, C., Millett, M. and Smith, I. (eds.), *Archaeology from the ploughsoil* (Sheffield: Department of Archaeology and Prehistory, University of Sheffield), 95–107.
Gardin, J.-C. 1958. 'Four codes for the description of artefacts: an essay in archaeological technique and theory', *American Anthropologist*, 60: 335–57.
   1985. *Code pour l'analyse des formes de poteries* (Paris: CNRS).
Garnier, E. 1880. *Histoire de la céramique* (Tours).
Geological Society of America 1948. *Rock-Color chart* (Boulder, Colo.: Geological Society of America).
Gifford, E. W. 1951. 'Archaeological excavations in Fiji', *Anthropological Records*, 13: 189–288.
Gifford, J. C. 1960. 'The type-variety method of ceramic classification as an indicator of cultural phenomena', *American Antiquity*, 25: 341–7.
Gillam, J. P. 1957. 'Types of Roman coarse pottery in northern Britain', *Archaeologia Aeliana*, 35: 180–251.
Gillin, J. 1938. 'A method of notation for the description and comparison of southwestern pottery sherds by formula', *American Antiquity*, 4: 22–9.
Gladwin, N. 1937. 'Petrography of Snaketown pottery', in Gladwin, H. S. (ed.), *Excavations at Snaketown*, Medallion Papers, Gila Pueblo, Arizona 25.
Glanzman, W. D. 1983. 'Xeroradiographic examination of pottery manufacturing techniques: a test case from the Baq'ah valley, Jordan', *MASCA Journal*, 2(6): 163–9.
Glock, A. E. 1975. 'Homo Faber: the pot and the potter at Taranach', *Bulletin of American Schools of Oriental Research*, 219: 9–28.
Glover, I. C. 1972. *Excavations in Timor* (Canberra: Australian National University).
   1990. 'Ban Don Ta Phet 1984–85', in Glover, I. C. and Glover, E. (eds.), *Southeast Asian Archaeology 1986*, British Archaeological Reports, International Series 561 (Oxford: BAR), 139–83.
Going, C. J. 1987. *The Mansio and other sites in south-eastern sector of Caesaromagus: the Roman pottery*, Council for British Archaeology Research Report 62 (London: Council for British Archaeology).
Goldmann, K. 1972. 'Zwei Methoden chronologischer Gruppierung', *Acta Praehistorica et Archaeologica*, 3: 1–34.
Goody, J. C. 1982. *Cooking, cuisine and culture* (Cambridge: Cambridge University Press).
Green, C. M. 1980. 'Roman pottery', in Jones, D. M. (ed.), *Excavations at Billingsgate Build-*

ings Triangle, Lower Thames Street, 1974, London and Middlesex Archaeological Society, Special Paper 4 (London: LAMAS), 39–80.

Greenacre, M. J. 1984. *Theory and applications of correspondence analysis* (London: Academic Press).

Greene, J. P. and Johnson, B. 1978. 'An experimental tile kiln at Norton Priory, Cheshire', *Medieval Ceramics*, 2: 31–42.

Greene, K. T. 1979. *The pre-Flavian fine wares*, Report on the excavations at Usk 1965–1976 (Cardiff: University of Wales Press).

Greenwell, W. 1877. *British barrows* (Oxford: Clarendon Press).

Griffin, J. B. 1950–54. *Prehistoric pottery of the eastern United States* (Ann Arbor: University of Michigan Museum of Anthropology).

Griffiths, D. 1978. 'Use-marks on historic ceramics: a preliminary study', *Historical Archaeology*, 12: 68–81.

Griffiths, N., Jenner, A. and Wilson, C. 1990. *Drawing archaeological finds* (London: Archetype Publications).

Grignon 1774. *Fouilles d'une ville romaine sur la montagne du Châtelet* (Paris).

Grimshaw, R. W. 1980. *The chemistry and physics of clays and allied ceramic materials* (New York: John Wiley).

Grivaux de la Vincelle, C. M. 1807. *Antiquités gauloises et romaines receuillies dans les jardins du Palais du Sénat* (Paris).

Groevius and Gronovius 1694. *Thesaurus antiquitatum* (Traj. ad Rhenum).

Gruner, D. 1973. *Die Berber-Keramik*, Studien zur Kulterkunde 33 (Wiesbaden: Franz Steiner).

Guiseppi, M. S. 1937. 'Medieval pottery in Kingston upon Thames', *Surrey Archaeological Collections*, 45: 151–2.

Günther, A. 1901. 'Augusteisches Gräberfeld bei Coblenz-Neuerdorf', *Bonner Jahrbücher*, 107: 73–94.

Guthe, C. E. 1925. *Pueblo pottery making, a study at the village of San Ildefonso*, Papers of the Southwestern Expedition, Department of Anthropology 2 (New Haven: Yale University Press).

    1927. *A method of ceramic description.* Papers of the Michigan Academy of Science, Arts and Letters 8.

Hagstrum, M. B. and Hildebrand, J. A. 1990. 'The two-curve method for reconstructing ceramic morphology', *American Antiquity*, 55(2): 388–403.

Hall, N. S. and Laflin, S. 1984. 'A computer aided design technique for pottery profiles', in Laflin, S. (ed.), *Computer applications in archaeology 1984* (Birmingham: Computer Centre, University of Birmingham), 178–88.

Hally, D. J. 1983. 'Use alteration of pottery vessel surfaces: an important source of evidence in the identification of vessel function', *North American Archaeologist*, 4: 3–26.

Hamilton, S. 1977. 'Excavations at Bishopstone', *Sussex Archaeological Collections*, 115: 83–118.

Hamilton, Sir W. 1766–67. *Etruscan, Greek and Roman vases from the cabinet of Sir W. Hamilton* (Naples).

Hamon, E. and Hesnard, A. 1977. 'Problèmes de documentation et de description relatifs à un corpus d'amphores romaines', in *Méthodes classiques et méthodes formelles dans l'étude des amphores*, Collection de l'Ecole Française de Rome 32 (Rome), 17–33.

Hampe, R. and Winter, A. 1962. *Bei Töpfern und Töpferinnen in Kreta Messenien und Zypern* (Mainz: Römisch-Germanisches Zentralmuseum).

    1965. *Bei Töpfern und Zieglern in Süditalien Sizilien und Greichenland* (Mainz: Römisch-Germanisches Zentralmuseum).

Harbottle, G. 1982. 'Provenience studies using neutron activation analysis: the role of standardization', in Olin, J. S. and Franklin, A. D. (eds.), *Archaeological ceramics* (Washington DC: Smithsonian Institution Press), 67–77.

Hardy-Smith, A. 1974. 'Post-medieval pot shapes: a quantitative analysis', *Science and Archaeology*, 11: 4–15.

Hargraves, L. L. and Smith, W. 1936. 'A method for determining the texture of pottery', *American Antiquity*, 2: 32–6.

Hart, F. A. and Adams, S. J. 1983. 'The chemical analysis of Romano-British pottery from the Alice Holt Forest, Hampshire, by means of inductively coupled plasma emission spectrometry', *Archaeometry*, 25: 179–85.

Haselgrove, C. 1985. 'Inference from ploughsoil', in Haselgrove, C., Millett, M. and Smith, I. (eds.), *Archaeology from the ploughsoil* (Sheffield: Department of Archaeology and Prehistory, University of Sheffield), 7–30.

Haselgrove, C., Millett, M. and Smith, I. (eds.) 1985. *Archaeology from the ploughsoil* (Sheffield: Department of Archaeology and Prehistory, University of Sheffield).

Haslam, J. 1975. 'The excavation of a 17th-century pottery site at Cove, E. Hampshire', *Post-Medieval Archaeology*, 9: 164–87.

Hayes, J. W. 1972. *Late Roman pottery* (London: The British School at Rome).

von Hefner, J. 1862. *Die römische Töpferei in Westerndorf* (München).

von Hefner, J. and Wolf, J. W. 1850. *Die Burg Tannenburg* (Frankfurt-am-Main).

Hendrickson, E. M. and McDonald, M. A. 1983. 'Ceramic form and function: an ethnographic search and archaeological explanation', *American Anthropologist*, 85: 630–43.

Hennicker, J. M. 1796. *Two letters on the origin of Norman tiles* (London).

Hermet, F. 1934. *La Graufesenque* (Paris: Ernest Leroux).

Heron, C. and Pollard, A. M. 1987. 'The analysis of natural resinous materials from Roman amphorae', in Slater, E. A. and Tate, J. O. (eds.), *Science and archaeology, Glasgow, 1987*, British Archaeological Reports, British Series 196 (Oxford: BAR), 429–47.

Hietala, H. J. (ed.) 1984. *Intrasite spatial analysis in archaeology* (Cambridge: Cambridge University Press).

Hilgers, W. 1969. *Lateinische Gefässnamen*, Beihefte Bonner Jahrbücher 31 (Düsseldorf).

Hill, H. E. 1983–84. 'Chemical analysis of pottery residues' *Bulletin of the Experimental Firing Group*, 2: 86–9.

Hill, J. N. 1970. *Broken K Pueblo: prehistoric social organization in the American South-west*, University of Arizona Anthropological Papers 18 (Tucson: University of Arizona Press).

Hill, M. O. 1974. 'Correspondence analysis: a neglected multivariate method', *Applied Statistics*, 23(3): 340–54.

Hinton, D. A. 1977. '"Rudely made earthen vessels" of the twelfth to fifteenth centuries AD', in Peacock, D. P. S. (ed.), *Pottery and early commerce* (London: Academic Press), 221–38.

Hinton, M. P. 1980. 'Medieval pottery from a kiln site at Kingston upon Thames', *London Archaeologist*, 3(14): 377–83.

Hirth, F. 1888. *Ancient porcelain: a study in Chinese medieval industry and trade* (London).

Hobson, R. L. 1903. *British Museum catalogue of English pottery* (London: British Museum).

Hodder, I. 1979. 'Pottery distribution: service and tribal areas', in Millett, M. (ed.), *Pottery and the archaeologist*, Institute of Archaeology Occasional Publications 4 (London: Institute of Archaeology), 7–24.

    1982. *Symbols in action: ethnoarchaeological studies of material culture* (Cambridge: Cambridge University Press).

    1986. *Reading the past: current approaches to interpretation in archaeology* (Cambridge: Cambridge University Press).

Hodder, I. and Orton, C. R. 1976. *Spatial analysis in archaeology* (Cambridge: Cambridge University Press).

Hodges, H. W. M. 1962. 'Thin sections of prehistoric pottery: an empirical study', *Bulletin of the University of London Institute of Archaeology*, 3: 58–68.

Holladay, J. S. 1976. 'A technical aid to pottery drawing', *Antiquity*, 50: 223–9.

Holmes, W. H. 1886. 'Pottery of the ancient pueblos', in *Fourth report of the bureau of Ethnology* (Washington), 257–360.

Howard, H. and Morris, E. (eds.) 1980. *Production and distribution: a ceramic viewpoint*, British Archaeological Reports, International Series 120 (Oxford: BAR).

Hughes, M. J., Cowell, M. R. and Craddock, P. T. 1976. 'Atomic absorption techniques in archaeology', *Archaeometry*, 18: 19–37.

Hulthén, B. 1974. *On documentation of pottery*, Acta Archaeologica Lundensia (Lund).

Hume, I. N. 1977. *Early English Delftware from London and Virginia*, Colonial Williamsburg Occasional Papers in Archaeology 2.

Huntley, D. J., Godfrey-Smith, D. I. and Thewalt, M. L. W. 1985. 'Optical dating of sediments', *Nature*, 313: 105–7.

Hurst, J. G. 1977. 'Annotations on Anglo-Saxon pottery', *Medieval Ceramics*, 1: 75–8.
   1982. 'Gerald Dunning and his contribution to medieval archaeology', *Medieval Ceramics*, 6: 3–20.

Ihm, P. 1981. *The Gaussian model in chronological seriation*, Proceedings of the 10th Congress of the International Union for Prehistoric and Protohistoric Sciences, Commission IV (Mexico).

Jacobs, L. 1983. 'Notes about the relationship between filler and clay, and filler and shrinkage', *Newsletter. Department of Pottery Technology* (*University of Leiden*), 1: 6–12.

Jacobs, M. and Peremans, P. 1976. 'De Studie van Archeologica op Schilderijen', *Handelingen der Maatschappij voor Geschiedenis en Oudheidkunde te Gent*, 30: 1–21.

Jenkins, J. H. B. 1908. 'The chemical examination of some substances from the Red Hills of Essex', *Proceedings of the Society of Antiquaries of London*, 22: 182–6.

Jewitt, L. 1878. *Ceramic art of Great Britain* (London).

Johns, C. 1971. *Arretine and samian pottery* (London: British Museum).

Jones, R. E. 1986. *Greek and Cypriot pottery: a review of scientific studies*, Fitch Laboratory Occasional Paper 1.

Jope, E. M. 1956. 'Ceramics: medieval', in Singer, C., Holmyard, E. J., Hall, A. R. and Williams, T. I. (eds.), *A history of technology* 2 (Oxford: Clarendon Press), 284–310.

Joukowsky, M. 1980. *A complete manual of field archaeology*, (Englewood Cliffs. NJ: Prentice-Hall).

Julien, S. 1856. *Histoire de la fabrication de la porcelaine chinoise* (Paris).

Keighley, J. 1973. 'Some problems in the quantitative interpretation of ceramic data', in Renfrew, C. (ed.), *The explanation of culture change* (London: Duckworth), 131–6.

Kempe, A. J. 1832. 'An account of various Roman antiquities discovered on the site of the Church of Saint Michael, Crooked Lane, and Eastcheap in forming the northern approaches of the new London Bridge', *Archaeologia*, 24: 190–202.

Kendall, D. G. 1971. 'Seriation from abundance matrices', in Hodson, F. R., Kendall, D. G. and Tautu, P. (eds.), *Mathematics in the archaeological and historical sciences* (Edinburgh: Edinburgh University Press). 215–52.

Kennedy, G. C. and Knopff, L. 1960. 'Dating by thermoluminescence', *Archaeology*, 13: 147–8.

Kerr, P. F. 1977. *Optical mineralogy* (New York: McGraw-Hill).

Kidder, A. V. 1924. *An introduction to the study of Southwestern archaeology*, Papers of the Southwestern Expedition, Department of Anthropology 1 (New Haven: Yale University Press).
   1931. *The pottery of Pecos*, Papers of the Southwestern Expedition, Department of Anthropology 5 (New Haven: Yale University Press).

Kidder, M. A. and Kidder, A. V. 1917. 'Notes on the pottery of Pecos', *American Anthropology*, 19: 325–60.

Kingery, W. D. 1982. 'Plausible inferences from ceramic artifacts', in Olin, J. S. and Franklin, A. D. (eds.), *Archaeological ceramics* (Washington DC: Smithsonian Institution Press), 37–45.

Kingery, W. D., Bowen, H. K. and Uhlmann, D. R. 1976. *Introduction to ceramics*, 2nd edn (New York: John Wiley).

Knight, C. 1841. *London. 1* (London).

Knorr, K. 1906. *Die verzierten Terra sigillata von Cannstatt* (Stuttgart).

Kramer, C. 1985. 'Ceramic ethnoarchaeology', *Annual Review of Anthropology*, 14: 77–102.

Krieger, A. D. 1944. 'The typological concept', *American Antiquity*, 9: 271–88.

Kroeber, A. L. 1916. *Zuñi potsherds*, Anthropological Papers of the American Museum of Natural History 18 (New York), 1–37.

Kunow, J., Giesler, J., Gechter, M., Gaitzsch, W., Follmann-Schulz, A. B. and von Brandt, D. 1986. *Vorschläge zur systematischen Beschreibung von Keramik*, Führer des Rheinischen Landesmuseums Bonn 124 (Köln: Rheinisches Landesmuseum Bonn/Rheinland Verlag).

Lasfargues, J. and Picon, M. 1982. 'Die chemischen Untersuchungen' in von Schnurbein, S. *Die unversierte Terra Sigillata aus Haltern*, Bonenaltertümer Westfalens 19 (Münster), 6–21.

Laubenheimer, F. 1990. *Le temps des amphores en Gaule. Vins, huiles et sauces*, Collection des Hesperides (Paris: Editions Errance).

Lauchert 1845. *Die römische Tongefässe und Legionsziegel der archäologische Sammlung zu Rottweil* (Tübingen).

Laxton, R. R. 1976. 'A measure of pre-Q-ness with applications to archaeology', *Journal of Archaeological Science*, 3(1): 43–54.

1987. 'Some mathematical problems in seriation with applications', in Ruggles, C. L. N. and Rahtz, S. P. Q. (eds.), *Computer and quantitative methods in archaeology 1987*, British Archaeological Reports, International Series 393 (Oxford: BAR), 39–44.

1993. *Seriation – the theory and practice of chronological ordering in archaeology* (Chichester: Wiley).

Laxton, R. R. and Restorick, J. 1989. 'Seriation by similarity and consistency', in Rahtz, S. P. Q. and Richards, J. D. (eds.), *Computer applications and quantitative methods in archaeology 1989*, British Archaeological Reports, International Series 548 (Oxford: BAR), 229–40.

Le Grand d'Aussy, P. J. B. 1782. *Histoire de la vie privée des Français* (Paris).

Le Patourel, H. E. J. 1968. 'Documentary evidence and the medieval pottery industry', *Medieval Archaeology*, 12: 101–26.

1983. 'Documentary evidence for the pottery trade in north-west Europe', in Davey, P. and Hodges, R. (eds.), *Ceramics and trade. The production and distribution of later medieval pottery in north-west Europe* (Sheffield: Department of Archaeology and Prehistory, University of Sheffield), 27–35.

Leach, B. 1940. *A potter's book* (London: Faber and Faber).

Leese, M. N. and Main, P. L. 1983. 'An approach to the assessment of artefact dimension as descriptors of shape', in Haigh, J. G. B. (ed.), *Computer applications in archaeology 1983* (Bradford: School of Archaeological Sciences, University of Bradford), 171–80.

van der Leeuw, S. E. 1976. *Studies in the technology of ancient pottery*, Unpublished dissertation (Amsterdam).

1984. 'Dust to dust: a transformational view of the ceramic cycle', in van der Leeuw, S. E. and Pritchard, A. C. (eds.), *The many dimensions of pottery: ceramics in archaeology and anthropology*, Cingula 7 (Amsterdam: Institute for Pre- and Proto-history, University of Amsterdam), 707–92.

van der Leeuw, S. E. and Pritchard, A. C. 1984. *The many dimensions of pottery: ceramics in archaeology and anthropology*, Cingula 7 (Amsterdam: Institute for Pre- and Proto-history, University of Amsterdam).

Lemoine, C. and Picon, M. 1982. 'La fixation du phosphore par les céramiques lors de leur enfouissement et ses incidences analytiques', *Revue d'Archéometrie*, 6: 101–12.

Lemoine, C., Walker, S. and Picon, M. 1982. 'Archaeological, geochemical, and statistical methods in ceramic provenance studies', in Olin, J. S. and Franklin, A. D. (eds.), *Archaeological ceramics* (Washington DC: Smithsonian Institution Press), 57–64.

Lewarch, D. E. and O'Brien, M. J. 1981. 'The expanding role of surface assemblages in archaeological research', in Schiffer, M. B. (ed.), *Advances in archaeological method and theory* 4 (New York: Academic Press), 297–342.

Lewis, P. H. and Goodson, K. K. 1991. 'Images, database and edge detection for archaeological object drawings', in Lockyear, K. and Rahtz, S. P. Q. (eds.), *Computer applications and quantitative methods in archaeology 1990*, British Archaeological Reports, International Series 565 (Oxford: BAR), 149–53.

Liddell, D. 1932. 'Report on the excavation at Hembury Fort, third season, 1932', *Proceedings of the Devon Archaeological Exploration Society*, 1: 162–83.

Liming, G., Hongjie, L. and Wilcock, J. D. 1989. 'The analysis of ancient Chinese pottery and porcelain shapes', in Rahtz, S. P. Q. and Richards, J. D. (eds.), *Computer applications and quantitative methods in archaeology 1989*, British Archaeological Reports, International Series 548 (Oxford: BAR), 363–74.

Linné, S. 1925. *The technique of South American ceramics* (Göteborg).

Litzel, G. 1749. *Beschreibung der Römischen Todten Töpfe* (Speyer).

Lobert, H. W. 1984. 'Types of potter's wheel and the spread of the spindle-wheel in Germany', in van der Leeuw, S. E. and Pritchard, A. C. (eds.), *The many dimensions of pottery: ceramics in archaeology and anthropology*, Cingula 7 (Amsterdam; Institute for Pre- and Proto-history, University of Amsterdam), 203–30.

Loeschcke, S. 1909. 'Keramische Funde in Haltern', *Mitteilunger der Altertums-Kommission für Westfalen*, 5: 103–322.

London, G. 1981. 'Dung-tempered clay', *Journal of Field Archaeology*, 8: 189–95.

London Museum 1940. *London Museum medieval catalogue* (London: London Museum).

Longacre, W. A. 1985. 'Pottery use-life among the Kalinga, Northern Luzon, the Philippines', in Nelson, B. A. (ed.), *Decoding prehistoric ceramics* (Carbondale: Southern Illinois University Press), 334–6.

Lucke, A. 1988. 'Brennversuche in Sinne experimenteller Archäologie', in Vossen, R. (ed.), *Töpfereiforschung zwischen Archäologie und Entwicklungspolitik*, Töpferei- und Keramikforschung 1 (Bonn: Rudolf Habelt), 128–41.

Ludowici, W. 1904. *Stempel-Namen römischer Töpfer von meinen Ausgrabungen im Rheinzabern* (Munich).

Lyne, M. A. B. and Jefferies, R. S. 1979. *The Alice Holt/Farnham pottery industry*, Council for British Archaeology Research Report 30 (London: Council for British Archaeology).

Madsen, T. 1988. 'Multivariate statistics and archaeology', in Madsen, T. (ed.), *Multivariate archaeology*, Jutland Archaeological Society publications 21, 7–27.

Main, P. L. 1981. *A method for the computer storage and comparison of the outline shapes of archaeological artefacts*, Unpublished Ph.D. thesis (London: Council for National Academic Awards).

1982. 'SHU – an interactive graphics program for the storage, retrieval and analysis of artefact shapes', in Graham, I. and Webb, E. (eds.), *Computer applications in archaeology 1981* (London: Institute of Archaeology), 75–82.

1986. 'Accessing outline shape information efficiently within a large database', in Laflin, S. (ed.), *Computer applications in archaeology 1986* (Birmingham: Computer Centre, University of Birmingham), 73–82.

Maniatis, Y. and Tite, M. S. 1981. 'Technological examination of Neolithic-Bronze Age pottery from Central and Southeast Europe and from the Near East', *Journal of Archaeological Science*, 8: 59–76.

Maniatis, Y., Jones, R. E., Whitbread, I. K., Kostikas, A., Simopoulos, A., Karakalos, C. and William, C. K. 1984. 'Punic amphoras found at Corinth, Greece: an investigation of their origin and technology', *Journal of Field Archaeology*, 11: 205–22.

Marby, J., Skibo, J. M., Schiffer, M. B. and Kvamme, K. 1988. 'Use of a falling-weight tester for assessing ceramic impact strength', *American Antiquity*, 53(4): 829–39.

March, B. 1934. *Standards of pottery descriptions*, University of Michigan Museum of Anthropology Occasional Contribution 3.

Marquardt, W. H. 1978. 'Advances in archaeological seriation', in Schiffer, M. B. (ed.), *Advances in archaeological method and theory* 1 (New York: Academic Press), 257–314.

Marsh, G. 1978. 'Early second century fine wares in the London area', in Arthur, P. R. and Marsh, G. D. (eds.), *Early fine wares in Roman Britain*, British Archaeological Reports, British Series 57 (Oxford: BAR), 119–223.

Marsh, G. D. and Tyers, P. A. 1978. 'The Roman pottery from Southwark', in Bird, J., Graham, A. H., Sheldon, H. L. and Townend, P. (eds.), *Southwark excavations 1972–1974* (London: Southwark and Lambeth Archaeological Excavation Committee), 533–86.

Mathew, A. J., Woods, A. J. and Oliver, C. 1991. 'Spots before your eyes: new comparison charts for visual percentage estimation in archaeological material', in Middleton, A. P. and Freestone, I. C. (eds.), *Recent developments in ceramic petrology*, British Museum Occasional Paper 81 (London: British Museum), 211–63.

Matson, F. R. 1951. 'Ceramic technology as an aid to cultural interpretation – techniques and problems', in Griffin, J. B. (ed.), *Essays in archaeological method*, University of Michigan Museum of Anthropology Papers 8, 102–16.

　　1952. 'The contribution of technical ceramic studies to American archaeology', in *Prehistoric pottery of the eastern United States* (Ann Arbor), 1–7.

　　1965. 'Ceramic ecology: an approach to the study of the early cultures of the Near East', in Matson, F. R. (ed.), *Ceramics and man*, Wenner Gren Foundation for Anthropological Research, Viking Fund Publications in Anthropology 41 (Chicago: Aldine).

　　1966. 'Some aspects of ceramic technology', in Brothwell, D. and Higgs, E. S. (eds.), *Science in archaeology* (London: Thames and Hudson), 592–602.

　　1981. 'Archaeological ceramics and the physical sciences: problem definition and results', *Journal of Field Archaeology*, 8: 448–57.

　　1984. 'Ceramics and Man reconsidered with some thoughts for the future', in van der Leeuw, S. E. and Pritchard, A. C. (eds.), *The many dimensions of pottery: ceramics in archaeology and anthropology*, Cingula 7 (Amsterdam: Institute for Pre- and Protohistory, University of Amsterdam), 25–49.

Mayes, P. 1961. 'The firing of a pottery kiln of a Romano-British type at Boston, Lincs.', *Archaeometry*, 4: 4–18.

　　1962. 'The firing of a second pottery kiln of Romano-British type at Boston, Lincs.', *Archaeometry*, 5: 80–5.

McCarthy, M. and Brooks, C. 1988. *Medieval pottery in Britain: AD 900–1600* (Leicester: Leicester University Press).

McMorris, M. R. 1990. 'The median procedure for n-trees as a maximum likelihood method', *Journal of Classification*, 7: 77–80.

McNutt, C. H. 1973. 'On the methodological validity of frequency seriation', *American Antiquity*, 38: 45–60.

van Mellen, J. 1679. *Historia urnae sepulchralis sarmaticae* (Jena).

Meyer, F. S. 1957. *Handbook of ornament* (New York: Dover).

Middleton, A. P. 1984–5. 'Examination of ash from the experimental firing group pottery bonfire held at Leicester in July 1984 and comparison with some archaeological ashes', *Bulletin of the Experimental Firing Group*, 3: 19–24.

Middleton, A. P., Freestone, I. C. and Leese, M. N. 1985. 'Textural analysis of ceramic thin sections: evaluation of grain sampling procedures', *Archaeometry*, 27: 64–74.

Miller, D. 1985. *Artefacts as categories: a study of ceramic variability in Central India* (Cambridge: Cambridge University Press).

Millett, M. 1979a. 'An approach to the functional interpretation of pottery', in Millett, M. (ed.), *Pottery and the archaeologist*, Institute of Archaeology Occasional Publications 4 (London: University of London Institute of Archaeology), 35–48.

1979b. 'How much pottery?', in Millett, M. (ed.), *Pottery and the archaeologist*, Institute of Archaeology Occasional Publications 4 (London: University of London Institute of Archaeology), 77–80.

1979c. 'The dating of Farnham (Alice Holt) pottery', *Britannia*, 10: 121–37.

1987. 'Boudicca, the first Colchester potters' shop, and the dating of Neronian samian', *Britannia*, 18: 93–123.

Millett, A. and Catling, H. W. 1967. 'Composition patterns of Minoan and Mycenaean pottery: survey and prospects', *Archaeometry*, 10: 70–7.

Millett, M. and Graham, D. 1986. *Excavations on the Roman-British small town at Neatham, Hampshire, 1969–1979*, Hampshire Field Club and Archaeological Society Monograph 3 (Gloucester: Alan Sutton).

Milne, G. and Milne, C. 1982. *Medieval waterfront development at Trig Lane, London*, London and Middlesex Archaeological Society, Special Paper 5 (London: LAMAS).

Moorhouse, S. 1978. 'Documentary evidence for the uses of medieval pottery: an interim statement', *Medieval Ceramics*, 2: 3–21.

1979. 'Tudor green: some further thoughts', *Medieval Ceramics*, 3: 52–61.

1981. 'The medieval pottery industry and its markets', in Crossley, D. W. (ed.), *Medieval industries*, Council for British Archaeology Research Report 40 (London: Council for British Archaeology), 96–125.

1983. 'The medieval pottery', in Mayes, P. and Butler, L. A. S. (eds.), *Sandal Castle excavations 1964–73* (Wakefield: Wakefield Historical Publications), 83–212.

1986. 'Non-dating uses of medieval pottery', *Medieval Ceramics*, 10: 85–124.

Mossman, B. M. and Selsor, M. 1988. 'A utilitarian pottery tradition and the modern Spanish kitchen', in Kolb, C. C., Lackey, L. M. and Kirkpatrick, M. (eds.), *A pot for all reasons: ceramic ecology revisited*, Special publication of Ceramica de Cultura Maya et al, 213–37.

Munsell Color Company 1975. *Munsell soil color charts* (Baltimore: Md.: Munsell Color Company).

Musty, J. W. G. 1974. 'Medieval pottery kilns', in Evison, V. I., Hodges, H. and Hurst, J. G. (eds.), *Medieval pottery from excavations* (London: John Baker), 41–65.

Needham, S. P. and Sørensen, M. L. S. 1989. 'Runnymede refuse tip – a consideration of midden deposits and their formation', in Barrett, J. C. and Kinnes, I. A. (eds.), *The archaeology of context: recent research on the Neolithic and Bronze Age in Britain* (Sheffield: Department of Prehistory and Archaeology), 113–20.

Neff, H., Bishop, R. L. and Arnold, D. E. 1988. 'Reconstructing ceramic production from ceramic compositional data: an example from Guatemala', *Journal of Field Archaeology*, 15: 339–48.

Nelson, N. C. 1916. 'Chronology of the Tano Ruins, New Mexico', *American Anthropologist*, 18 (2): 159–80.

Nicholson, P. T. 1989. *Iron Age pottery production in the Hunsrück-Eifel-Kultur of Germany*, British Archaeological Reports, International Series 501 (Oxford: BAR).

Nicholson, P. T. and Patterson, H. L. 1985. 'Pottery making in Upper Egypt: an ethnoarchaeological study', *World Archaeology*, 17 (2): 222–39.

Nicklin, K. 1971. 'Stability and innovation in pottery manufacture', *World Archaeology*, 3: 13–18.

Noritané, N., 1876–9. *Notice historique sur les arts et les industries japonais* (Paris).

Oakley, K. P. 1933. 'The pottery from the Romano-British site on Thundersbarrow Hill', *Antiquaries Journal*, 13: 134–41.

Obenauer, K. 1936. 'Petrographische Untersuchung der Keramik', in Buttler, W. and Haberey, W. (eds.), *Die Bandkeramische Ansiedlung bei Köln-Lindenthal* (Berlin: de Gruyter), 123–9.

Odell, G. H. and Cowan, F. 1987. 'Estimating tillage effects on artefact distributions', *American Antiquity*, 52 (3): 456–84.

Orton, C. R. 1975. 'Quantitative pottery studies: some progress, problems and prospects', *Science and Archaeology*, 16: 30–5.

  1979. 'Dealing with the pottery from a 600-acre urban site', in Millett, M. (ed.), *Pottery and the archaeologist*, Institute of Archaeology Occasional Publications 4 (London: Institute of Archaeology), 61–71.

  1980. *Mathematics in archaeology* (Cambridge: Cambridge University Press).

  1982a. 'Computer simulation experiments to assess the performance of measures of quantities of pottery', *World Archaeology*, 14 (1): 1–20.

  1982b. 'The excavation of a late medieval/transitional pottery kiln at Cheam, Surrey', *Surrey Archaeological Collections*, 73: 49–92.

  1985a. 'Two useful parameters for pottery research', in Webb, E. (ed.), *Computer applications in archaeology 1985* (London: University of London Institute of Archaeology), 114–20.

  1985b. 'Diffusion or impedance – obstacles to innovation in medieval ceramics', *Medieval Archaeology*, 9: 21–34.

  1987. 'The "envelope": un nouvel outil pour l'étude morphologique des céramiques', in Chapelot, J., Galinié, H. and Pilet-Lemière, J. (eds.), *La céramique (Ve–XIXe s.), fabrication, commercialisation, utilisation* (Caen: Société d'Archéologie Médiévale), 33–41.

Orton, C. R. and Orton, J. L. 1975. 'It's later than you think: a statistical look at an archaeological problem', *London Archaeologist*, 2 (11): 285–7.

Orton, C. R. and Tyers, P. A. 1990. 'Statistical analysis of ceramic assemblages', *Archeologia e Calcolatori*, 1: 81–110.

  1992. 'Counting broken objects: the statistics of ceramic assemblages' *Proceedings of the British Academy* 77: 163–84.

Papousek, R. A. 1984. 'Pots and people in Los Pueblos: the social and economic organisation of pottery', in van der Leeuw, S. E. and Pritchard, A. C. (eds.), *The many dimensions of pottery: ceramics in archaeology and anthropology*, Cingula 7 (Amsterdam: Institute for Pre- and Proto-history, University of Amsterdam), 475–526.

Partridge, C. 1981. *Skeleton Green*, Britannia monographs 2 (London: Society for the Promotion of Roman Studies).

Passeri, J. B. 1752. *Historia delle pitture in majolica fatte in Pesaro* (Venezia).

Peacock, D. P. S. 1967. 'The heavy mineral analysis of pottery: a preliminary report', *Archaeometry*, 10: 97–100.

  1969. 'A contribution to the study of Glastonbury ware from south-western Britain', *Antiquaries Journal*, 49: 41–61.

  1970. 'The scientific analysis of ancient ceramics: a review', *World Archaeology*, 1: 375–89.

  1977. 'Ceramics in Roman and medieval archaeology', in Peacock, D. P. S. (ed.), *Pottery in early commerce* (London: Academic Press), 21–34.

  1982. *Pottery in the Roman world: an ethnoarchaeological approach* (London: Longman).

  1984. 'Appendix 1. Seawater, salt and ceramics', in Fulford, M. G. and Peacock, D. P. S. (eds.), *The Avenue du President Habib Bourguiba, Salammbo: the pottery and other ceramic objects from the site*, Excavations at Carthage: The British Mission I, 2, 263–4.

1988. 'The gabbroic pottery of Cornwall', *Antiquity*, 62: 302–4.

Pearce, J. E. 1984. 'Getting a handle on medieval pottery', *London Archaeologist*, 5 (1): 17–23.

1992. *Post-medieval pottery in London 1500–1700, vol. 1, Border wares* (London: HMSO).

Pearce, J. E., and Vince, A. G. 1988. *A dated type-series of London medieval pottery. Part 4: Surrey whitewares*, London and Middlesex Archaeological Society, Special Paper 10 (London: LAMAS).

Pearce, J. E., Vince, A. G. and Jenner, M. A. 1985. *A dated type-series of London medieval pottery. Part 2: London-type ware*, London and Middlesex Archaeological Society, Special Paper 6 (London: LAMAS).

Perrin, J. R. 1990. *Roman pottery from the Colonia: 2*, The archaeology of York 16/4 (London: Council for British Archaeology).

Petrie, W. M. F. 1891. *Tell el Hesy (Lachish)* (London: Palestine Exploration Society).

1899. 'Sequences in prehistoric remains', *Journal of the Royal Anthropological Institute*, 29: 295–301.

1904. *Methods and aims in archaeology* (London: Macmillan).

Phillips, P. 1958. 'Application of the Wheat–Gifford–Wasley taxonomy to eastern ceramics', *American Antiquity*, 24: 117–25.

Picon, M. 1973. *Introduction à l'étude technique des céramiques sigillées de Lezoux*, Centre de recherches sur les techniques Gréco-Romaines 2 (Dijon: Université de Dijon).

1976. 'Remarques préliminaires sur deux types d'alteration de la composition chimique des céramiques au cours du temps', *Figlina*, 1: 159–76.

1984. *Problèmes de determination de l'origine des céramiques*, P.A.C.T. 10.

Pitt-Rivers, A. H. L. F. 1906. 'The principles of classification', in Myres, J. L. (ed.), *The evolution of culture and other essays* (Oxford: Clarendon Press).

van der Plas, L. and van Doesburg, J. 1987. 'Heavy minerals and feldspars in potsherds', *Newsletter. Department of Pottery Technology (University of Leiden)*, 5: 74–86.

Platt, C. and Coleman-Smith, R. 1975. *Excavations in medieval Southampton 1953–1969. Volume 2. The finds* (Leicester: University of Leicester).

Plique, A. E. 1887. *Etude de céramique arverno-romaine* (Caen).

Plog, S. 1978. 'Social interaction and stylistic similarity: a reanalysis', in Schiffer, M. B. (ed.), *Advances in archaeological method and theory* 1 (New York: Academic Press), 143–82.

1980. *Stylistic variation in prehistoric ceramics: design analysis in the American Southwest* (Cambridge: Cambridge University Press).

Ponsford, M. 1983. 'North European pottery imported into Bristol', in Davey, P. and Hodges, R. (eds.), *Ceramics and trade. The production and distribution of later medieval pottery in north-west Europe* (Sheffield: Department of Archaeology and Prehistory, University of Sheffield), 219–24.

Pottier, A. 1867. *Essai sur la classification des poteries normandes* (Rouen).

Rackham, B. 1948. *Medieval English pottery* (London: Faber).

Renfrew, C. and Sterud, G. 1969. 'Close-proximity analysis: a rapid method for the ordering of archaeological materials', *American Antiquity*, 34: 265–77.

Renfrew, C. and Cooke, K. L. (eds.), 1979. *Transformations – mathematical approaches to culture change* (New York: Academic Press).

Rhodes, M. 1979. 'Methods of cataloguing pottery in Inner London: an historical outline', *Medieval Ceramics*, 3: 81–108.

Rice, P. M. 1987. *Pottery analysis: a sourcebook* (Chicago: University of Chicago Press).

Richards, E. E. 1959. 'Preliminary spectrographic investigation of some Romano-British mortaria', *Archaeometry*, 2: 23–31.

Richards, J. D. 1987. *The significance of form and decoration of Anglo-Saxon cremation urns*, British Archaeological Reports, British Series 166 (Oxford: BAR).

Richards, J. D. and Ryan, N. S. 1985. *Data processing in archaeology* (Cambridge: Cambridge University Press).

Richardson, B. 1983. 'Excavation roundup, 1982 Part 2', *London Archaeologist*, 4(11): 288–91.

Richter, G. M. A. 1956. 'Ceramics: from *c.* 700 BC to the fall of the Roman Empire', in Singer, C., Holmyard, E. J., Hall, A. R. and Williams, T. I. (eds.), *A history of technology* 2 (Oxford: Clarendon Press), 259–83.

Rieth, A. 1960. *5000 Jahre Töpferschiebe* (Constance: Thorbecke).

Ritchie, W. A. and Macneish, R. S. 1949. 'The Pre-Iroquoian pottery of New York State', *American Antiquity*, 15: 97–124.

Roberts, J. P. 1963. 'Determination of the firing temperature of ancient ceramics by measurement of thermal expansion', *Archaeometry*, 6: 21–5.

Robinson, A. M. 1979. 'Three approaches to the problem of pottery fabric descriptions', *Medieval Ceramics*, 3: 3–36.

Robinson, W. M. 1951. 'A method for chronologically ordering archaeological deposits', *American Antiquity*, 16: 293–301.

Rossignol, E. A. 1861. *Des Antiquités et principalement de la poterie romaine trouvées à Montans* (Caen).

Rouse, I. 1939. *Prehistory in Haiti: a study in method*, Yale University Publication in Anthropology 21 (New Haven).

1960. 'The classification of artefacts in archaeology', *American Antiquity*, 25: 213–23.

1965. 'The New York planning conference', in Matson, F. R. (ed.), *Ceramics and man*, Wenner Gren Foundation for Anthropological Research, Viking Fund Publications in Anthropology 41 (Chicago: Aldine), 274–6.

Ruempol, A. P. E. and Dongen, A. G. A. van 1991. *Pre-Industriëlle Gebruiksvoorwerpen 1150–1800* (Rotterdam: Museum Boymans-van Beuningen).

Rye, O. S. 1976. 'Keeping your temper under control: materials and manufacture of Papuan pottery', *Archaeology and Physical Anthropology in Oceania*, 11(2): 106–37.

1977. 'Pottery manufacturing technique: X-ray studies', *Archaeometry*, 19: 205–11.

1981. *Pottery technology. Principles and reconstruction*, Manuals on archaeology 4 (Washington DC: Taraxacum).

Rye, O. S. and Evans, C. 1976. *Traditional pottery techniques in Pakistan: field and laboratory studies*, Smithsonian Contributions to Anthropology 21 (Washington DC: Smithsonian Institution Press).

Santley, R. S., Arnold, P. J. and Pool, C. A. 1989. 'The ceramic production system at Matacapan, Veracruz, Mexico', *Journal of Field Archaeology*, 19: 107–32.

Saraswati, B. and Behura, N. K. 1966. *Pottery techniques in peasant India*, Memoir 13 (Calcutta: Anthropological Survey of India).

Sayre, E. V. and Dobson, R. W. 1957. 'Neutron activation study of Mediterranean potsherds', *American Journal of Archaeology*, 61: 35–41.

Sayre, E. V., Murenhoff, A. and Weick, C. F. 1958. *The nondestructive analysis of ancient potsherds through neutron activation*, Brookhaven National Laboratory Publications 508.

Scheufler, V. 1968. *Classification system of pottery making tools*, Proceedings of the 8th congress of Anthropological and Ethnological Sciences Volume 3: Ethnology and Archaeology (Tokyo: Science Council of Japan).

Schiffer, M. B. 1987. *Formation processes of the archaeological record* (Albuquerque: University of New Mexico Press).

1990. 'The influence of surface treatment on heating effectiveness of ceramic vessels', *Journal of Archaeological Science*, 17(4): 373–82.

Schiffer, M. B. and Skibo, J. M. 1989. 'Theory and experiment in the study of technological change', *Current Anthropology*, 28: 595–622.

Schneider, G. (ed.) 1989. 'Naturwissenschaftliche Kriterien und Verfahren zur Beschreibing der Keramik', *Acta Prehistorica et Archaeologica*, 21: 7–39.

von Schnurbein, S. 1982. *Die unversierte Terra Sigillata aus Haltern*, Bonenaltertümer Westfalens 19 (Münster).

Schoolcraft, H. R. 1847. *Notices of some antique earthen vessels of Florida* (New York).

Schuring, J. M. 1984. 'Studies on Roman amphorae I–II', *Bulletin Antike Beschaving*, 59: 137–95.

Scott, Sir L. 1954. 'Pottery', in Singer, C., Holmyard, E. J. and Hall, A. R. (eds.), *A history of technology* 1 (Oxford: Clarendon Press), 376–412.

Sealey, P. R. 1985. *Amphoras from the 1970 excavations at Colchester Sheepen*, British Archaeological Reports, British Series 142 (Oxford: BAR).

Sealey, P. R. and Tyers, P. A. 1989. 'Olives from Roman Spain: a unique amphora find in British waters', *Antiquaries Journal*, 69(1): 53–72.

Shennan, S. J. 1988. *Quantifying archaeology* (Edinburgh: Edinburgh University Press).

Shepard, A. O. 1936. 'The technology of Pecos Pottery', in *Pottery of Pecos* 2 (New Haven).

   1942. *Rio Grande glaze paint ware, a study illustrating the place of ceramic technological analysis in archaeological research* (Washington: Carnegie Institute of Washington).

   1956. *Ceramics for the archaeologist* (Washington: Carnegie Institute of Washington).

   1964. 'Temper identification: technological sherd-splitting or an unanswered challenge', *American Antiquity*, 29: 518–20.

Shortt, T. P. 1841. *Sylva antiqua Iscana* (Exeter: Featherstone).

Skibo, J. M. and Schiffer, M. B. 1987. 'The effects of water on processes of ceramic abrasion', *Journal of Archaeological Science*, 14: 83–96.

Sklenář, K. 1983. *Archaeology in Central Europe: the first 500 years* (Leicester: Leicester University Press).

Smith, C. Roach 1854. *Catalogue of the Museum of London antiquities collected by, and property of, Charles Roach Smith* (London: privately printed).

Smith, M. F. 1983. *The study of ceramic function from artifact size and shape*, Ph.D. dissertation (Eugene: University of Oregon).

   1985. 'Towards an economic interpretation of ceramics: relating vessel size and shape to use', in Nelson, B. A. (ed.), *Decoding prehistoric ceramics* (Carbondale: Southern Illinois University Press), 254–309.

Smith, R. H. 1970. 'An approach to the drawing of pottery and small finds for excavation reports', *World Archaeology*, 2: 212–28.

   1972. 'The sectioning of potsherds as an archaeological method', *Berytus*, 21: 39–53.

Smith, W. 1816. *Strata identified by organized fossils* (London).

Solheim, W. G. 1960. 'The use of sherd weight and counts in the handling of archaeological data', *Current Anthropology*, 1: 325–9.

Solon, M. L. 1910. *Ceramic literature: an analytical index* (London: Charles Griffin).

Spier, L. 1917. *An outline for a chronology of Zuñi ruins*, Anthropological Papers of the American Museum of Natural History 18 (New York), 207–331.

Squier, E. G. and Davis, E. H. 1848. *Ancient monuments of the Mississippi Valley*, Smithsonian Contributions to Knowledge 1 (Washington: Smithsonian Institution).

Steinstra, P. 1986. 'Systematic macroscopic description of the texture and composition of ancient pottery – some basic methods', *Newsletter. Department of Pottery Technology (University of Leiden)*, 4: 28–48.

Steponaitis, V. P. 1983. *Ceramics, chronology and community patterns: an archaeological study at Moundville* (New York/London: Academic Press).

   1984. 'Technological studies of prehistoric pottery from Alabama: physical properties and vessel function', in van der Leeuw, S. E. and Pritchard, A. C. (eds.), *The many dimensions of pottery: ceramics in archaeology and anthropology*, Cingula 7 (Amsterdam: Institute for Pre- and Proto-history, University of Amsterdam), 79–122.

Stevenson, R. 1991. 'Post-medieval ceramic bird pots from excavations in Greater London'. *London Archaeologist*, 6(12): 320–1.

Stow, J. 1603. *A survey of London* (London).

Strange, J. F. 1989. 'Beyond socio-economics: some reactions to', in Blakeley, J. A. and Bennett, W. J. (eds.), *Analysis and publication of ceramics*, British Archaeological Reports, International Series 551 (Oxford: BAR), 23–30.

Streeten, A. D. F. 1980. 'Potters, kilns and markets in medieval Sussex: a preliminary study', *Sussex Archaeological Collections*, 118: 105–18.

    1982. 'Textural analysis: an approach to the characterization of sand tempered fabrics', in Freestone, I. C., Johns, C. and Potter, T. (eds.), *Current research in ceramics: thin-section studies*, British Museum Occasional Paper 32 (London: British Museum), 123–34.

Sullivan, A. P. 1988. 'Prehistoric southwestern ceramic manufacture: the limitations of current evidence', *American Antiquity*, 53(1): 23–35.

Swan, V. G. 1984. *The pottery kilns of Roman Britain*, Royal Commission on Historical Monuments Supplementary Series 5 (London).

Tarrell, J. and Osborne, J. 1971. 'Potsherd rim angles: a simple device', *Antiquity* 45: 299–302.

Tite, M. S. and Maniatis, Y. 1975. 'Examination of ancient pottery using the scanning electron microscope', *Nature*, 257: 122–3.

Tite, M. S. and Waine, J. 1961. 'Thermoluminescent dating: a re-appraisal', *Archaeometry*, 5: 53–79.

Tite, W. 1848. *A descriptive catalogue of the antiquities found in the excavations at the new Royal Exchange* (London).

Traunecker, C. 1984. *Code analytique de profils de céramique de l'ancienne Egypt*, Studien zur altägyptischen Keramik. Deutsches Archäologischen Institute – Abteilung Kairo (Mainz am Rhein: Verlag Philipp zon Zabern).

Trump, D. H. 1972. 'Aids to drawing: sherd radii', *Antiquity*, 46: 150–1.

Tschopik, H. 1950. 'An Andean ceramic tradition in archaeological perspective', *American Antiquity*, 15: 196–218.

Turner, J. D., Keary, A. C. and Peacock, D. P. S. 1990. 'Drawing potsherds: a low-cost computer-based system', *Archaeometry*, 32: 177–82.

Tyers, P. A. 1978. 'The poppy-head beakers of Britain and their relationship to the barbotine decorated beakers of the Rhineland and Switzerland', in Arthur, P. R. and Marsh, G.D. (eds.), *Early fine wares in Roman Britain*, British Archaeological Reports, British Series 57 (Oxford: BAR), 61–107.

Tyers, P. A. and Orton, C. R. 1991. 'Statistical analysis of ceramic assemblages', in Lockyear, K. and Rahtz, S. P. Q. (eds.), *Computer applications and quantitative methods in archaeology 1990*, British Archaeological Reports, International Series 565 (Oxford: Tempus Reparatum), 117–20.

Tyldesley, J. A., Johnson, J. G. and Snape, S. R. 1985. '"Shape" in archaeological artefacts: two case studies using a new analytic method', *Oxford Journal of Archaeology*, 4(1): 19–30.

Vince, A. G. 1977. 'Some aspects of pottery quantification', *Medieval Ceramics*, 1: 63–74.

Vossen, R. 1972. *Töpferei in Spanien*, Wegweiser zur Völkerkunde 12 (Hamburg: Hamburger Museum fur Völkerkunde).

Vossen, R. (ed.) 1988. *Töpfereiforschung zwischen Archäologie und Entwicklungspolitik*, Töpferei- und Keramikforschung 1 (Bonn: Rudolf Habelt).

Vossen, R. and Ebert, W. 1976. *Marokkanische Töpferei – Poterie marocaine* (Bonn: Rudolf Habelt).

Vossen, R., Seseña, N. and Köpfe, W. 1980. *Guia de los alfares de España* (Madrid: Editoria Nacional).

de Waldek, F. 1838. *Voyage dans la province d'Yucatan* (Paris).

Walters, H. B. 1908. *Catalogue of the Roman pottery in the Department of Antiquities of the British Museum* (London: British Museum).

Weaver, E. C. 1963. 'Technological analysis of prehistoric lower Mississippi ceramic materials: a preliminary report', *American Antiquity*, 29: 49–56.

Weber, T. 1719. *Uber die bei Giessen erwittern Urnis* (Giessen).

Webster, G. (ed.) 1964. *Romano-British coarse pottery: a students guide*, Council for British Archaeology Research Report 6 (London: Council for British Archaeology).

Wheat, J. B., Gifford, J. C. and Wasley, W. W. 1958. 'Ceramic variety, type cluster and ceramic system in south-western pottery analysis', *American Antiquity*, 24: 34–47.

Wheeler, A. and Locker, A. 1985. 'The estimation of size in sardines (*Sardina pilchardus*) from amphorae in a wreck at Randello, Sicily', *Journal of Archaeological Science*, 12: 97–100.

Wheeler, R. E. M. 1954. *Archaeology from the earth* (Oxford: Clarendon Press).

Whitbread, I. K. 1986. 'A microscopic view of Greek transport amphorae', in Jones, R. E. and Catling, H. W. (eds.), *Science in archaeology*, Fitch Laboratory Occasional Paper 2, 49–52.

White, K. D. 1975. *Farm equipment of the Roman world* (Cambridge: Cambridge University Press).

Wilcock, J. D. and Shennan, S. J. 1975a. 'Computer analysis of pottery shapes', in Laflin, S. (ed.), *Computer applications in archaeology 1975* (Birmingham: Computer Centre, University of Birmingham), 98–106.

   1975b. 'Shape and style variation in Central German Bell Beakers. A computer assisted study', *Science and Archaeology*, 15: 17–31.

Wilkinson, T. J. 1982. 'The definition of ancient manured zones by means of extensive sherd-sampling techniques', *Journal of Field Archaeology*, 9: 323–33.

Willey, G. and Sabloff, J. 1974. *A history of American archaeology*, 2nd edn (London: Thames and Hudson).

Williams, D. F. 1979. 'The heavy mineral separation of ancient ceramics by centrifugation: a preliminary report', *Archaeometry*, 21: 177–82.

Wilson, A. L. 1978. 'Elemental analysis of pottery in the study of its provenance: a review', *Journal of Archaeological Science*, 5: 219–36.

Woods, A. J. 1984–5. 'An introductory note on the use of tangential thin sections for distinguishing between wheel-thrown and coil/ring built vessels', *Bulletin of the Experimental Firing Group*, 3: 100–114.

   1986. 'Form, fabric and function: some observations on the cooking pot in antiquity', in Kingery, W. D. (ed.), *Technology and style*, Ceramics and Civilisation 2 (Columbus, Ohio: American Ceramics Society), 157–72.

Worrall, W. E. 1975. *Clays and ceramic raw materials* (London: Applied Science Publishers).

Yorston, R. M. 1990. 'Comments on estimating tillage effects on artifact distributions', *American Antiquity*, 55(3): 594–8.

Young, C. J. (ed.) 1980. *Guidelines for the processing and publication of Roman pottery from excavations*, Directorate of Ancient Monuments and Historic Buildings Occasional Paper 4 (London: HMSO).

Young, W. J. and Whitmore, F. E. 1957. 'Analysis of Oriental ceramic wares by non-destructive X-ray methods', *Far Eastern Ceramic Bulletin*, 9: 1–27.

INDEX